Critical acclai[n]
and The Wizard

I want to point my finger at YOU to absorb the wisdom of how common sense can beat the drums to regain America's leadership. This book is your call to serve your country for the common good and welfare of EVERY American. It makes sense!

– Uncle Sam

My torch is held high and brightly lit for Littman's brilliance in lighting the path for every American's pursuit of happiness and liberty for all by using common sense. I am cradling this book close to my heart as it beats life into our huddled masses.

– Lady Liberty

I am the Father of this country, while Littman's paper mache' creation impressively takes you by the hand to lead you to the future potential glory of a United America. **This is the first book which includes a $5 donation to BACK-OUR-VETS.** I can't tell a lie. It's a brilliant idea in an equally well told story.

– President George Washington

My role is to sew the stars and stripes together to flag your attention to how one warrior is waging a fierce war for his brothers and sisters in arms to receive the pay and benefits they courageously earned. Learn how Littman uniquely raises the flag 2 cents at a time for the benefit of 65 million of America's bravest.

– Betsy Ross

I would like to liberate myself from being plastered to this monumental seat at my Memorial and be able to run and buy Littman's "The Wizard of COMMON CENTS" that emancipates your mind to THINK. He writes about a Civic War that will engage you in the battle between the Red and the Blue states.

– President Abraham Lincoln

This wild ride through the countryside alerts you to the thunderous beat of stories which result in pure gold that our nation's future is ahead, so get mounted to strike it rich, using your God given COMMON CENTS.

– Paul Revere

Littman spins the web of citizens eating the manipulation of money powers that leads to controversy with the mix of parody and real-life political absurdities.

– President Thomas Jefferson

Littman writes his first book at age 87. He will guide you through the pages of turmoil from World War 2 to today's pioneering wisdom and newest technology.

– Davey Crockett

His prose of "War is for Peace" and his wise advice for using plain ordinary common sense for the common good creates a life preserver of long lasting prosperity for each and every class of American. This book has the clarity of purpose…to make every citizen proud to be an American.

– Eleanor Roosevelt

This book is your unforgettable travel guide to join the Billionaires Club by putting in your 2 cents for America's bravest. Open to membership no matter if you are rich or poor. Learn how to climb aboard this brand wagon to BACK-OUR-VETS.

– John D. Rockefeller

It's a real thriller...step-by-step this book will make your heart dance to Earl's cool common sense choreography. You will slide and glide through these memorable memoirs with unforgettable movements.

– Michael Jackson.

This book is a page turner with jagged edges to empower your mind – not to be missed. It's as tasty and as mouth-watering to digest as a sweet cup-cake.

– Dolly Madison

Earl Littman sets the bar too high for cinematic romance with his ever loving wife – Natalie. We should all be so lucky in legendary love!

– Casanova

Here I am chiseled in stone on top of Mt. Rushmore where I would much prefer to rush away from political stone-walling and learn more why Littman's book can carve out a new bully pulpit of monumental American greatness.

– President "Teddy" Roosevelt

It's been a long time since I have read anything else that will put a really big smile on my face like Littman's colorful portrait of each year since World War 2.

– Mona Lisa

I have a dream that Littman's thoughts on Common Cents will make common sense for the common good. I will buy that dream.

– Martin Luther King

Littman hit this one out-of-the-park!

– 'Babe' Ruth

Revolutionary thoughts to change America's thinking that "trickle-down" can be generated by any ordinary citizen- patriot like Earl Littman. His trickling ideas that create a towering wave storming our brains with mind-boggling plans to think about and consider employing for a more conscientious thoughtful public.

– President Ronald Reagan

Littman is throwing cartridges of bullets to strike out conspirators wanting to turn back the clock of progress. Common sense proves their game is over and out.

– Bob Feller

In this persuasive book Littman has launched a rocket ship of common sense ideas reaching to the moon which will land with impact on your mind, compelling America to explore new planets' for star reaching glory.

– President John F. Kennedy

Littman attacks with ferocity sensitive positions on abortion, gun control, minimum wage, amnesty, traitors, planned parenthood, climate control, border security, education and head start with simple common sense to challenge you to THINK about common solutions. You can trust my recommendation for this book.

— Walter Cronkite

This impressive book is a stroke of bright canvas filled colors which were painted on the failures and triumphs of Littman's personal lifetime experiences that will hypnotize you to use your own talents for common sense answers.

— Rembrandt

Littman's riveting book fires drones that fly and hit his targets with bulls-eye, uncanny accuracy. It's simply electric.

Thomas Edison

This patriotic author declares war on a do-nothing Congress' stagnation and draws a line-in-the-sand to use common sense to charge ahead and win the battle to restore America's greatness. Get out-of-your pathetic pot-holes and join this WW2 warrior's fight of the CENTury to BACK-OUR-VETS.

— General George Patton

Daring and remarkable...deeply effective — so rich-in-plot, addressing poverty, homelessness and never surrendering to a loss of hope.

— Bob Hope

The story telling is a bold and vivid epic adventure that is expressive with purpose. It's poignant message should never be lost.

– Amelia Earhart

An addictive book on the destructive influence of alcohol and substance abuse.

– Whitney Houston

A punch in the knows. A wallop to your head. A knockout to your social conscience. This book is a Golden Love Championship.

– Jack Dempsey

This man is a modest genius. I know best because we have lived, loved, laughed together for 65 years of a blissful marriage made in heaven. 26 million American military citizens who have honorably served our nation, along with their beloved families – totaling a majestic force of 65 million (one in every five families) can thank this American PREACHER for PATRIOTISM – the humble author of this soul-binding book for his untiring dedication and passionate effort to BACK-OUR-VETS.

– Natalie Littman

THE WIZARD OF
COMMON CENTS
One warrior's fierce battle of the CENTury

$9.<u>95</u> EBOOK
$18.<u>95</u> U.S.A.
$5 goes to
Back-Our-Vets™

A must read
for America's Patriots

EARL LITTMAN
America's PREACHER for PATRIOTISM

outskirtspress
DENVER, COLORADO

The Wizard of COMMON CENTS
One warrior's fierce battle of the CENTury
All Rights Reserved.
Copyright © 2014 Earl Littman
v4.0

Cover Image by Rebeca Porcara

Outskirts Press, Inc.
http://www.outskirtspress.com

ISBN: 978-1-4787-3164-1

Outskirts Press and the "OP" logo are trademarks belonging to Outskirts Press, Inc.

PRINTED IN THE UNITED STATES OF AMERICA

Inspired to remember all veterans and military troops, particularly the courageous secret combat warriors and respectfully America's fallen heroes.

Contents

Prologue: Reflections in the Mirror of My Life.......................i
The Wizard of Common Cents...1
I'm in the Navy Now..7
"Yes, Sir."..12
America. Home at Last...18
History from Natalie's Eyes...25
Job Search...28
The Music Man 34
The Bells Are Ringing 38
Home Sweat Home 41
New Job. New Place. New Career......................................45
Texas Here We Are: Lox, Stock and Bagels. 52
Time Out for a Commercial...55
Try to Guess Who… 60
Secrets Revealed 76
Charge Ahead...81
The Big Payoff 85
Now the Fun Begins...91
Barry the Hatchet..94
TexaGO 102

Nonprofits Are Humanly Profitable 108
GDL&W Is Out of My Life from Today On....................124
Let's Get Off the Bus and Take Another Look 140
Choice or Chance..148
Makes No Difference 155
*Blanton Bulletin 161
Latest Diary Entry...165
It Must Be Tuesday...177
Mess Call 182
Strike Out on Bourbon Street...............................186
Dying to Meet You..191
What a Beautiful Day.......................................197
Stormy Weather 203
Pop the Cork...207
Disappointments and Heart Breaks. 213
Time to Climb Back on the Bus 214
Be a Billionaire 233
To My Immediate Family. 242
If I Were King 243
Turn the Clock Forward 249
Love Letters...265
Games Lost 271
Two to Tango 285
The End Is Only the Beginning 298
Found the Money..304
The Tidal Wave of History 307
Steak of the Union 327
POST SCRIPture: Who Is the Wizard? 337

Prologue:
Reflections in the Mirror of My Life

How did I come to this point of my 87 years of living?

What path led me through the jungle to reach this point of wonder?

Was there a distant beacon light steering me through the treacherous waters?

I often ponder the mysteries that control our destiny to make each of us different than the other 7 billion people residing on planet earth. Why do I have a fire in my belly that burns daily to want to help 65 million people when I intimately know so few?

Intimately may be the key word to describe that we may not be friends or even acquaintances, but we share a common bond that makes us a family of brothers and sisters. Each of us served in the armed forces of our beloved country – the United States of America. It may have been in different times, during both wars and peace, and in various services such as the Army, Navy,

Marines, Air Force or Coast Guard as well as performing our unique duties for which we were trained to perform with honor and responsibility. Yet, we are a band of one--either a veteran or still serving in the troops--knowing we are each among America's bravest.

Today, when I look back over the years I continue to wonder in awe as to why I have assumed the role (no one asked me, nor do I deserve this honor) to be America's Voice for Victory for our Veterans which bears the burden of becoming the horsepower to raise billions of dollars to solve the problems of our veteran community.

Maybe I have to start at the beginning of when I think my life was being molded by something much greater than myself. My upbringing was probably a little more comfortable than most children, and I will admit we were a bit better off than many people during the depression years. Both my parents were immigrants from Europe who arrived as children and lived in poverty during their early years where they learned that life isn't always easy for everyone. From the time my father was a very young child, he labored and somehow learned to become a baker. Not just an ordinary youngster baking breads and cakes, but he progressed into becoming the head of the Mayflower Hotel bakery in Washington, D.C., and later simultaneously ran two large wholesale bakeries in N.Y.C. It was there he invented the chocolate-covered doughnut. During World War 2 at the request of the government, he developed the first cake mixes that were shipped overseas to serve our troops. During this time, my Mother had gone to work as a very young girl in a factory stuffing pillows with feathers to make a meager living contributing to her father who worked on a moving truck. She was blessed with extraordinary good looks and an outstanding personality that radiated warmth and charm. To meet her was to love her.

We lived comfortably in a beautiful home, and I never worried where our next meal would come from or if I wouldn't get an increase in my weekly allowance. I went to summer camp from the time I was 5 until I was a counselor at 17. Through all those years I couldn't help but observe that my family took care of our extended family. My father would hire brothers, uncles, cousins and their grown children to work in his food manufacturing factories, while my mother was involved with numerous religious and community charities by volunteering as well as offering generous financial support. Mostly she would shop groceries weekly not only for our immediate needs, but would load the car with every possible food that a family could ever eat. Then she would take me with her when she would drive and unload those bundles of love to our poor family members in different parts of the city. This kind of care and giving from the heart every week of the year left an indelible impression on my tender mind.

I'm listening to a ball game on the radio when the announcer interrupts and says, "We have been attacked and our fleet has been sorely damaged in Pearl Harbor." The world stopped! I was just 16 and immediately wanted to join the military. I was turned down with a "Young man, when you are 18 come back. We want you."

During those long war years the civilians at home sacrificed. Too many houses displayed flags hanging in their windows indicating with a gold star that someone, or ones, in service were fallen heroes. Almost everything was rationed and people had to stand in-line to get meat, sugar, rubber tires, gas, etc. Mom had left the kitchen to replace her husband or son who was off fighting a foreign war and she became "Rosie the Riveter." Everyone embraced the returning troops and not only did they welcome us home with a handshake, but they made every effort to help make the transition into civilian life easier for those of us fortunate to be sound of mind and body.

Compare that caring attitude with today. "Son, if you don't pay the monthly mortgage you are in default and you are on the street. I don't care if your wife is pregnant and you have two kids. You are OUT!" Things have changed, and I recognize that the laws have made the mortgage bankers blind to our veterans needs. This has increased our homeless numbers across America, resulting in divorces, and bankruptcies which may have been the cause of depression and alcohol and substance abuse. Maybe, possibly, even the cause of the rising suicide rate among veterans averaging a horrible 22 per day. This must be addressed, corrected and stopped!

I am not making excuses for anyone, as we all are different and circumstances can create unique problems, but as human beings we cannot turn our backs on those less fortunate than any of us…especially if they have sacrificed while honorably serving our country. We must remember they have courageously served each of us and we must stand-up tall to serve them. Isn't this why we are all commanded to be our brother's keeper?

You have not been totally blessed unless you have had the good fortune of being married to Natalie, my best friend and partner from the time we were literally children. How lucky was I to look across a summer camp campus and see the most beautiful girl in the world. As young as I might have been I quickly and wisely announced that Natalie (BooBoo) would be my wife. A decision I have never regretted and have been able to beam with pride and joy at her every step by my side.

In these turbulent times we have witnessed that too few couples ever find a marriage made in heaven like ours. God has been overly good to us, and in our own individual ways, I pray that we have done our best to be good to God, our loving family and this country we both cherish.

While facing the challenges of writing my first book I learned that my lifetime of varied experiences have taught me that most problems including both personal and political can be solved by using plain, ordinary common sense. In the following pages I will attempt to share my innovative ideas to use which I hope will get you thinking how you can use your common sense.

May we enjoy many productive years in our quest to bring to a successful fruition our shared desire to BACK-OUR-VETS - all 65 million and their families, - who deserve to depend on every American to help provide THE ARSENAL OF HOPE. That makes common sense.

    Earl Littman

> "Bullets are for battle. War is for peace.
> THE ARSENAL OF HOPE
> is a cartridge of caring and love
> to BACK-OUR-VETS."

The Wizard of Common Cents

1946 and Earl comes marching home from World War 2 to the loving arms of my Mom and Dad, and especially to Natalie, the girl I left behind two and half years back. She was even more beautiful now that she was a mature young lady of 18 with her natural blonde hair, green eyes and alabaster skin. No longer was her body that of a young growing girl, but she radiated a sexiness that was overwhelming not only for me, but simply to every man who passed by.

We would walk down the street and strange men's eyes turned. Once on Fifth Avenue in Manhattan as we were strolling along that busy street the famous TV actor and pianist Oscar Levant happened to walk by, he took one quick glance at Natalie and literally stopped in his tracks and exclaimed "WOW!" My father's friends would come to our home while Natalie might be visiting, and their tongues would be hanging out in envy. Who could blame them, because she was the most beautiful girl in the world who I had instantly fallen in love with when I first set eyes on her when she was all of 15.

But Natalie wasn't all I found wonderful in coming back to America. The country was joyous that they won the savage war over tyranny, and ended the horrors of the infamous holocaust where millions of humans were cremated into ashes. Their innocent existence had been turned into a forbidding smoke rising as a grey cloud twisting its crawling path into the heavens above.

Americans were rejoicing over having won a desperately hard fought victory, though the tears never stopped over the fallen heroes and the wounded, battle fatigued warriors. The small flags hanging in the front windows of homes across the land, with a blue star indicating the number of family members in the military, were being stored into memory boxes. We vowed never to forget or leave behind these draftees and military volunteers who saved America from a foe determined to conquer and change our democracy into a total dictatorship.

Mothers who had left the comforts of their homes to replace their husbands and sons going to war were busily leaving their roles as "Rosie the Riveter" to again don their aprons in the kitchens. Rationing of gas, rubber, sugar and other daily provisions were fading from the scene of obligation to help win the war, so Americans were beginning to feel all was right with a free and safe civilized world.

Yet, people of color couldn't eat in the same restaurant that served me, a white man, with open arms; they couldn't use the same public bathrooms; nor drink from the same water fountains; they were banned and not allowed in my classroom at school. Oh yes, ads for jobs read, "Jews need not apply," and the same discriminatory practice prevailed at hotels, as well as colleges and universities, with strict quotas to eliminate or reduce the number of Jewish students and faculty. Women worked under a glass ceiling in business so no matter how talented or smart they had to choose careers as secretaries, nurses or teachers.

Is this what my brothers and sisters in arms had fought to change?

No denying strides have been taken and made to alleviate and correct many of these blots on America, yet we must think and wonder: have we really changed what is in the hearts of many of our citizens?

Today it's 69 years later with discrimination still rearing its ugly head against people of different color; nationalities; sexual; religious; political persuasions; as well as denying women their right to choose. Hatred runs rampant against our President, our government and our basic American ideals and liberties. Have the hooded white sheets and the burning of crosses by the Ku Klux Klan been replaced, by jamming down our throats, new restrictive voting laws to reduce or eliminate the legal right to vote by all our legal citizens? Are women being forced to turn back into the alley ways to use garment hangers to abort an unplanned, or unwanted child, because parenthood clinics have been forced by some political zealots to close down their needed services?

In a land of plenty and abundance is there any reason to have people diving into garbage dumpsters in search of something to eat or literally thousands living on the streets where the rising heat of a sewer tries to keep them warm during winter's cold. While many of us have the luxury of sleeping in the comfort of a warm and cozy bed, too many others are finding refuge under bridges, sleeping on park benches or in the back of an abandoned junk car. Have you ever had to miss a meal or two then maybe you might remember the stomach pangs you felt which too many little boys and girls go off to school in the morning without having nothing to eat because there was not even a scrap of food at home. Those aches and pains burning in your little body keep you from paying attention to the teachers and your mind wanders rather than concentrating on what you are supposed to be learning and studying. Maybe you have a job as a cashier in a giant retail store; or preparing fast order food; or you are slaving throughout the night cleaning office after office, and your take home pay is hardly enough to cover the rent of a cramped-up apartment in a low-rent, crime-ridden part of town. Heaven forbid, you catch something and take sick and haven't any health or medical insurance. Worse yet, a damaging injury or a life threatening disease that will cost a small fortune to treat. Who do you turn to? Who will actually care?

Suppose you are one of the 65 million military members, or a veteran and their beloved families that fell on needy times. The VA repeatedly turned your claims down to help pay for the suffering and injuries of Agent Orange because they knew you were doomed to die early. Your mind is tormented and you can't think straight, memories haunt you during the night of the wounded and the fallen heroes that never escaped the non-discriminatory bombs and bullets, yet you feel guilty that you survived. Why you? So you turn to alcohol and then drugs to try to escape that never-ending nightmare which is a heavy cross weighing down your shoulders. You can't keep a job. Any job. You hang around the house useless to yourself and abusive to your wife and kids until your wife can't take another day.

She leaves taking the kids with her and she runs to her parent's home to try to find some peace and solitude from the man she once loved, worshiped and idolized who was her hero and now is a monster. You are alone with your only companions the bottle and the needle.

It doesn't take too much soul searching to realize that there are too many answerable problems ordinary citizens across America are facing daily. I say "answerable" because not everyone is under the same burdens…the same challenges that too many good people are fighting daily. Those of us who have been blessed to be able to avoid these troublesome cancers that are destroying the lives of so many need to take a moment to think what else can we, should we, be doing to help to relieve the misery and despair of our fellow countrymen?

I am not so blind as to not recognize that many Americans have opened their hearts and pocketbooks to help those less fortunate among us for which I can only say God Bless, and wish there were many more of you. However, is that enough when with more money we could provide additional professional help for the mentally and physically wounded. With more care and concern for one- another we might help raise the standards of life so that no one is left wandering the streets of a life of bewilderment, frustration and devastation.

A strong America shouldn't be dumbing down education; fighting proven climate changes; watching our streets, roadways and bridges crumbling apart; allowing other nations to advance beyond us with more innovative technology; developing faster and safer means of transportation; leading in science, research and medical improvements while we wrestle in our government how not to lead, but to stop our space on planet earth from moving forward as the returning giant of progress.

It's time for me to stop complaining, and to share my humble thoughts on creating the Grandest Generation, but where should I begin?

I'm in the Navy Now

I make no claim as to be a "brain" with a record of scholarship achievements from some of the world's finest educational facilities. My schooling consisted of attending public elementary, middle and high school. I was lucky I didn't flunk finger painting in kindergarten, and my grades were very ordinary. An occasional "A" in subjects I liked, and a barely passing grade in math and foreign languages in which the teachers were being overly generous. I preferred sports, and later as I grew more mature in my likes I discovered girls, but was too shy to know why or how I was attracted to them.

When World War 2 suddenly interrupted America's daily routine of living I was 16 years old, and rushed to the Marine recruiting office to be turned down with the advice to return when I reached 18. My Dad proudly showed the letter to all his business clients from the Marine Commander thanking me for prematurely volunteering, while my Mother breathed a deep sigh of relief. Meanwhile, I was a freshman and then a sophomore attending New York University who was embarrassed that my best friend Sonny was now a U.S. Army parachutist, and Seymour, my closest cousin was serving in the army. I believed that everyone was looking at me, a relatively tall, thin teen-ager, as a draft dodger or a reject as being 4F (physically unfit) to serve our country. The day I turned 18 I volunteered to join the Navy and was on a troop train to the Sampson Naval Base on the Great Lakes for basic training. Immediately, previous life experiences dramatically changed like a blindfold being removed from playing pin-the-tail-on-the-donkey during childhood games.

Like most kids of the time I had lived a very isolated life. Almost every other boy and girl that I knew were carbon copies of me. We were basically all the same skin color, lived with Mom and Dad and had a brother or sister or two, went to the same religious schools, played stoop ball or other school yard activities, and held birthday parties at home under strict parental supervision. Along with my friends we waited every afternoon for the "Good Humor" man to come driving down the street while ringing his car bells to alert us to get ready to enjoy the chocolate covered popsicle we quickly devoured trying to get down to the stick which would indicate if we won a free ice cream treat.

On the train, rumbling north to become a real U.S. sailor, I looked at the other young boys, who were soon to become men, and immediately noticed some of those guys looked and acted differently than all my old friends. Not everyone was white skinned, and their civilian clothes didn't all come from our neighborhood department store. Suddenly, a new world was opening to a spoiled kid from Manhattan Beach, a secluded, residential island off Brooklyn, separated by Sheepshead Bay and boldly shoring the Atlantic Ocean.

I'M IN THE NAVY NOW

In those days rumors would run rampant among the wealthy families living in Manhattan Beach soon after the military had taken over the country club facing the Atlantic that German submarines were seen lurking off the shores. The war was suddenly in our backyard while I am off to boot camp.

"Hi. My name is Earl. I sure am excited about being in the Navy. What's your name and where are you from?"

"You said you're a farm boy. What do you actually do?" "You milk cows! We get our milk in a bottle delivered by the Sheffield man who drives a black wagon drawn by a horse."

And, so it went talking the time away with black, city and country guys some of which had either just finished high school or dropped out. Most expressed total surprise I already had two years of college. "Whatcha' some kinda' genius?"

"Naw, it's just that Nu Yawlk schools are crowded so they skip you ahead to get rid of you," was my simple excuse for not wanting to look too smart or different than all these other young recruits. Try to be one of the guys was my adopted motto, and do what they do...until I quickly learned that wasn't really my style.

It didn't take long to observe when we had a few precious minutes to relax, almost everyone would light up a cigarette or want to gamble at playing card games. Without exception they drank coffee by the tank-full. From the time I was in junior high school where I wanted to play basketball the coach had admonished us to never use any tobacco product with nicotine such as cigarettes, cigars or smoke a pipe; nobody is to have caffeine like in coffee, and never drink alcohol which is beer, liquor or whiskey. If he found you didn't follow his rules, you would be kicked off the team no matter how good a player you were.

Maybe at that early age I was impressionable but I did take him seriously. I made a silent vow that I would not break his code of conduct. Navy, or no Navy, I decided I will do my own thing and not give a darn what all the guys would think. It turned out to be a tough decision for a young 18 year old trying to be one of the boys. They giggled, smirked and laughed at my unusual behavior, and must have agreed among themselves that I was a sissy, and not a "real man". The taunting might have gone on the first few weeks while I was beginning to think maybe these guys were meant to be real Navy men and I must be a wimp. Yet, I stuck to my guns (which sounds like an unintended pun) and never did I go back on my word...until many years later when I would indulge in a really dark beer after running a long and difficult foot race or marathon, and needed to restore the carbohydrates in my tired body. Another time, during my first two years in college I wanted to impress the girls so I took up smoking a pipe to appear sophisticated and worldly. After cleaning the pipe stem a few times with what looked like a long toothpick that had white hairs growing on it, and witnessed the nasty looking tobacco stains I put the pipes away for good. I must confess I also cheated with abusing alcohol during a religious holiday service when having wine was part of the meal. I didn't actually drink the cup of wine, but would put my finger into the glass and then into my mouth for a brief taste. Other than those few infractions I have maintained my vows for over 73 years, and frankly have no regrets while Marlboro, Johnny Walker and Starbucks have never noticed a decline in sales.

Please don't have the mistaken impression I am always Mr. Goody Two Shoes. Somewhere along the line I must have taken a solemn oath to never let anything but chocolate enter my mouth, be it cake, cookies, candy or ice cream.

"Yes, Sir."

At boot camp I was no hot shot with a rifle in comparison to those farm boys who grew-up hunting and shooting, yet I was able to hold my own especially when it came to running around the grinder even while wearing heavy boots and carrying a heavy back pack. I don't remember ever complaining about boot camp, the food or being away from home even though I occasionally would run into a relative that was married, and was totally upset to be away from his wife and family. It paid to be young and stupid because you knew no better.

What I quickly learned was how to behave properly in the Navy system which was to play by their rules written and withheld. Just before we were finished with our basic training we each were called in for a private interview. The person in charge had a dossier detailing our backgrounds both in civilian life and what we might have accomplished during boot camp. I guessed what he might be asking of each of us, "If you have a choice what would you like to be doing in the Navy now that you completed boot camp?" My mind was racing and thinking should I tell him the truth that I would like to be sent to officer candidate school. Instead I took a deep breath and said, "Sir, I will do whatever the Navy wants me to do." He held back a smile, reached for his pen and wrote out his decision which was that I would be assigned to become a hospital corpsman. It didn't take much wonderment to understand why he would have come to that conclusion. When he saw I had two years of college before enlisting he must have assumed that I probably would be able to learn and understand the medical procedures and drugs to be used, so I was designated to become a medic.

Within a few days I was saying goodbye to the friends I had made during those cold January and February days working around and on the Great Lakes. I was headed to much warmer San Diego, California, to learn the skills and responsibilities of being a corpsman while training in the Balboa Hospital. It was truly a blast as San Diego attracted a bevy of Hollywood stars to entertain the troops weekly which made me feel like every weekend was attending a Broadway show and the price was right. I have to admit I felt like I was right at home, but wishing my best girl Natalie would be with me holding my hand, and singing along under the bright moon hanging over the outdoor theatre.

It didn't take long and again I was called into a private meeting with an officer who said, "Littman, I see you were a member of the St. George swimming team while you were in high school." I modestly replied, "Yes, sir," to which he simply said, "Good. I am sending you to UDT in Florida." After mumbling another "Thank you, sir" I left his office not knowing what the heck he was talking about, nor where I was being sent in Florida. I placed the manila envelope under my arm and headed back to my room where without hesitation I opened my instructions as to when and where I was to leave and my destination was Ft. Pierce.

I arrived at Ft. Pierce to find a sign indicating UDT stood for "Underwater Demolition Team". Wow, I didn't think I was brave or courageous enough to do that kind of special work, and couldn't you get hurt or killed? There's no earthly reason for me to describe or go into the details of this training, but it didn't take too long when I thought my body would soon be growing fins. It wasn't too much time after that our group was narrowed down to just two teams of 100 men who were given very special and totally secret training as special combat naked warriors. If I were to elaborate or tell you more I would be forced to kill you. I can say we were assigned to the Pacific and it was an honor to perform our responsibilities to lead the way for our Marines and soldiers. I am the most blessed person to have returned after my tour of duty alive and unharmed physically. Unfortunately, only God knows why too many of my brothers in arms were maimed or became fallen heroes only to leave their blood on foreign shores. Before we left to return to the USA we had to swear and take an oath never to reveal what, where or when we carried out our missions. We were instructed that our records would be permanently altered so that no friend or foe would be able to trace our roles in this war, and that we were advised never to talk about our special service, and to not contact one another as long as we lived for we would be tempted to reminisce and someone may overhear our conversation.

There was many a time during these past 69 years I was tempted to drop a hint or two. Many of our dearest friends had also served during World War 2, and when the guys got together they might start talking about their military experience and exploits. I would listen intently, and with great admiration for their various courageous accomplishments. Everyone was a giant of a hero in my eyes, and I took pride in their service for our country as we all served in different ways. "Hey, Earl, you were in the Navy. What did you do?" I always responded with the same words, "I was a medic". That was it then, and it's the same simple answer today.

I would be remiss not to share with you some memories that remain in my mind and heart. As a medic I was not to directly engage in battle with the enemy. According to international law I could carry a side arm to use only in the case I was in direct and immediate threat of being killed in combat. My conscience is clear that I never shot anyone, but did shoot many a morphine injection in the attempt to help alleviate the pain of a wounded comrade. Our missions were kept so secret that we were never told in advance as to which place, island or country we would be headed until we were aboard a helicopter, destroyer or submarine that delivered us as close as possible to where we had been trained to perform our clandestine duties.

It's really better to keep secrets within a trusted few dedicated patriots.

There's another point I would like to share. I was brought up to obey the Ten Commandments, the ten laws of moral and religious conduct given to Moses by God: Exodus 20:2-17. There are times in our lives when by force or nature we are confronted with circumstances which may be beyond our control. I was luckily spared having to violate the sacred commandment "Thou shall not kill".

Please do not get me wrong. I respect and honor every military man and woman who performed whatever was their task in order to preserve the freedoms of our county while trying to eliminate the evils of our enemies.

Within my body my heart still weeps and bleeds for those wounded in battle that as long as they live to wear the purple vest indicating they are a wounded warrior. How can you ever, ever forget America's bravest fallen heroes who gave their lives for their country? How can we ever forget those who never returned alive to their loved ones? Their memory is a Gold Star on a monument recognizing their sacrifice while a spouse, parent or close kin forever bare an irreplaceable hole in their hearts. They are gone, but hopefully never forgotten by a grateful America.

Very recently my son admonished me that it has been over 69 years since I served, so what is the harm in letting people know more about my experiences in the South Pacific fighting the Japanese forces. My response was simply to remind him that when his Mother and I got married we took a vow to love, honor and obey and have always tried to live a life abiding by those simple commandments. God willing, we will be celebrating our marriage vows of 65 years within less than a month from this writing. Why would I not want to keep my solemn oath with our country?

Let me acquaint you with some background information which will become important as the accordion of my life story later unfolds.

Across my desk I daily stare at two things. One is a silver framed full color photograph of Natalie when she was probably in her late thirties. Grace Kelly and she were amazing look a likes. Absolutely beautiful women that could steal anyone's heart. The other item is a small easel backed poster which always reminds me, "Change is the law of life. And those who look only to the past or present are certain to miss the future." – JFK.

I think admirably of President John F. Kennedy particularly when he delivered a speech in 1961 challenging America that we will dedicate our nation to 'go to the moon! We accepted the challenge and America WE DID IT! What many others may have forgotten is that JFK also promised to begin a new command in the military that he said were standing on the shoulders of the secret combat warriors of World War 2. These clandestine sea, air and land warriors were to be called "SEALS."

Which brings me to what happened next.

America. Home at Last.

I am no longer a Navy hospital corpsman, a medic, listening for the desperate scream " Doc, man down". I am dressed in civilian clothes, finally wearing brown shoes, and am a hopeless P.O.W.

"A Prisoner Of Worship," united again with the most beautiful girl in the world who I worship with my body and soul at her feet. It's been a two and a half year separation with one visit when I was on the East coast in Atlantic City and the other in a hospital on Long Island where I was a patient just weeks before being discharged. There is probably little to compare to young love and the mystery of getting to know and understand one another. It's like finding a treasure of a book in which every page opens a wondrous miracle of newly discovered wealth.

It wouldn't really surprise me that if you met this beautiful blonde that you might think she must be as dumb as she is attractive. Many a school teacher may have had that first impression as they would review her written compositions. Typically they would call her up to their desk and say, "Miss Jacobson, I believe you must be cheating to get a 100% score on this paper. These answers are too perfect!"

Then that shy little girl would reply, "Excuse me, Ma'am... I can prove to you that I never cheat." Without blinking an eye Miss Natalie would quietly repeat every word, paragraph for paragraph, including identifying the commas, punctuation marks and every period from the assignment book. The teacher would be astounded by her photographic memory and amazing record of always earning "A's" throughout her school years. It also stood her in good graces in learning French and Spanish as learning languages always came easy as a cool breeze in a hot Texas summer. Our good Parisian friends Jaque Harland and his wife Brigette always would welcome talking with Natalie in their native language, and repeatedly remarked that she was the only foreigner that spoke like she was born with a French spoon in her mouth. The skill with languages has come in handy for Natalie as the years have gone by. She may hear a song sung once and remembers the words forever and a day where I forget them before the song is ended.

So back to finish our junior and senior years of higher education. Natalie to Hunter College, and I returning back to the School of Business at N.Y.U. When I was 17 I had applied to the Wharton School of Business in Pennsylvania, and was told I would be admitted; however, my Mother suggested I go to an in-city school as I would soon be going into the service and she preferred I be at home before leaving. It's hard to believe how numerous young men and women were returning home after World War 2 with so many wanting to get a college degree. In order to help control the tsunami wave of entrants all the schools gave priority acceptance to those whose studies were interrupted by serving in the armed forces. Much to my disappointment at the time, no school other than N.Y.U. would accept me, so I approved the decision and it was back to Washington Square for the next two years.

Thank you G.I. Bill for the $475 per year to completely cover tuition and books! Unlike today where students are buried in debt which may take years, or forever, to get the loans paid off. I recently read in amazement that the N.Y.U. tuition has sky-rocketed to $28,000 per year. Thank heaven I was there during the late 1940's or I would still be a student wondering if I would ever be able to pay my debt.

These were a very strange two years after being away as an enlisted man conducting activities which previously were un-imaginable. The other students were either too young to have been in the military or others of us were twisted with memories which we would have preferred to forget to be able to concentrate on the books. The professors were generally bor-ing, like wooden sticks, who didn't have the passion of officers who had the lives of the men under their command in their hands. My mind constantly wandered, and I would watch the clouds floating like eagles outside the windows while wonder-ing where they would be drifting around the world. Will those pillows of white fluff carry rain drops to let fall over London, or were they destined to block out the sun over Alaska? The only classes I really enjoyed, and paid attention, were where we discussed advertising, marketing and sales promotion. The pro-fessor was enthusiastic and created a challenge to my psyche. Will I ever be able to overcome the hurdles using written words and pictures to create interest, deliver the benefits of the prod-uct or service, and move the reader to taking action? Could I ever write simple, understandable copy as if I were talking to one individual, rather than the masses, to convince that person to go out and buy whatever I was selling? It certainly sounded easy enough until we had the assignment to write a print ad or radio commercial.

For over two previous years I was writing love letters to Natalie or keeping my parents up to date as to what life in the Navy was all about. There were no limits on how much space or time was allotted with these all too familiar missiles. I wasn't busy trying to "sell" anything, but mainly motivated to alleviate any fears my family or Natalie may have from reading the war news.

You might say I was a zombie going from class to class making little impression upon my teachers or fellow students. I played a little basketball with the School of Commerce team and Natalie was my constant companion attending the games and carrying my gym bag. We took dancing lessons in our free evenings and on weekends. Not to think we would ever be "Dancing With the Stars," but it was a legitimate excuse to be holding each other close while dancing cheek-to-cheek. Our instructor was a suave looking Latin who would repeatedly admonish Natalie to stand-up tall, lift and push out your chest and let the world know how magnificent you look.

My grades were abominable, but I couldn't care less as I was constantly back in the South Pacific yet trying to hide my thoughts from everyone else. It was my way of coping. I smiled and "acted" like any other normal person while my stomach was turning in trying to relive a tension I tried hard to hide. Finally, it was time to graduate, and to this day I wonder why

I never could build-up the courage to attend that celebration which my class-mates talked about incessantly with vigor and anticipation. Was it an inner fear that receiving that Certificate was insignificant in comparison to a flag draped coffin being sent home to a despairing loved one and family?

There is something I have skipped over which earlier also made an indelible impression on my mind and impacted my life from that moment on. It was probably my fourth or fifth week in boot camp and we had gotten permission to call home. Naturally, I called Natalie, and her aunt Stella answered my ring.

"Hi Stella, it's Earl. May I please speak with Natalie?" A quiet, somber voice said "No." Immediately my mind raced ahead, thinking that Natalie fell in love with a mid-shipman from Annapolis, so all I could stammer out was, "Any reason why she won't talk to me?" Then Aunt Stella whispered into the phone, "Her father just passed away." I had only met him once, and knew he was in his very early forties, so I was in shock at this unexpected news. I quickly hung-up the phone and dialed my folks to share the calamitous news which brought about the most unusual response. Without any hesitation, my Mom and Dad took on the responsibility of adopting Natalie as if she were their birth daughter. They recognized that financially Natalie's family would be devastated as Mr. Jacobson was just a Federal employee in a less than meaningful job. They lived in a third floor walk-up apartment occupied by both parents, two daughters and an aunt sharing the small space.

My folks first met Natalie while she was all of 15. The advertising club at N.Y.U. was sponsoring a fund raiser and was selling tickets to a Broadway musical show called "Pajama Game." I bought two tickets, but didn't have a date. Suddenly I thought about the especially pretty girl at summer camp, but didn't know if she would have any idea as to who I was. I was acquainted with one of Natalie's friends from summer camp and asked Corky to call her to see if she might accept a call from me. "Yes," Corky reported that same evening, so I took a great big breath and dialed Natalie's phone. She quickly accepted my invitation to join me Friday evening to attend the show, however because I didn't know the part of the city where she lived, I brazenly asked if she would meet me at the theatre, but I promised I would drive her home.

Friday night I nervously got to the theatre early to plant myself in front of the box office to be able to look at both ends of the street where there were subway exits. It was a cold December evening and the snow started falling heavily when I spotted a young blonde girl wearing a leopard skinned coat walking toward me. It was like a scene from a Norman Rockwell painting and in that instant I knew I was falling head-over-heels in love. After the show I drove her back home and we climbed the fake marble stairs up to the third floor apartment door. I bravely leaned over to say goodnight, and give her a friendly kiss on the cheek when Natalie leaned back and accidentally rang the door bell. The sudden noise of the bell made me jump away and my hand accidentally hit the pearl necklace she was wearing. The string broke sending all the pearls tumbling down the staircase clanging merrily as they went. One after another, apartment doors for three floors suddenly sprung open and the mothers started yelling "Natalie, are you all right?" I was so embarrassed all I could do is hurriedly rush down the staircase to get into my car to escape into the black cover of the night.

The next morning while I am eating my 'Breakfast of Champions,' Mom cheerfully asks, "How was your date last night?"

"Mom, that's the girl I am going to marry!"

After stifling a funny laugh she responded, "Earl dear, there will be hundreds of girls before you are ready to marry."

Just then my Dad walks in and overhears the conversation and he chimes in, "Well son, if you think this young lady is so remarkable then why don't you invite her to the house so that we can meet her?"

I didn't hesitate to run to the phone, "Hi Natalie, can you come to our home this Saturday to meet my folks? They said they would love to have you visit. I can pick you up and drive you down here. O. K.?"

Before you know it, Natalie and I are sitting in my living room with my Mother and Dad along with my seven year younger brother Jerry. After some chit-chat my Dad says, "Natalie, Earl says you would like to be a professional singer. Do you mind singing a song for us?" Here is the cutest, little 15 year old girl, who replies, "I would be happy to, and leaves her chair to stand in the middle of the room."

Without a single moment of hesitation Natalie belts out, "I want to get married. I want to get spliced. See my friends knotted, potted and riced..." the hit song from Pajama Game which she and I went to see only days before. I can never forget what happened next. My Dad turned to my Mother and said, "Cele, that IS the girl Earl will marry." The rest is history.

History from Natalie's Eyes

My friend Corky who was two years older than me, and a mentor to my counselor-in-training at Camp Brookwood in Glen Spey, N.Y., kept telling me all summer about this cute guy on the Boy's campus who was also a counselor. She felt that we would really like one another. Unfortunately, I was in "Kiddie Kastle" situated atop of the hill at Procter and Gambles' former estate, and for one reason or another our paths never crossed all summer.

I was kept too busy taking care of my little 4 to 6 year old charges or socializing with the camp waiters during the evenings of those happy summer weeks. One night in late November Earl called to ask me out. I had been pre-warned by our mutual friend Corrine (Corky) and I accepted his invitation to see a Broadway show. The only drawback was that my parents didn't know him, and he was coming from an island off Brooklyn where he lived. It would be difficult for him to pick me up and for the two of us to make the show schedule.

I don't know how or why till this day I prevailed on my parents to let me go by subway train and meet him at the theatre. But after my Mom spoke to Corky and got her questions answered - both she and Dad consented.

The theater wasn't too far from the subway stop and the walk was short. The snowflakes had begun to fall and as I rounded the corner there was Earl, all rosy cheeked from the cold, dressed in tan corduroy trousers and tan cashmere jacket, and looking clean-cut and very handsome waiting patiently to meet me.

The show had marvelous songs and the lead female star Gertrude Neissen was a 'wow'! I walked out having picked up a few catchy tunes, singing softly...didn't want Earl to think I was a nutty, immature girl of 15. However, with his shared love of music it didn't take long and I was emoting, and he was doing a Fred Astaire imitation down Broadway.

Having just met him, I remember being so enthralled with the evening and my date that we held hands so tightly as if our fists were locked together. Earl drove me home, as promised, and we parked the car at the curb, and he walked me up the three flights of stairs. We really didn't want to say goodnight and end the evening, but as he reached over to give me a kiss and tell me he would call, the pearls I wore (which were snap-ons) broke, and one by one went thumping down the marble stairs. Neighbors immediately began to open their doors to see what mayhem was going on, and when my Mother opened the door Earl who was mortified uttered a fast goodnight and left.

I was busy recounting the evening to my parents and sounding like I was truly smitten when the phone rang. It was Earl asking if I would consider coming to his home and meeting his family. Again I had to ask for permission, but since I was still gushing over all of his attributes, somehow my Dad said he wished he had met this boy, but trusted my judgment.

Off I went to my first look at Manhattan Beach, the quiet island off Brooklyn.

I remember that his family lived in a very beautiful two story home on an esplanade street, and I was immediately impressed by the warmth and friendliness of his folks and kid brother. As we sat around, visiting some cousins came in and again all the introductions were made.

Earl's Dad casually said, "Natalie, I understand you like to sing- would you sing us a song?" Not taking time to think, with no further ado, I got up and sang the song I had been humming since the night Earl and I attended the Broadway hit show. " I want to get married, I want to get spliced, etc." never ever thinking of the implications.

I believe Earl's Mother had a surprised look, but his Dad became my staunch ally and continued that way until the day he died."

Job Search

Turn back the clock to the spring/summer of 1948. Hunter College and New York University are now stored away as alumni memories as it's time to go out into the real world to search for a job. Send out the resumes. Make the phone calls. Knock on doors.

Meantime Natalie and I become engaged and she is wearing the most beautiful engagement ring that my father could afford to buy for me to present to her. We are both gloriously happy as we prepare for the wedding during the upcoming December holiday season. Natalie borrows a beautifully pearl-studded wedding gown from a girl friend, and has it expertly tucked-in here and there to be form fitting. She gets a job with Paramount Pictures to be a secretary to Barney Balaban the head honcho in their New York offices because she not only speaks fluent French, but her good looks portray a look of Hollywood ultra personified. It's a temporary job to Natalie as she's more interested in the wedding day.

Meanwhile, I am wearing out my shoe leather going from one

ad agency to another, from one recruitment agency to another, from one library to another researching potential businesses or agencies that may want to hire an inexperienced nobody with little attributes other than having a magnificent looking fiancée.

There was a silent code among most of us in college that we wouldn't get married until we graduated. We said no kids, no shot-gun weddings, just abstinence, limited to holding hands and stealing kisses. This wasn't based on religious doctrine. It was just plain old common sense. To keep ourselves occupied we would go out on double dates with longtime buddies and their significant others who were usually engaged to one another just like us. Our delays in actually getting married was that we were all looking for jobs, or had just started a new one, and were waiting to see how things might progress before announcing the wedding date.

After most of the big, well-established advertising agencies either never responded or turned me flat down, I finally cracked the door open with a relatively small agency located on the 34th floor of the Empire State Building. They specialized in doing barter advertising with hotels and vacation resorts which primarily were in Florida. It wasn't the job I had hoped for, but it was an opportunity for me to learn and have some experience I could add to a woefully short business resume. To show how totally unaware of the real business experience of working in an ad agency, within the first few days I was introduced to the lady who was the bookkeeper. Today she might be called the Senior Financial Administrator, but things back then weren't so fancy-schmantzy, but simply down-to-earth.

The lady was very nice and explained the standard ad agency billing procedures and how they earned net revenue. Most every agency at the time earned 15% commission paid by the media to the agency for the ads they placed with the print publications (newspapers, magazines and outdoor billboards) or radio stations (TV wasn't invented for commercial use yet), and the production of the ads was based on our time and cost of materials at 17.65% to earn the net 15%. I was a total nincompoop in school when it came to math, and why we were charging 15% on media and 17.65% on production to earn 15% was beyond my comprehension. Hadn't we told our clients we earn 15% of what our billing is to them so why the two different figures? Were we being dishonest? Could we go to jail for fraud? The lady was about to jump out of the 34th floor window at my ineptitude in understanding basic arithmetic, but she patiently kept trying to make me understand this simple concept before thinking she ought to take pity on me by throwing me out the window as well as ending my brief advertising career.

Much to her surprise, as well as the two brothers that owned the place, I soon caught on to how the barter system worked and was progressing along nicely, but my young mind and creative juices weren't being challenged. However being young and hopeful, I began looking for another opportunity which struck me like a Mohammed Ali blow to the head.

What's to stop me from getting a really big and famous national advertising account?

Out of sheer naive understanding of how to acquire new business, I decided I would call on the American Tobacco Company as there were few bigger national advertisers. I bravely walked to their headquarter building, went inside, got on the elevator and pressed the button to their executive floor.

The office seemed as big as a football field where I was greeted by the receptionist who asked with whom I had an appointment. I responded with one of the most famous business names of the day, and chairman, "I would like to see Mr. Vincent Riggio." "Do you have an appointment?" she asked, to which I responded, "I will wait." With a slight shrug of her shoulders she motioned me to sit in one of the couches lining the room.

I walked past the other more mature, well attired gentlemen also waiting, and sat down alone to think about what I might say to Mr. Riggio. There were end tables between the couches, and in clear crystal glass containers were cigarettes which all the other people were using to casually blow Lucky Strike smoke signals into the air. "Should I or shouldn't I?" kept running through my head, and I finally decided I would get sick and start coughing my lungs out if I tried one cigarette.

The hours were clicking away as one person after another disappeared into Mr. Riggio's private chamber. I was sitting there all alone wondering if the staff would all soon go home, the receptionist said, "Mr. Riggio will see you now. Please go into his office, and wait for him to greet you."

Oh, oh, had I made a mistake? Maybe I should just turn around and get on the elevator and disappear, when I said to myself, "He can't be worse than a Jap with a bayonet charging directly at you, knock on the wood panel door, turn the knob and walk in. So what if your knees are shaking like a shimmering bowl of Jell-O?"

Two steps more , and I am in the office looking across at a man sitting behind a mahogany desk bigger than my car. He picks his face up and looks directly at me and I see an exact replica of my father. Small of stature, wiry build, thinning gray hair and piercing, intent eyes who after sizing me up-and-down smiles, and says, "Please sit down young man and tell me what you want."

I am totally taken aback and forgot the speech I was practicing in my mind while in the waiting room, and was able to simply blurt out, "I want your advertising business." Mr. Riggio didn't burst out laughing or fall to the floor with cardiac arrest. He simply explained how important advertising was to all his brands, and he had to have the biggest, best, brightest, and most experienced advertising agencies devoted to help sell their many brands. He patiently went on to explain the American Tobacco's needs to remain the dominant factor in his industry. Then this titian of industry said something which I can never wipe out of my mind. "Son, I admire your spirit and courage to do what no other young person has ever done by calling on me unannounced, so I will give you an opportunity to work with us. I want you to have the chance to work with us by representing our foreign language newspapers in America. We advertise in the Italian, Polish, Irish, German, French, Jewish, Catholic, Latin and other secular newspapers, so tomorrow call my secretary, and she will give you the name of the man I want you to see in our advertising department. Thanks for your visit, your service, and Good Luck."

I couldn't believe it then, and I still wonder at my good fortune now. By then it was late of day, so I hurried home and could hardly wait to get into the office in the morning to report my unbelievable success. I didn't know, or care, how much money this would bring into the agency. All I could think of was how important it would be to have the behemoth American To-bacco Company as a client.

"Unbelievable!" That was exactly how my bosses reacted when I retold this meeting with Mr. Riggio.

"Incredible! Earl, are you drinking? Dreaming? What kind of cock 'n bull story is this? Forget it and get back to work. Now!"

Shaken and disappointed I decided at that moment I needed out of this place, to look for a new job where doubt would be replaced with trust, and search for that illusive rainbow leading to a pot of gold.

The Music Man

It wasn't a leprechaun but opportunity soon landed in my lap. I went to work for another independent agency which was run by a husband and wife team who had a stable of relatively large clients mostly in the fashion business. The companies they represented weren't the giants such as Coca-Cola, General Mills or Ford Motors, but their roster included Madame Alexander Dolls, Wonder Bras, a relatively famous new panty hose Danskin, and other brands that most people would recognize.

In very short order I realized that the two principals were as phony as a three dollar bill. They feigned an English brogue and dressed accordingly though they were born and raised on a street with a tree in Brooklyn. The lady always wore a wide brimmed hat and I can't remember if she ever took it off either in the office or out. They claimed they were Christian Scientists, and to prove it to the troops at Christmas time, if any employee were to receive a gift of a bottle of spirits the agency owners would confiscate the bottle, and made a great show of spilling the gift of alcohol down the sink.

I just was never comfortable with their ethics or moral code of conduct. I did enjoy though working on some of the clients such as Goshen Manufacturing, which was located in Indiana, and manufactured sturdy wooden ladders and the very popular garden swings of two benches across from one another that had a charming green canvas roof. Thomasville Furniture in the Carolinas was another of my accounts, and the trips to the furniture markets were exciting.

I was responsible for acquiring the Cashew Nut Manufacturers Association account, and loved writing the radio commercial and producing it. ("Down in the tropics where cashews grow, where the sun shines and the trade winds blow..."). Then I was responsible for acquiring an inexpensive wine product Chateau Martin that I also created the radio campaign... ("I'm nuts about the Chateau Martin wine, 'Z' flavor and 'Z' taste so divine..."). Irving Berlin, Cole Porter and the Gershwin brothers never had to worry about their latest Tin Pan Alley rival.

Much to my surprise, the agency management didn't complain about the revenue this wine company generated, but I felt this was a bit two-faced. Money talks.

I have to admit I tried as often as possible to go to all the meetings which another account executive had with his client the manufacturer of the Wonder Bras. The models were all young and attractive so the meetings turned pleasure before business. It's been years since, but I can never forget the owner's unique name – Hy Pilot, nor those beautiful, half-dressed girls who never even asked my name.

Public morals then were much more stringent than today. The

agency designed a full page ad to run in LOOK Magazine. They posed a woman lying on her back with her legs spread apart as if she were riding a bicycle to show the first seamless Danskin panty hose. The ad never ran because the magazine publisher censored it as being too risqué. Lady GaGa would have GaGagged at a similar prudent ruling today.

One time the big boss asked me to accompany him on a new business presentation to Midas Watch Company on Fifth Avenue. We had a film presentation which he wanted to show so I was to carry the large projector which weighed more than my 150 pounds.

In those days a film projector had two reels. One on top which held the film and the other at the bottom of the projector was for rewinding the film. The film was carefully placed behind a spring loaded metal cover onto two rows of small sprockets in front of the bulb which would project the pictures on a portable screen which I also had schlepped to the meeting.

I hooked up this complicated monster, plugged in the electric cords and speaker, waiting for my bosses English accent to command, "ROLL it, Earl."

I did.

The film was not tied in properly to the bottom reel so it sure did ROLL--- all across the prospective clients' Oriental rug making a horrendous heap-of-a-mess as well as messing up the important new business presentation. I was embarrassed. I had no legitimate excuse and my boss was furious. My days at that agency were numbered and I never heard that foul language from anyone since leaving the military service.

I started looking for a new job, and somehow good fortune was working for a newlywed guy who could use a break.

Thank you, God.

The Bells Are Ringing

How could I ever have missed telling about the happiest day of my life? The day was set as December 21, 1948, for Natalie's and my wedding day. We were two excited young people making all the usual arrangements such as who was to be the best man and the bridesmaids, the ushers as well as the caterer, and what appeared like a mountain of minutiae to be done in preparation. The choice of the groom's best man was easy as I always looked up to my Father's youngest brother who was a popular athlete playing baseball and ice hockey in high school, and in Brooklyn College where he was a pole-vaulter.

Natalie had it equally easy as her younger sister Seena was an equally easy choice to be her best maid. Natalie's bevy of stunning sorority sisters from Delta Phi Epsilon were chosen to be bridesmaids.

The caterer was also an easy decision as her Mom was related to one of the largest and most outstanding caterers in New York City who would create a marvelous meal yet, would keep the cost most affordable recognizing the financial state of Natalie's widowed mother.

Remember it was late December and the weather decided to play fun and games by snowing up a storm and blanketed the East coast. My folks had bought a home on top of a hill in West Hempstead, Long Island and there was a long, very long, curving drive from the street to the front door of the house. We were snowed in with no way out to attend the long anticipated wedding. My Mom called the highway patrol and relayed our predicament. They responded that they would clear the street and then the drive to the highway leading us back to the city, but there was no way they can clean off the snow on our private drive from the house to the street. Earl came to the rescue on the morning of his wedding day, by shoveling, shoveling, and shoveling what seemed like tons of snow off the drive way to allow our auto to get down to the street where the giant snow plow led us safely to the highway of escape to Brooklyn and the place of the wedding ceremony.

Not very long after the organ struck up I was walking down the aisle in my rented tuxedo with my mother and dad in tow. I towered over both parents, especially with the tall top-hat I wore so that in looking at the photographs it looks like I am carrying two pieces of luggage down the carpet while wearing a nervous looking smile.

On the other hand, Natalie was radiant with her cheeks rosy from blushing with joy and her Uncle was proudly doing the honors. Every guest was standing and you could hear the murmur of whispers repeating, "Have you ever seen such a lovely bride? She is prettier than any picture. My God she IS beautiful beyond belief."

The rest of the ceremony is still a jumble in my mind. My heart was beating so loudly I thought no one, including me, could hear the Rabbi as he made the blessings. When it came to placing the ring on Natalie's finger my hands were shaking so much I thought she will be the first bride wearing a marriage ring on her left thumb. When I heard everyone shout "Mazel Tov" (good luck) after I smashed the napkin wrapped glass placed on the floor with my right foot. I had hit the glass so hard that I could only limp for the next week. The shock of the glass shattering under my foot made me realize we were now 'Mr. and Mrs.' I wasn't too shaken-up that I didn't plant a great big kiss on her lips while the audience started clapping so loudly you would have thought we had just won the Super Bowl, World Series and the Noble Peace Prize.

Later that evening the two married lovers checked into the luxurious EsSEX Hotel, across from Central Park while the snow danced its magic through the moonlight. It was a day and night we will always remember, and treasure its romantic memories. However, my back still aches from shoveling that Mt. Everest of snow just 65 short years ago.

Home Sweat Home

Now that we are two it's time to think of a house. We found our small cottage about half-a mile away from my parent's home on the hill in the town of West Hempstead, Long Island. Unlike today, this new development in a suburb of N.Y.C. was a former potato farm that a developer planned a single row of newly built homes soon to be occupied primarily by ex-G.I.'s. Today's price for a similar home might be in the $250,000 range where our 4% interest G.I. Bill mortgage, with no money down cost (how can we afford it?) $14,500. Every home looked fairly much alike, with a ground floor for living, and a stairwell leading up to an unfinished expansion attic that some day in the future might be converted into bedrooms for the yet unborn children to occupy. Many of the twenty or so families living on Redmont Road were a few years older than Natalie and me, but we all shared an experience of having served during the war. Our neighbor directly across the street was working at Cunningham and Walsh, a major ad agency, and there was one more guy engaged in advertising so there was a built-in comradeship for the young kid who was breaking into the advertising world.

Down the street there was the nicest of couples that had just purchased a Charles Atlas retail franchise. Just next door on our right, the man worked in the garment industry in sales. Every woman was a stay-at-home Mom...not all mothers, as yet, but give them time.

Behind us was a big piece of land with a lone home occupied by a former Air Force pilot now employed by a commercial airline. No home builder developer had bought his land at the time which eventually gave way to the bulldozers clearing the towering trees for more growth and prosperity.

As you walked into our home through the fire engine red painted door, the stair well going upstairs was on the right, and you immediately were in the living room on the left. We had been gifted a hand crafted cobbler's bench which sat in front of the brick fronted fireplace. The rest of the furniture, three red wood outdoor lawn chairs with green canvas cloth pillows on which to sit, was all we could afford. You were lucky if the iron springs didn't catch your pants, or skin, while you were trying to get out of the chairs. We were living dangerously.

Attached to the living room was our dining room that had a painted white wainscot. I have forgotten how we scraped up enough money to have the walls covered with a colorful paper depicting an outdoor hunting scene, but since the room was so teensy-weensy it couldn't have cost more than a small wedding gift. My parents had bought six black dining room chairs with gold trim for us which we still use in our current dining room though they have been recovered more often than a movie star's face lifts. We had an all-white, sterile looking kitchen with a GE refrigerator that had the round cooling coils on top, and a free standing oven and range. The largest room was our bedroom. No, it wasn't the Master Bedroom. It was the ONLY bedroom of size. My folks generously came to our rescue by providing the bed with headboard, two end tables and two dressers which we still cherish as they enjoy a place of honor in our current master bedroom. There were two closets and one bathroom plus another itsy-bitsy closet size and guest room. This was our honeymooner's castle in the burbs.

To get to work in the big city you had to drive, or get a lift, to the quaint little railroad station in what might be called down-town W. Hempstead, which consisted of the lone (I was about to write "loan") neighborhood bank. Fare on the "rarely-on-time" Long Island Railroad was $60 a month, which bled our anemic wallet when my salary was $65 gross per week. How did we ever get by without food stamps, or other welfare bene-fits? We pinched every penny until Abraham Lincoln screamed in pain. We walked when we could have driven so as not to burn gas. We ate at home, and listened to the radio instead of heading to the movies unless it was Thursday night when they gave you free dinnerware, one piece at a time. We skimped and saved, we sweated every penny spent, and we were in love.

We thanked our lucky stars that when we closed our G.I. home loan at the bank, the banker generously offered that we could pay the interest monthly and forget the principal which he knew his bank would get back whenever we sold the house.

As I fondly look back at his unexpected generosity, understand-ing and concern, for a veteran and his young bride, it made the sacrifice of time serving our nation our finest reward.

May our savior rest in eternal peace.

Somewhere inside my body someone must have planted the spirit of entrepreneurship. During whatever spare time I could muster I decided to invent, produce, and market some consumer products which I dreamed would make me rich. Unlike my home in Manhattan Beach that had city sewers, our new country home depended on a cesspool. I learned quickly that they could clog and to remedy the situation would take a ton of money.

After doing some research I discovered that yeast could help dissolve human waste. Why not package powdered yeast and sell it as "NO-CLOG"? Televisions were just being introduced into the consumer market, and they all had screens. Why not create a window cleaner and sell it as "SKREEN CLEAN"? Every lady wore white gloves and the men all had brown leather gloves. Why not produce a glove cleaner, and sell it as "GLOVE LOVE"?

I took a few bucks of money put-aside from my Navy days and bought some ad posters inside the Long Island railroad passenger cars to help build brand identity for "NO-CLOG." In very short order I received a cease and desist from a company making a product for cleaning commercial laundry equipment called 'No-Klog.' They threatened to sue, which shattered my poor-man's dream of becoming the next Procter & Gamble.

New Job. New Place. New Career.

I read in the classified section of the "New York Times" of an opportunity to be an Advertising Director of a major manufacturer of building products in Pittsburgh, Pa. I applied as I thought it would be a smart career move to have both agency and client experience. At the same time, I had come to the realization that the Mad Men world in New York wasn't necessarily my cup of tea. Drinking, smoking, running around chasing broads wasn't my game. The falsehoods, cheating, stabbing you-in-the-back lifestyle was gnawing at my conscience. Maybe I needed a change.

Maybe it's me that's wrong. Every one of my family, friends, and business associates keeps on saying, "If you can't make it here, you can't make it anywhere." Am I running away only to make a bigger mistake? I'm puzzled, confused and worried terribly what to do.

Much to my great surprise the owner of the company in Pittsburgh called to say they were looking to replace their current advertising person, and would I really be interested in moving?

Before he could hang up the phone, I was getting my air ticket to Pittsburgh. When we met he offered me $15,000 a year to start. I was in hog heaven, because the advertising campaign for the esteemed WALL STREET JOURNAL read "If you want to make $15,000 a year read the Wall Street Journal."

I was now to be a proud middle class American.

Meantime, a lot was happening with the Littman's. On March 13th, 1950, the stork delivered our daughter Erica and quickly made a return trip to help make a happy foursome with the arrival of baby Bonnie on June 18th, 1952.

I had to move solo to Pittsburgh to begin the new job at Jones & Brown, and find a home for my growing family. The day finally arrived for Natalie and our two little girls to fly into the Pittsburgh airport. I eagerly waited at the cyclone fence separating me from the arriving airplane when it taxies up to the gate. Most of the stream of passengers debark by climbing down the long flight of metal stairs when a very harried looking Natalie finally appears in the door way cradling baby Bonnie in one arm and leading little Erica with the other hand. Her purse and diaper bag are slung over both shoulders. She struggles slowly down the stairs one hesitant step at a time when suddenly the crowd gathering at the gate to board for the next flight loudly gasps.

What happened was that Natalie's pink under- slip was literally slipping from her waist down, past her knees, to her shoes as she was protecting her two girls from getting hurt while deliberately descending to the waiting tarmac below. I didn't know if I should run away or run to her to help. I chose to take both the kids from her arms as she slipped the slip into her hand bag. We kissed and moved on to our new home.

Not knowing very much about Pittsburgh, I decided it might be best to rent a home in Mt. Lebanon. It was a fast-growing area where many young families, who had been born and raised in the bustling city of Pittsburgh, had decided to emigrate as it was close enough to be near their families, yet it had the feeling of country living. The rental home was plain vanilla, and was situated on the main road leading in and out of Mt. Lebanon. We didn't waste much time or money in trying to make it any more than a temporary nest to stay while scouting for something more cozy and permanent. Our effort paid off quickly and we moved into a very lovely home situated on the top of the hill for which Pittsburgh was famous. Walking those hills was what accounted for all the ladies having firm and beautiful legs. Not that I ever noticed.

We had a fenced in yard in which two little girls could romp around in safety. What really was nice is the homes on the street were occupied by young couples with small children, Having kids at that stage is a magnet drawing each family to bond as one. The young mothers would gather like bees to honey and formed a colleague of fast friends with mutual interests. Though we haven't lived there since the mid nineteen fifties, Natalie and some of the now mature ladies continue exchanging news via telephone every week. They no longer talk of little babies, but great grandchildren, and the universities their grandsons and granddaughters attend.

The city of steel had opened its heart to my family for which we remain grateful.

Jones & Brown was a surprise. Pittsburgh was their main office, but they had manufacturing plants in Indiana and Puerto Rico where they made asphalt-coated siding which was called "Inselbric." The products were sold nationally through independent siding contractors and home remodelers. We had our own corporate sales force headed up by an imposing gentleman of Dutch heritage named Bill Sauer. He was tall, wide as a football tackle, and had blue eyes which cut like a laser tool. His voice was like a thunderstorm which could rattle your bones. He took an immediate dislike to me as he was both friend and admirer of the previous advertising director whom I replaced. Bill didn't talk to me. He scowled. He frowned or rolled his eyes at every suggestion I offered. He made my every day at the office as uncomfortable as possible until one day I was so fed up with his cruddy attitude I blurted out an old Navy expression, "Go blow it out of your ditty bag." Instead of getting mad, Bill roared back, "I was wondering when you would talk back to me?" with which he started laughing, his baby blues flashing like a signal light, and gave me a big bear like hug. From that moment on he was my best friend and mentor.

Bill would ask me to go with him on sales calls. I would be ready to present my business card to try to impress our prospect, and he would admonish me to never do that again. "Why, Bill? Then he knows my name." to which he would say, "Yeah, and he plays with your card the rest of the meeting instead of looking directly at you and listening to what you have to say." I never made that mistake again. One time we were calling on a large building materials distributor who during the course of the conversation asked what we know about one of our major competitors, The Cellulose Company. I immediately tried being polite and jumped in with, "They are a fine, large company with a great line of products…"

When we got back in the car Bill turned to me and blisterdly said, "Next time someone asks about any of our competitors don't you ever say anything. Not a word. Keep your damn mouth shut. Tight!"

"But, Bill, I was trying to politely tell him my opinion. What harm could that do?"

"Kid, did you ever think he might hate the company you name because they had an argument or something worse? You just confirmed that you and he disagree. Next time stay quiet, and let the question die."

A confrontation like that would bring out the Dutchman in him, and his face would turn beet red and bloated, but that too soon passed as I learned a valuable life-time lesson from an experienced "hard knocked" street salesman that had been successfully fighting fires with his bare hands. Another lesson he taught me was where to sit a customer we were taking to lunch. He always took the seat against the wall and made sure the guest was directly across the table from him where his eyes were either on Bill or the blank wall behind him. He wouldn't allow the guest to be distracted by who else was coming into the restaurant, or anything to disrupt his attention from their conversation. Lessons taught and learned by me who was his sponge.

Bill could be the sweetest, most grandfatherly person every time he would meet my two little girls. "Here's some money,

Erica and Bonnie, to buy yourselves some ice cream or candy.
Uncle Bill loves you."

Jones and Brown had an advertising agency, and the principal
was a friend of our President. I didn't know how the gentleman
would act toward the new advertising director. His name was
Julius, and he didn't look or act like the account executives
I knew in New York. He was just an ordinary guy, without
any airs, who could have been my next door neighbor in the
dress business. But, I soon learned he was smart and knew our
business as well, or better, than anyone working a longtime at
Jones & Brown. He took me under-his-wing and diligently
taught me the ropes of how to get things done so that they
would be approved, as well as liked, by top management. We
didn't do a lot of direct consumer advertising except for producing co-op ads placed by the dealers featuring our products.
I quickly learned how to make each ad produce sales otherwise
holy heck would be ringing over the telephone. Our customers
weren't sheep. They were roaring lions. We produced all kinds
of promotional materials the sales reps would use in consumers' homes to turn a lead into a profitable immediate sale. There
were no computers, or means of producing sales literature electronically. You had to develop a "pitch" that would work in
full-color printed literature guaranteed to open doors, and you
better be good at selling these pieces during sales meetings to a
rowdy bunch of know-it-all, door-to-door bangers. I was learning a different style of advertising created in a crucible of fire,
and if it didn't produce sales, you can bet your life you would
be tossed into those flames and be fired…for real!

Within the first two years of being ad director at Jones & Brown
I had entered a contest sponsored by the Industrial Advertising

Association, and amazingly was notified I was to be named: "The Industrial Advertising Man of the Year." I couldn't wait to run down to the President's office on the floor below to announce my good fortune. Patsy R. looked at me and shook his head, "Oh sure. It's just a gimmick to get you, and the company, to make a donation. Kid, don't be so gullible."

I was still smarting from his remark and rebuke when the invitation arrived welcoming me to attend a dinner in my honor, and receive the $1,000 check. I kept the money, and took the Award Certificate to hang in the empty space that my College Degree should have filled.

Jones & Brown had been formed by two partners (neither name being Jones or Brown) who many years later after they were both multi-millionaires had a SPAT. No, it was more than that. It was an all-out WAR. One partner, Patsy R. continued running the business, while an armed guard was posted daily at our front entrance to bar the errant partner from entering the building. It felt as if I had never left the South Pacific, because you were under instructions that if you were ever seen or found talking to the "bad guy" partner it meant automatic job dismissal. No discussions allowed. You were gone and soon forgotten. Could that have been what happened to my predecessor who no one ever spoke about after my arrival?

By this time, I was beginning to know what it was like to be an advertising director in a bureaucratic organization, and more or less repeating the same assignments, with the same company for the rest of my business career until retirement. This isn't what I had dreamed I wanted to follow as my hair turned gray, so I welcomed an unexpected phone call.

Texas Here We Are: Lox, Stock and Bagels.

"Hello, Earl, you old son-of-a gun. You gotta' remember me. Vernon, who used to work at Jones & Brown in sales. You know the good lookin' sonov'-a-bitch, woman chaser (laughs hysterically). I'm here in good 'ole Texas. You know, Houston – and I'm working for some giant company – Consolidated General Products, they make all kinds of shit, like venetian blinds, all kinds 'a window coverings, attic fans, aluminum boats, and they're going to start making asphalt and aluminum siding to compete with that screwed up armed camp Jones & Brown. Our big guy, Mr. James tells me…they need an advertising big shit, so I recommended you. You and your family. How'r the kids? And your doll wife will love it here. Real down-to-earth, friendly conservative folks, not like that steel trash in Pittsburgh."

What do I have to lose, so I went home and broke the news to Natalie. "Earl, if that's what you want to do, then go down and visit with that Mr. James and see what he has in mind and what his offer might be. You have had your belly-full where you are now. The girls and I will do whatever you think is best."

TEXAS HERE WE ARE: LOX, STOCK AND BAGELS.

Can you wonder why I love her?

It's a Sunday. Next thing you know I am landing at Hobby Airport in Houston. The door from the plane opens wide. And you immediately get a blast of hot, humid air which reminds you of crossing the Equator. Jump in a cab and look out the window at this strange land. Disappointedly there are no cowboys, no cattle nor any desert, not even a horse to be seen, but what are all those ditches on the side of the streets? Don't they have any sewers?

The taxi takes me to a beautiful Colonial mansion with white soaring Grecian columns which is Mr. James address on River Oaks Boulevard. I approach the front door and ring the bell. A starched white clad maid peeks out from around the door and says, "Are you Mr. Littman? Mr. James was expecting you, but he's not home. He is at his place on Clear Lake and asked you to come to his office tomorrow morning at nine when he would like to talk with you."

Here I am, stranded in a strange city wondering about the Texas famed hospitality?

Who does this Mr. James think he is? Maybe he's the for real JESSIE James.

Next morning I get to the honest-to-goodness Mr. James' offices which are a series of five story yellow brick buildings that look like an old school, and are located in an area known as The Heights. The campus impressively fills-up a whole city block. There are lots of one story homes surrounding the place occupied by what obviously look like salt-of-the-earth blue collar families. Consolidated General Products main entrance is located in the major building topped with a square brick tower holding a giant clock that announces every hour with a bell like sound. I go in and ask to see Mr. James and am told he is waiting to see me. I think, well this is a little more promising than yesterday which encourages me to enter this elusive personal domain of Mr. James.

(He's not Jesse as he isn't wearing the expected black mask.)

We introduce ourselves, and I receive no apology for yesterday's mishap except a lame excuse that he had gone out on his yacht to go fishing with his family since the weather was so welcome. We get down to discuss business and Mr. James explains that he has three different advertising agencies representing his various business enterprises, and if I would open my own agency in Houston, I can take over all of the Consolidated advertising business.

Is this how dreams come true? My own advertising agency! I pinched myself, put out my hand to shake his, and was able to get out a whisper: "We've got a deal."

As I left the place to get a cab back to the airport, I remembered an old Western movie where the cowboys sang: "Yippee-ky-yay." I started singing the Yippee song all the way back to Hobby Airport...or, should this happy camper say, "Heavenly Airport?"

Time Out for a Commercial

While tossing and turning last night thinking about writing this memoir, or is it an auto-biography which was supposed to be a persuasive piece on politics and the miss-Stake of the Union, what would happen if my great-grandchildren ever read this book?

Let's assume instead of being three and six years old they were in high school and found these pages hidden in the back of a closet collecting a cover of dust. Would they understand that in my 87 years on earth things had changed so much that it was difficult to lift and search your memory to remember how it used to be?

Could they actually imagine me going to school sitting at a wooden desk with an open ink well in the upper right-hand corner where we would dip a feathered pen from which to write? This primitive pen was replaced with a Waterman's fountain pen where we dipped the point of the pen into the ink well, pulled a little lever on the side of the pen which filled the barrel with ink from which to write. Then someone invented the Bic ball point pen where we dropped in a small wire-like cartridge that would write without liquid ink. It wasn't too much later that we had a funny looking machine called an Underwood typewriter where you pressed keys that had letters printed on them to spell out and print whatever you wanted onto a single piece of paper. If you needed copies you would use a blue sheet of carbon paper making sure you didn't get the blue carbon smeared on your fingers because it was tough to wash off. This was soon replaced by an electric IBM typewriter which could speed-up the process of printing, until lo-and-behold a young Turk in California, working out of his home garage, develops something called the computer that revolutionizes the whole world of communications.

Meantime things were rapidly changing in the auto industry. As a young boy, the first cars I remember had to be cranked-up to get the motor to start coughing before working. That was grown-up work because the crank, unless the right amount of pressure was applied, could back-fire, and hurt or break your fist or arm.

I can remember that our family was one of the first in our neck-of-the-woods to have a luxury automobile other than the Henry Ford tin-lizzy. It was a big, black Packard, with giant size headlights, and an ornate chrome ornament on the front hood. To drive it, you had to put your foot down on one of the floor pedals and pull on a floor shift to make it go either front or backwards. The tires were huge and had gleaming white side-walls. Everywhere we went people would stop and look and want to feel this sturdy car made of real steel. What really made eyes turn and mouths gape was that my Mother was one of the first ladies that learned how to drive. We also owned a small car called the Sunbeam. It was painted yellow as the sun and sat two; but best of all for a young kid, it had a rumble seat in which you pulled open the back of a rear trunk, climbed in and sat in the open with the wind blowing through your hair while either freezing or sweating depending on the weather. Rain was when you ducked inside.

In our luxury Packard there was no air conditioning except to crack open a side vent window. We rolled the windows up and down by turning a small lever inside the car. To indicate you were going to make a turn, you put your arm out the window and pointed whether you were going left or right. I can't remember having a built-in radio until many years later, and GPS was the furthest thing from our minds.

To plan a trip, you used a road map which the local gas station was glad to provide so the glove compartment was always stuffed full with every brand of gas maps. The price of gas went from a nickel a gallon to an astronomical 25 cents a gallon. Today I break into a case of hives while watching the gauge on the gas pump climb above $3.50 a gallon before I have to drive to the bank to be sure my credit card will be honored. Did you just ask me, "What's a credit card?"

Probably, though many things had changed, the waging of war was most dramatic. When America was first discovered by foreigners, the Indian natives were using bows and arrows to hunt or fight one another. We introduced rifles and battle has never been the same. Try to imagine what a native American warrior in those years might think if he saw one of today's armored tanks firing multiple ballistics for miles with pin-point accuracy; or a jet airplane flying at sound-breaking speed, or helicopters able to fly horizontally, or up-and-down vertically like an elevator rising just on air. Instead of animal skin covered canoes carrying native warriors, we have replaced their boats with battleships or air carriers capable of delivering death at unbelievable distances. Could they ever believe man could live and travel underwater for days and weeks covering thousands of miles in a submarine to deliver a torpedo that can instantly destroy a ship as large as a floating city?

More personally, what would I have given if the clumsy, big box of a radio we lugged onto the beaches of the island we were attempting to liberate during World War 2 might have been able to send a satellite signal to a surgeon that could have guided me to help save a courageous wounded warrior's life.

The conduct of war changed civilization 360 degrees when America dropped the nuclear bombs on two different cities in Japan causing mass devastation and untold deaths in 1945. Japan surrendered and ended the war. And, now through even more sophisticated technology someone sitting in an isolated facility in Houston can electronically maneuver and direct a drone to target and kill a single terrorist leader who is hiding somewhere on the other side of the earth.

Children, I am not complaining. I am simply reporting that from time immemorial life and civilizations have changed for both the greater good as well as unfortunately the bad. I, along with probably billions of earth's inhabitants, would prefer to change the world for the better.

I am counting on your generation to do your part in finding a just peace worldwide where we are all neighbors living in harmony, and respect for each other. Impossible? Not really when you think how each generation has matured to make positive changes for our greater good.

Try to Guess Who...

A true story which best illustrates how evil intent can also be harnessed to bring happiness, peace and joy to every living being. Before Germany, under the despicable dictatorship of Adolph Hitler, openly declared war against most of Europe, he was befriended by one of his country's leading munitions manufacturers who was married to one of the world's most beautiful women, a German – secret Jewess.

The manufacturer and Hitler became great friends and shared many a fine dinner feast together while the munitions manufacturer was always accompanied by his trophy wife. While he engaged Hitler with his dream of creating missiles that would be able to be controlled to hit defined targets, his beautiful wife sat there looking dumb and would never utter a word. She actually hated her husband for embracing Nazi doctrines. He finally locked her in his castle, and she was forbidden to leave until one day she drugged her maid, stole her clothing and escaped the confines of the prison like castle.

I won't bore you by going into long details of how this brilliant young and beautiful lady invented the technology for wireless transmissions that had the unique capability of using various non-detectable codes to deliver missiles, or messages, to single receivers wherever they were located.

By this time she had moved to Hollywood, California where Louis B. Mayer of Metro, Goldwyn, Mayer hired her to appear in her first film where she ran through the woods, and swam across the waters totally naked. The censors banned this shocking film which only created a greater demand for people to want to see this nude goddess. Her popularity soared.

Meantime America had entered into World War 2, and this young actress went to Washington where her patented invention of fool-proof wireless delivery of everything from torpedoes to bombs was employed against Hitler's and Hirohito's military armies that was instrumental in achieving victory for the Allies.

Today our cell phone, or any other wireless device, depends on the benefactor and developer of the patent owned by one of America's most famous and legendary actresses – Hedi Lammar.

The moral of this story is that things we accept today as being common place have been standing on the shoulders of other common place products over years long past. It is each civilizations choice to choose what is harmful or will bring lasting peace and comfort.

My solemn prayer is that you and your generation will choose wisely for the greater good of all.

Kick the Can

Pardon the interruption, but I just had to tell you the true story of Hedi Lammar. Every chapter of our lives is standing on the preceding chapters, and how they influence and guide you into the future of the unknown. To get back to my memoirs, I have just decided to accept Mr. James' proposal to take over the advertising account of Consolidated General Products in Houston.

Monday morning and I drive over to Consolidated General and walk in my shined shoes into the building and follow instructions to meet Mr. James in his office promptly at 9 a.m. Before the minute hand touches nine I entered into Mr. James' lair. He introduces me to his step-son James (Jimmy) Coston who handles advertising for all divisions of the company. Seems like a very nice guy. I am guessing Jimmy is about my age, and I can see by the ring on his finger he's married.

"Thank you for this opportunity, Mr. James. It is very much appreciated. I promise to give this my full commitment to make a successful contribution to your many companies. Since I am so new to Houston I would appreciate your advice as to where I should set-up the office to my advertising agency. I would like to get that accomplished very quickly so that I can begin to concentrate on your business."

Mr. James responded, "I have anticipated this, so I have arranged a very nice office for you on the third floor of this building. Jimmy will show you the place."

I was taken aback by this reply, and if I had been smart enough to recognize what it meant, I would have immediately figured 'Earl, what INDEPENDENT advertising agency have you put your foot into?' Jimmy and I trot out the door, and go to my new advertising agency, on the third floor, that didn't come equipped with a private telephone number, or a private secretary. By the time Jimmy and I discuss the basics, and he leaves for lunch, dusk had risen on the horizon, and I realize I have been duped to sell my soul to become another glorified corporate advertising director. Right there and then I make up my mind to not fret, but make the most of this opportunity one way or the other. I have the $1,250 a month to look forward to, I have my wife and the two little girls to think of, and a challenge to do the best I can in a city that I don't know where downtown is related to my motel room, which is somewhere that I parked my car after arriving in Houston two days ago.

If a dog actually works, I was one. I put in the hours and the effort to meet the challenge, and maybe because I had little social distraction, I stayed busy putting all the bones together to get some real advertising done. I began meeting the media, printers, artists and production people while learning more about each of the Consolidated Manufacturing businesses. Jimmy

and I were getting along famously as he was a big help knowing the Houston advertising community, and certainly knew
the products and brands of the family business. My one major
outside occupation was to find a home for my family as soon
as possible and have all three of my loved ones join me. This
was no easy task. Wherever I looked, the homes were too rich
for my blood and brood. With no zoning laws, I found potential homes to buy surrounded by undesired neighborhoods, or
schools. One weekend I decided to look outside the immediate city, so I drove down Main Street, just past the Shamrock
Hotel, and the beginnings of the Medical Center. Within a few
short streets I was in the open country of a few small stores, a
popular restaurant, and on the right a very small amusement
park that consisted of pony rides for the little ones. On the
left of Main Street there were continuous flat fields with black
pumps dotting the landscape like birds pecking the ground
looking for worms, but these were pumping oil. Finally, just
off to my right were three or four rows of new homes. 'New'
meaning they were built over the past five or less years. I pulled
into a small unimpressive building marked "REAL ESTATE."
When I walked in the door they must have guessed that God
had just delivered a messenger of money since I said I am new
in town. The gentleman showed me a few of the homes for sale
while he was touting their virtues. So far, I wasn't buying, until
he opened the door to a home with a swimming pool, and a
children's play house just off the back porch with a corrugated
yellow plastic roof. The girls will love it-so I bought it! Only
later to discover that I may have paid $10,000 more than the
other homes in this distant sub-division. Of course, the owners
who sold the house were so thrilled they moved to California
to probably retire as millionaires. I hope they have remembered
the donor of their largesse.

Actually this home on Stillbrooke Drive was very nice and comfortable. The neighbors in those more friendly days would walk from home to home and knock on the door without being afraid to not be made most welcome. There were lots of young kids to play with, and the schools were new and the teachers were bright. What then was considered the outskirts of Houston, today would be part of the inner city, and the oil pumps have been replaced by the Astrodome, Reliant stadium and hotels, motels and much more significant apartments and homes, with a wide array of all types of eating establishments and big box stores. I never claimed to be smart, but if I were, I should have gone to work as an agent for the real estate firm that took me on that home ride.

One great benefit that I could never have imagined at the time was that my immediate neighbor on our right was a home builder. He was struggling to make a go of things as he was building more expensive homes in the neighborhood just north of ours. He was lucky to sell two a year but he was averaging just one that just about scratched out a living for his young family of five. One evening I walked around our fence to talk with him to suggest he start building a lower priced home in a nearby open field, and that I would do his advertising and promotion. I named the homes, "Viking Homes" and bought junior billboards on the major streets leading to this pioneer community. Each billboard had a giant cutout of a full-fledged Viking in full regalia standing on top of the boards. They caught everyone's attention, as well as the high school kids that would climb up high and steal them as trophies. This created lots of free publicity as the media enjoyed reporting these Viking thefts. Sales didn't just boom-they were a boon to the builder who from that humble beginning became one of the largest residential builders in Houston. In a few short years he retired and reportedly moved to buy Fort Knox.

Where did he get the money to start these low priced homes on land he had to buy? I had introduced him to one of our banking clients who gave him the boost and that's the rest of the story.

Getting back to me at Consolidated General Products, after maybe a year I thought we had everything running smoothly and there were no complaints. Little praise, but the checks kept us alive and living. Meanwhile I was getting a little restless to want to build a real independent advertising agency. I did what the Navy had trained me to do which was to engage in some quiet, secret explorations of the landscape to see if there was anything worth capturing. Within a relatively short time I captured enough clients to get the attention of other agencies who were wondering who is this unknown scoundrel and what magic is he weaving? The secret was that I had broken the traditional code of charging 15% commissions on the media. I instituted a fee system and was able to sell my prospects. This was fairer for both them and me as I was being paid for services rendered by the hour, and results attained. Within a relatively short time I had gained eleven clients including Consolidated, yet my operation was relatively clandestine without having to resort to storming the beaches dressed in brown swim shorts, fins and a backpack filled with medical supplies.

Some of my erstwhile agency competitors must have been concerned that I was upsetting their cherished cart of 15% commissions based revenue, and went screaming to the American Advertising Agencies Association in N.Y.C. They sent their financial wizard Harry Paster to put the fear of God into this little country 2-person ad agency who was down in the weeds scaring everyone. Harry was a nice man whose head was about to explode at my flawed "let the best math win" philosophy. He must have flown back to the Big Apple to report I didn't take his bite.

Jimmy Coston and I were getting along famously and one day he invited me to be his guest at a party. One evening after we both left the office, Jimmy drove me in his car to some place that I didn't recognize. We went inside and entered a large gym sized room that men of all ages were sitting around in folding chairs. Each guy was holding a beer or hard liquor drink in their hands, and music was playing softly. Jimmy and I sat down next to one another and Jimmy ordered a drink and I asked for a Coke. The music got much louder and a few barely clothed ladies came out on the floor while gyrating to the beat of the music. Interesting! Until one buxomy broad takes off whatever little she was wearing and heads right towards me. Her more than ample busts are weaving from side to side as she dances closer. I am turning redder than a STOP sign. When she pushes her boobs practically into my nose I jump up and run out the door. Jimmy quickly follows while laughing out loud. "I knew you were a prude, but you just made me lose $10 because I was holding the money over your head." Together we both laughed all the way home. I had simply thought what had attracted that lady to me was my eyes being crossed while staring, and tongue hanging out in amazement.

During World War 2 the government would run ads that said, "Loose lips will sink ships." My ship was about to sink as the secret of my gaining other new clients probably leaked out to

Mr. James. He summoned me into his office and threatened to throw me out on the street unless I gave his business my 100% attention. I wish today I simply stood up straight and would have said something like, "Sir, I am marching out of here and screw you." Instead I did what I thought was proper and said that I understood his request, but thought I had to follow my dream to try to be as successful as he has been in his business career. We agreed that I would leave to establish an independent business, and I would continue to work for Consolidated, without the $15,000 annual guarantee. So be it – either now or never.

Natalie never shed a tear, or said, "You are too impulsive for your own good. Think of the kids and me...do we have to be homeless and hungry just to soothe your own vanity?" Instead she stood straight and tall as a trooper and said, "Earl, I know you are capable and will make a go of this venture."

I found an office in a two story building on Montrose which was in those days one of the premier streets where formerly some of Houston's most prominent families resided among the tall palms lining this wide boulevard. What attracted me to this singular location was that just within blocks some of the largest advertising agencies in the country had housed their local offices. But, the real allure was that this office had a large showroom window facing the highly trafficked street. I wasn't aware that any other ad agency in the country had a street level showcase to promote their clients products and services, so I signed the lease...with my fingers crossed behind my back.

Talk about being wet behind both ears! We needed a name for our new advertising agency, and we settled on calling us

Abbott and Earl. There was no Abbott, but in our innocence we thought by being one of the first names in the advertising section of the Yellow Pages our phone would ring off the hook with client prospects. The majority of our calls were from people trying to sell us their services, or reminding us to pay their bills that were getting so late that even the date had expired.

Both of our girls were now in school, so I prevailed on Natalie to come in for a few hours daily to answer the phone and do a little typing if I had to be out on business. I noticed that many of the male media sales reps would like to come in just to see Natalie. None of them were blind, so who could blame them for looking? We kept getting a little busier, but not making enough money to more than keep us alive and dreaming. Came the holidays and Natalie needed more time to prepare the festive meals and take care of the girls who were on school break. We decided to hire a temporary for those few days. Krin Holtzhauser came to work and stayed much more than 20 years.

One day, unexpectedly the phone did ring without someone pleading to be paid, or trying to sell us their Brooklyn Bridge. It was a man who introduced himself as Henry Dannenbaum asking to speak with me. Before grabbing the phone, I knew who he was though we had never met. Mr. Dannenbaum was a partner in the oldest and most recognized independent advertising agency in Houston - Goodwin, Dannenbaum. "Good morning, Mr. Dannenbaum. Please let me save you some trouble. If you are calling to invite me to join The Houston Advertising club, or wanting a donation for some worthy cause, I just am not able to help you." He didn't hang-up. He just laughed loud and clear. "I could have expected that answer after hearing and checking you out. I want to buy your lunch and see if you would be interested in joining Goodwin Dannenbaum as a partner."

"Sir, when and where? How soon?" (Drowning sailors are happy to grab a life saver).

"May I see you tomorrow at noon at Rudi's?"

That was the pinnacle of restaurants which I was hoping to be able to take Natalie for some momentous celebration if we ever struck it richer than working pay day to payday. It hadn't happened yet, but at least I would get the chance to check Rudi's out.

"My great pleasure to meet you in person, Mr. Dannenbaum." That was the beginning which changed our fortunes and launched a real professional advertising career. Over lunch "Henry" laid the deal out on the table for me to digest. His agency was getting old and stodgy. They were stuck in the mud and couldn't get the wheels moving forward. He felt they needed a fresh breath of air and invited me to come in and be the third partner. I stopped eating. I was afraid I would put the fork in my eye. Henry said, there would be two requirements. I needed to meet his partner John Paul Goodwin, plus invest $25,000. I not only had stopped stuffing my mouth with delicious food, but thought I would have cardiac arrest."

$25,000!!! "Thank you, Mr. Dannenbaum, but I must decline. Even $2,500 would be more than I could swallow."

"Earl, we have the solution. We will simply draw it out of your paycheck and you can take 5 years, or more if need be."

KICK THE CAN

"Henry, when can I meet Mr. Goodwin?"

The next morning I drive up to this old converted mansion in what might have been, a long time ago a nice neighborhood. Today it contained a supermarket of small businesses, a museum and many social charities filling these remodeled homes. Inside, Goodwin Dannenbaum was nothing impressive except the people. John Paul and Henry occupied what was probably the former living room. John Paul was a distinguished Southern gentleman who was born and raised in Shreveport, Louisiana. His father was the publisher of the major newspaper. John Paul spent his early career as a Shakespearean actor and was the first voice heard over Houston television in the earliest days of that new media. His diction was as perfect as his flowing gray hair. He was a stickler for precise grammar. His tone of voice was deep and mellow and as practiced as if he were always performing on stage. Very impressive to see and hear.

What impressed me most is that he also thought we could all work together, so we had a deal and I was the new partner.

I was introduced to the staff, one by one. Probably a dozen in all. The copy writers and financial people, with the few media buyers occupied the main two story building along with the partners who were mostly responsible for acquiring and handling the clients. In the rear of the building, over the three car garage, in the former servant quarters, was home to the artists, production people, and Bob Dannenbaum, a tall, unassuming, spectacled young man who was Henry's son and responsible for research and marketing. There was no way not to notice the large man who was in charge of the art department. He was aptly named – Walter Lodge. Large in size, very large both in height and width, as well as talent with a booming girth of personality.

Probably the gem of all the people was a lady named Anna Jane Wingfield. As quiet as her manner her unique capability as a writer shouted across the land. In my whole advertising career I never met anyone more capable of putting words into arrows that pierced your heart. Words were the instrument she played to make you want to dance, sing and especially buy whatever she was being paid to sell in print.

If there was one word to describe Anna Jane it would be "TAL-Lented."

Henry and John Paul decided to change the name of the company and decided this old firm would have a new name: Goodwin, Dannenbaum, Littman & Wingfield, Inc., a mouthful to say the least. They included Anna Jane in respect for her word smithing, and my "take it out of his paycheck" bankrolling the business.

Our big clients included O.J. Beauty Lotion which was the invention of a Shreveport pharmacist who happened to live next door to John Paul's parent's home. When John Paul graduated college, Mr. Parham, the founder of O.J.'s, asked him to start a business in which they painted the sides of thousands of drug stores with the O.J.'s logo and bottle. From there, as the business flourished, they went to mass media advertising with John Paul delivering the radio messages. Our next most important client was the Capital National Bank that Henry watched over like he was the father and the bank was his most precious child. They were among the top four banks and had a network of correspondent banks across East Texas. There was Transcontinental Pipeline which served people from Texas up to New England. A close friend of John Paul's and valued client was Gitting's. Bachrach and Paul Linwood Gittings were probably the two most noted portrait photographers in the nation. You weren't a 'somebody' until you had a Gitting's portrait hanging in your home or office.

The mother of all the clients was Foley's Department Stores which was relatively new, but recognized as the biggest potential for advertising growth, plus Gulfgate Mall which at the time was the largest in Houston, and the bell weather for others around the country. I was asked to work with Henry on Capital National Bank, and be responsible for Foley's, but my main role was to become the rainmaker to find and close new business.

Henry Dannenbaum who had fished me out of the sea of drowning in mortgages and bills to keep our little family away from eventually begging on street corners, was a native of Houston. His father was a former judge who went to Washington, D.C. as either the attorney general, or assistant. I have forgotten. He somehow got into a fight with the administration and returned to Houston a broken man. Meanwhile Henry was at the University of Texas studying to become an attorney in his father's footsteps when that plan was shattered by the episode in Washington. Somehow Henry opened a small gift shop in downtown where he met John Paul and they both decided to open an ad agency with the O.J.'s account as the foundation. Henry was tall, very thin and very well put together, extremely intense and overly protective of his bank client. He lived in Sugar Land in a charming home overlooking the lazy blue waters swimming down Oyster Creek. I loved him for his kind and caring ways. Almost every evening on his long drive home to Sugar Land, he would stop at my home in Willow Bend to give both Erica, Bonnie and our little guy Michael a hug as if he were their long lost grandfather.

Henry would love taking Michael into his arms and then lifting them overhead as if he was going to shoot a three pointer across a basketball court. Then he would let Mike fall and catch him as Henry would laugh while Mike would echo back with a giggle. Thank heaven Henry never thought he was Joe Namath throwing a 'Hail Michael' downfield for a touchdown.

It wasn't too long after I joined GDL&W that Henry asked us to come to his home to spend a Sunday afternoon. After lunch Henry invited me and the kids to go out in his rowboat. I volunteered to row, but he insisted I watch the children and he would row us up and down the shore to look at the houses and wave to the people. I can't account for how long we were on the waters when Henry turned pale white and said, "Earl! Hurry! Take the oars" and keeled over. I screamed at Erica and Bonnie to watch over Mike and started to row as fast as possible to get back to Henry's home. I pulled the boat up onto the shore, got the kids out and started yelling to Natalie and Henry's wife to call an ambulance quickly.

I took Henry' pulse, but could hardly feel a beat. I dragged or lifted him to the dry land, and carefully placed him down on the grass, and waited frantically for the ambulance to get him to the hospital. Sugar Land in those years was nothing like it is today. It was small and the ambulance arrived within just minutes. The attendants put Henry on a stretcher and with sirens wailing rushed him to the hospital. Unlike modern medicine the care of heart patients was nothing like it is today. Within two to three days he passed away hitting his family like a sledge hammer. All his agency associates and clients, many of whom were his best and most loyal friends were shocked as well. I was lost as taps was being played again in my mind especially to lose a mentor and man whom I respected, admired and truly worshipped.

All we can do is resume life as always. I have seen better days, but I have also seen worse.

A secret which we kept among ourselves in the agency family was that John Paul was a hopeless alcoholic.

Secrets Revealed

Upon Henry's untimely death, I became President of GDL&W, and Bob voluntarily left the agency to move to Chicago. I never knew his real reason for making that decision, but suspected that he may have thought he should have inherited that role. Bob was more in keeping with the test and measure philosophy of conducting advertising, where I was hell bent for leather to produce the best creative product, and let the consumers be persuaded to buy our messages to create sales. I was determined to make the rain fall in torrents of new and bigger clients flowing into our shop.

Who was right? We both were had we sat down and used our common sense to compromise. I should have known that the King of Madison Avenue – David Ogilvy preached, "The most important four letter word in advertising is TEST." My ignorance wasn't bliss.

Many families have things hidden in their closet they would prefer to be kept quiet, and I should not be revealing John Paul Goodwin's illness publicly. I do so primarily to reveal that the most brilliant and capable of people can be destructive of others, as well as themselves, due to an addiction. There were many embarrassing incidents where alcohol took over as alco-HOLD on the imbiber.

The creative team and I were meeting with our client that operated a national chain of fast food hamburger stores while quietly discussing our latest advertising campaign when who burst into the room unannounced, but John Paul. With his most dramatic flair he announced 'that your hamburgers aren't worth eating. They are either under or over cooked, and no real Texan would ever eat such shish-ke-blah.' Silence fell as the advertising director stood-up ready to walk out after hearing the wrath from our Chairman. I stopped him, and quickly escorted John Paul out the door. I came back into the stunned conference to offer my excuse by explaining, "John Paul has a rare disease which requires that he go to the hospital every Wednesday to have his blood exchanged, and this is Wednesday which puts him in a foul mood. We express our regrets."

Where did this whopper of a lie ever come from? But, it saved the day, and the client.

Another time, which cost us dearly, was when John Paul was in his car and tried backing out of a carport that had many automobiles lined up under a common roof supported with poles between each car. John Paul rammed the poles as he put his car into reverse causing literally a domino effect as the roof came tumbling down on a string of automobiles. We paid dearly, and then purchased a new car that came with a full time driver to tote John Paul around safely without causing harm except to our treasury.

O.J.'s Beauty Lotion was headquartered in Shreveport and John Paul always looked forward to meet with his longtime client, and very close friends. However, it wasn't only business but too frequently it would be a binge. One time the two of us took the trip. After a very successful meeting we got back to the airport to wait for the plane to take us home to Houston. I sat down in the waiting lounge to read a book while John Paul disappeared with the excuse he was going to the restroom. They announced the plane had arrived. I look around and John Paul is nowhere to be seen. The other passengers are beginning to get aboard. No, John Paul! I rush to the bar and he is stooped over the counter with drink in hand. "Hurry, John Paul, or we will miss our flight." I help him weave his way onto the plane. I get him seated and move forward not to be seen with him. From Shreveport to Houston he was loud, making one fuss after another. The passengers were obviously upset, and the poor hostess had more than enough on her hands to try to quiet him down. I felt lucky that he wasn't arrested for disturbing the peace with his loud utterances to cause a piece of the plane fall off just to find some quiet place.

During the war I had witnessed guys drinking to calm their nerves, or possibly help forget what dreaded dragons they were facing. Now I was involved with a normal, highly respected businessman going through the same torment. Both times I was totally ignorant of how to be of any real help. Was this why someone high above was leading me down this blind path? Would my future have the blind-fold removed from my eyes so that I might become curious to see the cure for this gripping disease?

Our ad agency enjoyed the usual ups-and-downs of most agencies, with fortunately more ups. We were being rewarded with wonderful new clients, which created more jobs for the talented people who joined our staff. Pete Barthelme joined us and he and I worked closely together as he became the Creative Director. Pete came from a long line of brothers who were noted authors, and he had their DNA in abundance. For Stran Steel, a major manufacturer of pre-engineered steel buildings, I suggested a slogan, "Do Something Constructive." Pete would take those three words and turn it into ads which stood high above the crowd of their competitors. His talents were extraordinary and I embraced them whole heartedly. Usually, but not regularly, we had the common sense to differ, but compromise for the common good of the client and the agency. What good is it if you lose the client and it makes the agency suffer? It's better to argue, fight, express your views and listen to the other party. Then agree to agree and move forward.

I don't want this to sound like it's easy and it's just magic. I recognized the internal resentment I was creating by receiving more public credit than I deserved for the work and growth of GDL&W. Success isn't possible without the brain power and labor of the full staff. No one person deserves the total adulation and awards bestowed-- including David Ogilvy, Mary Wells Lawrence or my acquaintance Lois Wise who created "With a name like Schmuckers it has to be good." My favorite person Anna Jane Wingfield despised that I would sign my letters, "Have Happiness Today," and had bumper stickers printed with this slogan. We are all different, and many at GDL&W may have thought I was being too egotistical by stealing the lime light. I believed I was simply trying to create a brand difference by employing creACTive® as a way of explaining our ads create action – sales!

Therefore, I have learned my lesson and will not extol the growth and virtues of GDL&W as you may mistake our progress due to MY cracking the whip over the crew as we sailed on forward. However, GDL&W stormed the beaches to gain a foothold in the tough and turbulent jungles of advertising. There was always a hidden land mine to be destroyed if we were to make any progress. Some sniper was lurking who would like to drop us dead in our tracks, so we had to find how to maneuver around them to come out victorious. To some extent we did more often than not, but I won't take you through all those missions, but try to highlight what unusual artillery we built for our disposal.

Charge Ahead

When Natalie and I gambled and started our own agency – Abbott & Earl had a great front with our showroom window, but a very sparse actual office. Goodwin Dannenbaum's offices were more reminiscent of a 1940's movie – old, tired and worn.

It was time to take the bull by the horn and move ahead to new and better office space. Before we rented the second floor of a brand new building that our Y.P.O. friend Gerald Hines was building on Highway 610 South, just off Westheimer, I consulted with our long time accountant and friend David Miller.

"David. What do you think? Should we take the plunge and rent there?"

"Earl, jump on this. If you hesitate a moment there will be a long line of people wanting that space and prime location."

We did, and we moved, but not before decorating the interior to be different for that time, day and age. Today it will not sound too daring, but it was a pace setting office for the time.

Between each office, from door-to-door, and floor to ceiling, were large black and white photographs depicting the tools of our trade, typewriter keys, pencil points, the lens of a camera. It made a striking display around that full floor of space. We hired an interior decorator that was a friend of Anna's who also worked for a client of ours in the office equipment and furnishings business. I bowed reverently to all her suggestions until it came to the choice of floor coverings in the conference room. She suggested a sisal rug, and I balked, or should I say barked "No way." I thought I had checked this out and learned that the heels of woman's shoes could get snagged in the openings, and that if anyone were to spill a coffee or a drink, there was nothing to keep the liquid from spreading. I insisted we have solid carpeting installed, which from that day on both Anna Jane and her decorator friend swore I was their fatal enemy. So be it, but as time proved my decision was the right one, but you can't regain the confidence of one when it is damaged and lost.

We should have sat down and found a compromise to assuage both parties. I was guilty of not using common sense that would have kept the important bridge of friendship flowing for many future years. Before our five years lease was up, the Hines Group told us they were selling the building and would we agree to sell our interest in the property. We jumped at the opportunity, and immediately started looking for new office space. This was our chance to do something truly unusual that could be a monument to our foresight. Not too far distant was an empty piece of ground on which an acquaintance was planning on building two five story office buildings. Would we be interested? You betcha' life if we could have control of the exterior building design as we didn't want to move into another cookie-cutter square building without any significant differences to set it apart. We helped the architect with our suggestion to build a totally exposed elevator extending vertically off the front of the all glass building. Done!

Next was how to make our third floor a WOW after someone stepped off the elevator. The results gained a front page picture on ARCHITECTURAL DIGEST, and a page after page article showing our unique office design. Best of all, in my opinion, was when our client Mrs. Oveta Culp Hobby, the publisher of THE HOUSTON POST, and former Secretary of the WASPS during World War 2, made a special point of visiting to take a tour of our open concept with no wires being visible. When we were finished going from office to office and were sitting in our creACTive conference room, Mrs. Hobby turned to me to ask permission to have her architects visit because she was planning a new office complex. She couldn't have paid a bigger compliment for us daring to be different than any other ad agency in the country, including 99.9% of corporate America.

I won't extol all the virtues of the NEW G.D.L.&W. offices as that would take up this full book, however I will try to describe our creACTive conference room which was a 36' foot circle in the middle of the office floor. The exterior walls were covered with panels of aluminum encrusted with brass protrusions and colored stones such as emeralds and rubies. This masterpiece was created and designed by Pebworth, a noted sculptor known for his giant works in Hyatt Hotels and pieces hanging in art museums. He outdid himself for the entrance where the door handles were individual pieces of art that reached out to say "grab me." The inside of the room contained a thick round black marble top table floating on a hidden base which also hid all the electronics which remotely operated the presentation

⌒ 83 ⌒

materials. The walls were covered in white fabric that acted as screens on which to project images. There were 12 red covered plush chairs for people to use sitting around the conference table. Plus, there was built-in seating around the full circumference room of the circular room which also was covered in the same red fabric as were the chairs. Behind the walls were a series of 36 slide projectors that pierced through small windows in the walls and could surround the room with instantly projected inside views of any store, mall, room or any exterior location such as a baseball field, a travel location or simply a beautiful scene atop a mountain.

It gave us the opportunity to practically demonstrate the real 360 degree life experience of a visitor being in a supermarket as we talked with a consumer products manufacturer of food products. It worked well for our clients, such as Ranch Style Beans, or Pearl Beer. It brought real drama to the Gordon's Jewelers management as they were automatically transferred into one of their stores in a shopping mall. It was advertising Disney Land which helped us land more business. We also let many a charity group use these facilities at no charge. Our creACTive room featured an old-time silver plated cash register to remind our staff and clients that nothing happens until we help create a sale with our innovative advertising.

The Big Payoff

Things had changed for the better since the day I had been chosen to receive the God given opportunity to join Henry and John Paul with their total staff of 12. Now GDL&W had multiplied by ten times in the number of people employed. We were fortunate to have retained some of the original client roster and had added many sterling new clients. My horoscope read that I was one fortunate guy to have a wonderful family, a lovely home, and a thriving business.

Then lightning strikes. Suddenly America was hit and fell into a deep economic depression. Good paying clients either cut back or fell by the wayside. Our broad portfolio of financial and real estate clients was particularly devastated, and we along with them were feeling the pinch like a punch in the face to bankruptcy. Rich Witmer, our treasurer, may he rest in peace, would storm into my office saying, "Earl, we can't pay our bills. We need to call it quits. Let's take bankruptcy to avoid our creditors."

"Not as long as I live. We will tighten our belts and fight to the bitter end. Hear me, we are not quitting."

Rich would leave my office shaking his head, and I would wonder, how long can I remain so stupid to keep fighting blindly on? Lots bigger and stronger companies were taking down their shingles, so what is going to save us? I kept praying to myself, but it seemed that my line to God was cut-off for not keeping the long distance phone bill current.

I had forgotten that months earlier we had received a request for a proposal from an advertising consultant out of Chicago. He never identified the client he was representing only to describe them as being a major retailer of consumer bulk and packaged goods. It was my responsibility to answer every RFP, so I spent a few days trying to answer this lengthy inquiry. The guessing game began among the troops. Who was this mystery retail client? One person said, "See's Candy." Others counted "Hickory Farms Hams" while others guessed it must be "Baskin Robbins." Weeks and months went by, without hearing a word, and I forgot about this as just another waste of time.

As was my bent, I was out on the road searching for new business without much luck when my phone rang while I am in a hotel in St. Louis. "Earl, guess who the prospect is that the Chicago consultant was helping to find a new ad agency?"

"Stop fooling around. Tell me is it Hickory Farms, Baskin Robbins or whomever?"

"Hold onto your seat. Matter of fact you better sit down. (a long pause). It's Texaco, and they want to come in to see us tomorrow. Pack up your bags and fly home tonight!"

By dawn's early light I was back at my desk in the office going through my mail and messages waiting for the troops to arrive. We soon gathered around the table in the creACTive room and there was an obvious air of excitement and anticipation.

"What's the game plan Earl? What should we arrange to show these Texaco folks?"

"Nothing" was my response. You could hear the gasps of surprise.

"Nothing?"

"Earl, have you lost your cottin' pickin'mind? This is the biggest account we have ever pitched and we are going to sit here and do nothing. You must have lost your marbles on your way home last night!"

"Come on Earl, we have got to show them our sample reel at least."

"Listen to me. They have been in-touch with 40 agencies across the country. Who the heck are we to try to impress them with our accounts, no matter how great we think our stuff is? Play it cool, and listen to what they have to say. I will take full responsibility if we look like fools who don't want their business."

With heads down, while wondering why we would want to turn Texaco away, my team walked out the door with a disgruntled and amazed look. They were very aware we would always pull out all the stops to try to land new business – large or small. What has happened to old Earl?

That very afternoon, at the appointed time two gentlemen from Texaco came through our open doors. They were ushered into the creActive room, offered something to drink, and I opened the presentation by simply stating our thanks for taking the time to meet with us this afternoon.

Without a minutes hesitation I then stated, "Gentlemen, we know this has been an arduous search to pick the right advertising agency for your business. You have probably been over-loaded with seeing all sorts of wonderful advertising campaigns, and heard all sorts of ideas thrown out at you. I know you wouldn't be here unless you already thought we were qualified and capable of working with Texaco. I simply promise that GDL&W will do and get done whatever Texaco needs. It's a promise you can bank on that we are dedicated to execute to the very best of our capabilities…and we will work, wherever in the world you trust us to represent you."

Dead silence. The two guys look at one another, and one quietly responds, "We would like you to meet our head honcho, Glenn Tilton. If he is available can you meet with him?"

"Of course, just tell us when and where."

Maybe a total of 30 minutes had passed and out they go. No thumbs up, because we are not sure they weren't using an excuse to get out of this nut house as quickly as possible.

Before the work day was over, I received a phone call saying, "Mr. Tilton would like to come by your agency before noon tomorrow. Will that work for you?"

Thank you God, is all that I could think while waiting for tomorrow to hurry up and come.

Sure enough, at 11:45am the two gentleman come back along with a handsome, bright young man that all you had to do was take a quick look, and believe, "Fast track, on his way to doing great things and achieving a world of success." We sat down and chatted for thirty minutes as you could see he was getting the lay of the land and confirming in his mind if there could be a marriage. He suggested we go to lunch, and Barry Silverman, our recently appointed President, and I hopped into my car to meet the three Texaco executives at Richard's a nearby restaurant.

We ordered lunch though I don't know if I ate a morsel. I was too busy listening to what Glenn (we are first names by now) has to say while carefully watching the three Texaco guys body language. This was all happening just three short days before the Christmas vacation. " If Texaco wants us to have representation in Detroit to handle their auto racing sponsorships we will be there. If they need us to be in Los Angeles to work with Texaco on their boat racing programs then count us in. We are ready to roll-up-our-sleeves to assist your special events wherever you need our assistance. GDL&W promises to be your right arm...and your left arm, too, when or where ever we can be of help to Texaco."

Glenn simply turns to his two co-workers and says, "Let's get started with our new advertising agency immediately."

Barry and I get into my car to return to the agency. "We both asked the same question to one another.

"Do you think he really means it? This is too incredulous." We could never have gotten a bigger, more welcome surprise gift for the Holidays.

I had to rush home to give Natalie a great big kiss. The agency won't be going bankrupt. They won't foreclose on our home. Our kids will have something to eat and no living in a culvert. It's Hanukah and Christmas all rolled-in one great big package of joy and happiness.

Now the Fun Begins

Holiday or no holiday we have got to get this bus on the road to fulfill our spoken word. Barry and I are in the office and beginning to shift into high gear. To fulfill our promise to Glenn Tilton and Texaco we need to fill some additional chairs with the addition of some new people. Come hell or high water, rain or snow, holiday or regular work day, we will get this mission accomplished.

We go through the file of resumes and get on the phone calling these folks wherever they may be which isn't as easy as it sounds, as it's holiday and they may be out of town. We are playing phone detective searching for missing bodies to come to work as quickly as possible. If we make contact, we invite them to come in for an interview to work on the Texaco account. That peaks a lot of interest as Texaco is the power house that powers the gas and oil consumer business as they have 33,000 service stations around the world. The Havoline brands and products are prominent among the leaders in the business. Almost everyone we are able to contact knows that having worked on the Texaco account is a shiny gold star on their resume. There are some takers willing to get paid for flying back to Houston to be interviewed for this plum job.

Very quickly we have added 14 new faces. Three were former employees we recently had honorably discharged due to our forced cut-backs, and the other eleven would be coming in to attend boot camp. We knew that some wouldn't be able to cut muster, but we had to give them the opportunity to prove their worth while we continue scouting for additional help.

This experience of practically going under to join Davey Jones' locker, and then suddenly being rescued by the Texaco helicopter emergency team brought me to my senses. How close I was to be standing on the unemployment line with my hand out. Would I be able to feed the kids with food stamps, and how could I get them medical aid if someone caught some disease? Will anyone, anyone provide a roof over our heads to keep out the rain, heat and roaches from crawling over our bodies? Where will the kids go to school if we are always on the run to keep from being homeless or starving into human walking skeletons?

I learned from practical experience this type hardship can happen to anyone no matter whom they are, how well educated or successful they might have been. What employer will want to hire someone who lost their business, their home, their lifestyle and is now at the doorway to retirement? It's cheaper, and safer to hire a young and eager beaver than to give this old fart a chance to start anew. Just THINK. It could happen to you. We fortunately escaped that dangerous knife by the skin of our teeth, but what would have happened if we hadn't been saved by the hand of God? I am going to join hands with Him to try to help others avoid a similar fate...if given the opportunity, I will get on the expressway to speed to be of whatever help I can offer...so help me.

Now, there's Texaco to absorb into our culture, and take care of our other clients. I still need to do my rainmaker dance to continue to attract new business. Having won the Texaco account is like wearing a chest full of medals and battle ribbons of merit to boast of your victories. We are now in a better position to attract other more prestigious clients. I forget about all those lost battles in trying to capture Conoco, Exxon and Tenneco. GDL&W caught the brass ring on the Merry-go-round of advertising. The other agencies in Houston, and the other 39 competitors, must be wondering what did that little known shop in the no-where of advertising agencies do to capture the King of the 'Bests'?

I was convinced we had the people and the talent to do our job. We will now be capable of adding any talents that we may need to keep our promise to Texaco. Earl, get back to steering the boat and head for the open seas where you can search and seize as there are lots more big fish to fry.

As time will tell -- a whopper of a <u>big</u> mistake!

Barry the Hatchet

Previously I mentioned Barry. I can't recall now, exactly when I hired this young man to come work at GDL&W. I must have been impressed enough to invite him to join our agency though he had no prior applicable work experience. I did learn he was a University of Texas grad, and I was aware of his well regarded family through a number of my friends. His full name is Barry Silverman, and for a young, attractive bachelor I wondered why the girls hadn't hooked him as yet.

When I was making client calls I would ask Barry to tag along, and invited him to sit in on many a new business presentation. In some small way I was mentoring him as if he were my own son Michael who was busily climbing his own career ladder in California advertising agencies. Mike Littman started in the mail room of Davis, Johnson and Colombatto in Los Angeles. The principal, Bob Colombatto, was one of my dearest friends. We had met through a professional association in which we were both members - the Affiliated Advertising Agencies International. Of all the thousands of men and women I have encountered toiling in the field of advertising, there was only one inimitable Collie. He was one smart cookie. He looked the part and acted like Mr. Hollywood. His ties were never fully wrapped in a bow. His clothing was impeccable. Born of Italian heritage his waving blond hair and good looks made you think he must have just flown in from Sweden. Nobody had a better sense of humor, which was proven time and time again, as no one ever felt offended when Collie spoke and would throw in a few choice words that would make a drunken sailor cringe. Everyone just knew it was Collie trying to give "color" to his witty remarks. The ads he created for his agency's clients were funny, yet always found a unique way to find their way to make the viewer respond positively to his message. It was a special talent that he had whether he was selling packaged horse manure or getting people to go to Santa Anita race track, or to place their money with his bank client. As you might expect, his always sunburned wife Dee Dee was a native Californian, and did more than justice to looking and playing the part. They lived in a magnificent home overlooking the blue waters of the bay until Dee Dee suddenly passed away to be soon followed by Collie. To lose such precious friends at an early stage in their joy filled lives brought home the fragility of all human beings no matter how blessed and full their lives may have been.

Natalie and I feel comforted to have travelled from Houston to visit with Collie just days before he was no longer able to continue living as being my dear friend whom I idolized. Bob "Collie" Colombatto will always remain my hero - a true creative giant worthy of being a towering advertising legend.

Finally, when I thought Barry was groomed and ready to take on a major account responsibility, I introduced him to the management of Foley's Department stores which was a long time client and dominant retailer. Foley's were pioneers in TV advertising, and had the evening news locked-up on the leading news program which enjoyed the largest daily audience. Ms. Gene Key Monigold was our senior contact on Foley's, and was responsible for the creative production which was a herculean job. She and her staff produced a minimum of two 30-second TV spots every day of the week that were fresh, attractive and timely. Being a large, diversified department store we could be promoting furniture and mattresses, the latest woman's fashions, or Van Heusen shirts for men, always with a fresh twist and a flair to be original, tasty and persuasive. Everyone was familiar with Foley's advertising so it became a calling card for GDL&W. Barry was assigned to take over my responsibilities of supervising the account and working with their management, oversee the media buying, work with the vendors co-op budgets, and account billings. Barry soon was working in conjunction with the large Foley in-house advertising, marketing, sales promotion, and event planner departments. It was within six months that the wicked witch that headed the department, who had replaced Lee Dubow with whom I had a most harmonious relationship, irately called me. She insisted that I fire Barry, and replace him immediately. She spit cuss words out adamantly so no amount of gentle persuasion could convince her to try and patiently work things out in order to smooth her ruffled feathers. In my attempt to calm and end her displeasure, I agreed to assign another Account Executive to replace Barry Silverman. Coincidentally, it was another Barry. This time I nominated Barry Smith. Barry was a smart, tough and very aggressive person that I thought might be able to handle foul-mouth "Ms. Misery."

Whenever the guys at GDL&W would decide to play a game

of tag football against one another, this Barry Smith always seemed to take personal delight to see if he could knock me on my ass. No one else ever tried to hit me so hard before. Once when we were playing and I saw him purposefully coming at me, I lifted my knee and hit him where it hurt enough for him to have to bend over in pain. That ended that parade until his voice lowered down from a high soprano back to a normal baritone.

We continued to work with Foley's as their chairman and president recognized the value of our agency/client relationship, and the contributions we were making to their success and bottom line. Both gentlemen were constantly in our corner and always actively assisted us in getting additional Federated Department stores in non-competing markets to become GDL&W clients. That is the reward of gratitude for performing consistent results which rang their cash registers.

Some time went by and things with Foley's appeared to be as regular as my Patek Philippe wrist watch when some of the team working on the account started to whisper behind closed doors they thought some hanky- panky might be taking place with Barry Smith and the Kueen Kong. I didn't doubt the possibility after observing how overly ambitious and conniving Barry could be. Barry and the dragon lady were allegedly plotting to steal the business away from GDL&W.

You don't go running to top management to make accusations you can't prove, and if I were wrong we would appear to be paranoid fools, so we kept quiet and patiently watched what might unfold. Nothing happened until Macy's came into the scene and bought Foley's which included taking the rug out from under our feet by assuming the advertising. Things like that happen in business, so you tighten your belt and take pride in the fact that we had a long, successful and mutually profitable marathon relationship with Foley's and their staff including many of their loyal buyers, department managers and the professionals engaged in their marketing efforts. Foley's was responsible for GDL&W achieving the reputation nationally as being the experts in department store advertising. No complaints. Only compliments as we were forced to close that long chapter in our history.

To continue the Barry Silverman story, after he was kicked off of the Foley's team he became an indispensable employee working hard to prove he was meritorious by helping to build our business. He remained one of Houston's recognized outstanding bachelors who would make a great catch for some lady fishing in the sea of potential husbands. Meanwhile Barry was having the time of his life dating famous movie and entertainment stars and many of the lovely models we used in our ads. I enjoyed listening and learning about his numerous conquests while occasionally eating my envious heart out.

Sorry Natalie, please skip over this remark which I meant in jest.

Each year the major television stations would invite the management executives and the media buyers from the bigger advertising agencies to their studios to put on a big presentation introducing the networks newest line-up of TV shows. While attending one event where the station's news anchors were on the stage introducing what was supposed to be the next big block-buster show that would bury the competition. I couldn't help paying particular attention to one outstanding blonde lady who all ready was a recognized super-star news anchor. She was perched on a tall stool with her legs crossed. She was not only brilliant, and attractive, she was a raving beauty that exuded charm and charisma. I soon returned to GDL&W and I spotted Barry.

"I just saw the girl you should court and marry. If I wasn't in love with my wife Natalie I think I would be knocking her door down."

As luck would have it, the jewel I found in the rough and tumble TV studio, turned out to be married. It may be hard to believe, but not too long after Barry (and all of Houston) learned she had gotten a divorce. Mutual friends told each one individually they knew the perfect partners so they introduced them, and Barry and Sharah have been married a good number of years. Another marriage made in heaven.

But back on earth things weren't turning out quite so rosy.

It wasn't the first time while running Houston's oldest and largest independent advertising agency that one of my associates got overly cozy with one of our best clients. They would form a marriage between one of our Account Managers and the client to start a new advertising agency by taking a big chunk of our business. The first time I can recall was when our Senior Account Director and Bud Adam's chief of operations of the Houston Oilers football team decided to team together and run with the ball, while also taking the new Quick Kick beverage which was to take the place of Gatorade, by forming their

THE WIZARD OF COMMON CENTS

own ad agency. It didn't take too long before that dream team went down in quick defeat while we lost a great client, and a good friend in Bud Adams who was the handsomest of Naval officers during World War 2.

We lost George Mitchell's entire stable of businesses which really hurt because we lived through the hardest of times when trying to convince Houstonians to move 25 miles north to live in The Woodlands. Pulling a reluctant dog by his collar might have been easier. It took trial and error to finally crack the ice where the FHA stopped threatening to foreclose on the property. One of the ladies in our public relations department was also a Galvestonian and had a family relationship with George that proved attractive so they pulled the Mitchell business, and it landed in her lap. She took one or two of her assistants to help start the business which fortunately for them and George Mitchell proved very successful.

The third and most devastating case was an internal coupe. I should have learned a long time back that we are all greedy and selfish, and want what is best for us personally without regard to who may have been responsible for their success.

You may already be asking, "Why didn't you have non-compete contracts with your key people?" I just never believed in them, as I thought they violated free enterprise where everyone supposedly has the right to choose, including employees. My experience, after having worked at three agencies, was to voluntarily leave their employ if I felt uncomfortable. If my new employer had a conflict with the past agency, I didn't want that to be a hurdle for me in signing on with the new shop. So, I was responsible for creating decisions which proved harmful and costly when people left our shop with one or more of our accounts, or what happened next.

Wouldn't it be nice if greed was prohibited by Congress? That is a pipe dream if you ever heard one.

TexaGO

Glenn Tilton wanted GDL&W to assume the Texaco account at the first of the New Year, and there were only three days to the Christmas holiday in which we kept a small staff on hand primarily to handle emergencies.

Barry and I decided we had to stay and work during the holiday. We needed more people rather instantly to work with auto racing in Detroit, and for the boat projects on the west coast. We divided the project of looking in our resume files to see if we could find people to fit Texaco's needs. Barry searched folks that might have racing car experience, while I looked for account people that sailed or boated. Our art director and broadcast production manager were asked to try to find people that will fit the missing holes they might need in their departments. To expedite things, because of the holiday, we offered interested potential employee prospects bonuses and travel expenses if they could come in immediately for an interview. Some accepted while others promised to meet the first week of the New Year. We did make some quick decisions to fill the empty chairs knowing full well they might not be the right people, but we felt obliged to demonstrate that we had Texaco's best interests at heart. As time went by we made some necessary changes to insure we had the best people possible to fulfill our obligations to this gigantic client. Bruce Eskowitz was one of the best choices we could have made, as over time, he became an anchor of trustworthiness and capability on working with some of the toughest assignments in the area of entertainment shows which Texaco would sponsor. Jake Elliott, who was our Public Relations director took an active part, while Barry was the day-to-day conduit with Texaco.

In the beginning I took it upon myself to try to travel and visit with the major Texaco operations across the country and meet with the managers and key staff people. I enjoyed every minute of meeting those dedicated people and took great satisfaction when they would remark, "Texaco has had other advertising agencies over the years, but this is the first and only time we have ever met the chairman personally. Thanks for taking the time to come and visit with us Earl."

Now when I look back at these visits a long way from home I wonder if being a good politician was also the cause of my ultimate downfall. Rather than holding hands daily with the key Texaco contacts in Houston I was absent, and a quiet revolution began taking place. Barry assumed that liaison role and became buddy-buddy with the key guys that were responsible for the agency-client relationship. True, I did have some enjoyable contacts at the big presentation meetings with Texaco and especially with Glenn Tilton and his wife, but my hands-on daily involvement was being dissolved into becoming just a forgotten figurehead. I wasn't being invited to daily meetings or discussions about the Texaco creative product. Each day

I felt like I was a visitor rather than chairman of GDL&W. There was an obvious chill surrounding me, and I wasn't smart enough to correct what was happening. Maybe I felt if I did anything drastic it would harm the Texaco business which now represented possibly 80% of our total revenue. Texaco had become the big gorilla in our agency, and the people most closely associated with the business were anxious to keep this animal trainer outside the cage.

Things had gotten so strained that when NASA was searching for a new agency they called GDL&W to set-up an appointment. Until that point I was always the one in charge of new business and directed the presentation and proposal effort.

Without sounding too egoistical there would be independent surveys in the Houston area judging the capabilities of the advertising agencies. Invariably Earl Littman would consistently come out on top to be judged the best presenter in the Houston region. Barry was busy hurrying around to organize the presentation to NASA and was obviously frustrated when he saw me and asked if I would pitch in and do something which would impress the NASA people when they were to visit the agency. I got to work immediately and visited with a display house to help us create an entrance into the creACTive room that would knock their NASA socks off their feet. We created a 3D display of an Astronaut that we hung over the entrance door as if he were floating in space.

When our NASA visitors started entering the room the rockets on the backpack of the Astronaut belched out smoke and the display moved forward as if it was moving around the world. Appropriate music played over our sound system so that it created the atmosphere that the visitors were also flying in space. Barry had to admit it was a sensational visual introduction to set the scene for receptivity. Old Earl was not included in what the agency was going to present or who was to deliver which part as I was being deliberately ostracized. I swallowed my hurting pride and let them do whatever they had planned. It bombed! NASA selected another agency which was no great surprise without the orchestra maestro leading the show.

Any baseball manager would want to have Babe Ruth go up to bat to try to win a crucial game. Instead they let this Babe sit on the bench while they struck out.

Obviously it was mutiny for the pirates bounty since we were secretly approached by a giant international advertising agency that was interested in buying GDL&W, who was confidentially negotiating with Barry and a few of his cohorts. I was locked out of these clandestine meetings which were held behind locked doors. The purchaser was primarily interested in acquiring the big plum Texaco account as our wide variety of real estate, banks and retailers were probably of little interest. At no time was I ever involved, or invited to meet the legion of visiting executives representing the buyer. Only after the deal was consummated did I officially learn the agency had been sold, signed and delivered.

The next morning I was sitting with our Comptroller while he was explaining the terms of the purchase when one of the acquiring agency executives walked in, and we were introduced to one another. We talked briefly in general terms, and the new agency representative never asked me what I intended to do now that I was no longer going to be associated with the advertising agency I helped build over the past 35 years. Showing his real lack of interest as he must have thought that I was reaching the ripe old age of 65 I would want to retire and go leisurely off into the sunset. We simply wished each other good luck, and I walked out. The very same afternoon I asked the Comptroller in to visit for a minute and what he shared with me was indicative of what had been happening behind the scenes. He told me that when I left the morning meeting, the visiting guest turned to him and said, "I am shocked. Earl is nothing like the monster we were led to believe he was. He appears to be a real gentleman."

The end of an era for Earl and GDL&W.

How did I feel? Disappointed, of course, but not as upset as you might imagine.

We are all human beings subject to different frailties. It's fairly natural to want the best for yourself. To want to succeed by hook-or-by-crook people will climb over others backs to get to the top of their mountain. I've witnessed people hating their boss for no reason at all except a hidden amount of jealousy thinking he or she is no smarter or better than me. There are some Americans that hated Presidents Lincoln, Roosevelt, Kennedy and Reagan yet never met them personally to learn what kind of men they were, and what motivated them to perform their notable deeds and noble accomplishments.

President Obama receives hate mail, and threats on his life. He's accused of being a socialist and communist, and not being a born American, but do these accusers have anything but conspiracy theories to convincingly prove otherwise? Nelson

Mandela is eulogized as being the world shaker in bringing human rights to his country, yet he spent years in prison for his beliefs and he too was accused of being a despised Marxist, communist and socialist. We learn that life must go on and try to do your best by avoiding the ruts which if they get deep enough become graves of regret. I may be down, but I am not out. There is always another challenge to conquer. It's time to bury the hatchet, and move on.

Nonprofits Are Humanly Profitable

"Hello. Please let me introduce myself to you. My name is "Champ" Champion, who formerly was the V.P. of Operations at GDL&W that Earl mentioned. I am now president of a major engineering company, but I feel compelled to tell you more about GDL&W which Earl may have skipped boasting about. First, let me explain that the agency had grown considerably from when Earl first came aboard, and he was the main reason why. He knew how to shake the trees so that the apples would fall at his feet. At the time he first entered the doors of Goodwin Dannenbaum, they had been well established, but were going nowhere. They needed a fresh shot-in-the-arm of youthful vigor and vitality which Earl could inject in huge doses. He is one of the most unusual people I have ever been associated with during my long business career.

When I first joined GDL&W they had a head bookkeeper Mildred Edwards who was a blazing red head, slightly pudgy lady, and Rich Witmer was the Treasurer. He wore two hats, as he also was an account supervisor over their large number of financial clients. Rich was also a talented piano player who was always called into duty to play at our Christmas and other parties. Mildred was married to Lee and you never saw a more incongruous looking couple. She was short and round while Lee was tall and thin as a rail, but they were extremely happily married. Rich Witmer and his lovely wife Gayle had a large family and they were so proud that one of their sons was now a priest and their other children were also doing well in their private lives. Both Mildred and Rich, along with Anna Jane and many others were 20 year veterans of GDL&W. Mildred, Rich and I took care of the agencies finances. Math and algebra were foreign languages to Earl. That was not Earl's bag. He was good at lots of things, but financial matters and working mechanical objects were beyond his capabilities. He never learned to type, but used up mountains of yellow pads writing letters, presentations, and his famous speeches which his secretaries would type, and then Earl would make mountains more of corrections until he felt comfortable with the structure and sound of the words.

He had brought Barry Silverman into the business a few years before I joined. It was obvious that he was teaching and training Barry to be his successor and when he thought Barry was ready he appointed him as president. Remembering the deal which Henry Dannenbaum and John Paul Goodwin offered Earl to get him to join their agency he asked Barry to buy into GDL&W for $25,000. Barry refused to accept the offer, and maybe this is where Earl might have made a mistake. He let Barry stay on without ever having to put a penny into the treasury. Who knows?

Barry had different attributes than Earl. He was much more hardnosed when it came to money. He would be tough on slow paying clients and would be ruthless when it came to negotiating questioned bills with suppliers and media. It was a good balance between the two of them. Earl thrived on the creative end of the business, and was a whiz when it came to attracting new business, and had the uncanny knack of knowing how to close the deal.

Like almost everyone else we would wonder what made the guy tick. He wouldn't get to be buddy- buddy with anyone as he always seemed to be too busy to make close friends. His lifestyle was the opposite end of the expected at the time. He was a gym rat who early every morning would leave his house to run a minimum of 8 miles, and late that night, after helping with the dishes and putting the kids to bed he would run a repeat 8 miles. Then on the weekends he might run a competitive 5k, or 10k, or half-marathon or complete one of his 39 marathons. This was long before jogging, running or lifting weights, spinning or kayaking was generally practiced by every Tom, Dick and Harry. We knew he had served in the U.S. Navy during World War 2, but he wouldn't talk about what he did other than to say he was a hospital corpsman- a medic.

He was a maniac about work. You could find him first to arrive and last to leave the office. He loved what he was doing, and would find it difficult not to want to butt into what the staff he had hired was doing with producing the ads. Let me share a perfect example. At the time the Houston Police Department was in shambles and public disgrace as a result of a few errant cops tying handcuffs behind the back of their prisoner Joe Torres. Then they threw Torres into the Bayou to drown. When this evil deed came to light of day, the Police Chief was fired and a new, Chief Pappy Bond was put in the job with the whole department bearing the Torres shame. Pappy decided to try to change the image of HPD, so he sent out a request for a proposal to all the Houston based advertising agencies. We naturally responded and started to brain storm what we were to propose. It would be Earl's responsibility to lead the team to make the actual presentation. The creative team would discuss and show Earl what they had in mind, and he repeatedly would shake his head, and say, 'That doesn't make me love a cop. Do something that is meaningful!' The creatives would leave his office muttering obscenities to themselves, and thinking 'slave driver...it's simple to say "no."

That evening Earl was looking through a magazine and came across an ad that basically said if you care for a child then donate money to help feed a kid in Africa. A light bulb went on in his head, and in the morning he rushed into the creative director's office and said, "Try doing a bumper sticker that says 'THE BADGE MEANS YOU CARE'." Now it was the copywriter, art director, and the creative department director who said, "What we showed you is much stronger."

"DO IT", Earl demanded, but he knew that he wanted an official HPD badge to be shown with the copy. Police Officers are not allowed to let anyone have or wear their official badge so how were we to get one to photograph for the bumper sticker design? If you have ever heard of luck, or fate taking place, it readily fell in our laps. Earl's secretary was Carol Kelley who was a young carbon copy of his wife, Natalie. Carol had blonde hair, blue eyes where Natalie's were emerald green and they both were sweet, charming and unassuming. Carol was single, and had a handsome boyfriend who was a Police Officer in the drug division. They were scheduled to go out together that evening so Earl prevailed on Carol to invite the officer to come and pick-her-up at work where we might take a few minutes to photograph his badge. It worked, and off the young couple went. After they enjoyed dinner, the officer dropped Carol off at her home and left to conduct that night's assignment.

Officer Kilty drove his unmarked car up to a shabby apartment in the shady side of town and climbed the stairs to find the apartment at the top where he knocked on the wooden door, "POLICE" he shouted. The response was a shotgun blast through the door that struck Officer Kilty directly into his body. Office Kilty then tumbled down the stairs where he died.

It was just days after that horrible incident that Earl and the GDL&W team were in the Riesner street headquarters of the Houston Police Department where they were ushered into a small conference room. Sitting around the long wooden table were eight uniformed officers with close cropped hair, and a balding Pappy Bond at the far end of the table. There were three green shaded light bulbs hanging down from the ceiling, and the only natural light was a thin string of windows placed high enough that you couldn't look out nor could anyone look in. Earl described it as being in a Nazi P.O.W. interrogation room.

Earl began the presentation, and quickly got to the point where he was showing the design with the proposed new theme for the Houston Police Department. THE BADGE MEANS YOU CARE was in bold white letters against a dark blue background, and to the far right was the exact photograph of the HPD badge.

Before Earl could mutter another word, Chief Pappy Bond loudly shouted his interruption, "Who wrote that?"

Not knowing if Pappy was pleased or angry, Earl stuttered, "It was someone back at our office, sir."

Pappy banged his fists on the table hard enough to rock the room, and said; "Well you go back and tell that someone that is EXACTLY what I want every member under my command to think, believe and act that way."

Softly, Pappy then asked, "Where did you get that badge? I can't read the numbers from here."

"Sir, it belonged to Officer Kilty."

Need I tell you anymore? The agency had 2,000 bumper stickers printed within the first week, and the figures would climb daily as practically every car in the region, especially the pickup trucks were proudly displaying "THE BADGE MEANS YOU CARE." It was one of the longest running advertising campaigns in Houston's history, and every once in a while you might still see that bumper sticker on an old car riding down the street.

One of Earl's proudest moments came when he picked-up the phone and the voice on the other end said, "I am a Captain with the Canadian Royal Mounted Police. May we please ask permission to use the theme "The Badge Means You Care?" This was just one of many other police departments that asked for and were granted permission without his agency asking for compensation.

Jake Elliott, who headed up our Public Relations department, would always comment, "Earl has never met a charity he wouldn't have us work for without the agency asking to be paid."

I am not certain I can even remember the number of non-profit organizations for which we worked. Before I joined GDL&W I know they helped the NAACP because Earl was totally against any racial discrimination, and he was the first white person to be honored for his work in Houston to end black injustice. He also served on The Texas Southern University Foundation board helping to raise needed finances for that institution. We helped a few black people to run for political office and he would always promise them that due to prejudice they may not win, but the campaign would be of such high standards that they would probably get a good job in Washington. This happened more than once. Earl's great disappointment was that he never had the personal pleasure to meet Congresswoman Barbara Jordan whom he admired, not only for her strong beliefs, but for how she expressed herself. He would try to remember while giving a speech to follow Barbara's style of pausing, and then repeating what she had just said for emphasis of the point she was delivering to her audience.

Though, to the best of my knowledge, Earl never took speech lessons, and didn't attend speech contests in school, yet he was always attuned to what the great speech makers of his day were able to convey.

He admires Presidents Roosevelt and John F. Kennedy, not only for what they expressed, but how well they did it. They had the ability to wrap their audiences around their fingers and

I think that Earl would like to have had that same capability. Another person he greatly admired was the Rabbi of the Temple that he attended. I never met the Rabbi, though I can picture him from Earl's admiring descriptions. His name was Robert Kahn. He was strikingly tall and ruggedly handsome. He would start each sermon with a story that anyone could relate to as he described any family with the usual problems everyone faces over a lifetime. The sick child, the loss of a job, the bout with cancer, a marriage gone astray, kids off to college, an empty nest, an empty heart, the death of a loved one or the birth of a newborn, the gay son or daughter, a fallen hero never to hold again a son or daughter joining the military and what might happen. Then he would relate it to the history found in the Torah with a message that would take hold of your heart so that when you left the Temple you were inspired to be a better person, and do what you can to make this world a better place. I understand that when Rabbi Kahn would end the service he would raise both arms and with words of old he would recite the blessings, and wish for peace among all nations and people. Earl would say, "It was like God was speaking."

Another attribute that Earl admired his Rabbi for was his service during World War 2. He was able to assimilate and make his presence not only known, but admired by everyone in the general community.

If Earl had any ambition, it would be to try to emulate and follow his esteemed Rabbi's path of leading a good and productive life with putting family first and foremost. This may have been why he was attracted to joining the Anti-Defamation League (ADL) when two of his acquaintances from Temple suggested he might be interested. The Anti-Defamation League was one of the oldest Jewish organizations fighting against hate and discrimination for all people. He joined, and in a very short period was elected as Chairman of the Houston Chapter. If you would ask Earl what were the outstanding highlights of those years in office he probably would tell you that he was invited to meet with the Executive Committee of the Houston Chamber of Commerce to confront them with his argument to drop the oil embargo on Israel. It helped work as the oil baron's recognized his points that as Americans we have an obligation to work with the only Democracy in the mid-east, and not against them.

If you want to call it a highlight, Farankhan was an outspoken Jew hater and stood for everything negative – discrimination, hatred, bigotry. He was going to be in Houston trying to rally his storm troopers. One of the radio stations asked him to appear on their station and engage in a debate with someone having contrary viewpoints. He refused to appear directly with anyone else in the station confronting him face to face especially if that person were Jewish. Earl was asked if he would like to try to counter Farankhan's biased statements, and would he be willing to be interviewed in the lobby of a popular hotel in Houston away from his counterpart in the radio studio. Earl agreed and met the challenge. He never made claim that he won the argument with someone whose mind was demented, and filled with hatred. But, it wasn't too long later that Farankhan was no longer a threat on this earth to people of goodwill.

When Earl had just gotten started in Houston he hired a temporary to come to work. Over the years, more than twenty, this lady- Krin Holtzhauser became a media maven and was active in the national association of women in media. She served as national president and brought glory to herself as well as GDL&W. On numerous occasions Earl would be asked to speak to the various AWRT chapters across the country. He was in hog-heaven having his own harem of admiring women hanging on to his every word.

Incidentally GDL&W was one of the first, if not the first in America, to be acknowledged as giving the most opportunity to women in business. More than 50% of the GDL&W department heads were women as Earl believed the ladies best understood and related to consumers who accounted for most purchases at retail. He understood and recognized that a female's capabilities can, and will crack the glass ceiling which businesses held over their heads to keep them down in the firm.

There's another story you might like to know. GDL&W represented the largest supermarket chain in the area – Weingarten's. It was possibly some time in the 1970's or early 80's when a Mrs. Barbara Falick, who was the wife of the supermarket's president called, and asked Earl if she and a few ladies could come by to speak with him. You don't turn the wife of a major client down, especially when you know that Barara Falick was a Weingarten before she married Harold Falick. It didn't take much later when Mrs. Falick visited and introduced Earl to Mary Keegan who was a well recognized civic leader, Sister Francis , and Lillian Pasternak who happened to be a friend of his wife Natalie as they both worked helping the blind. Mary Keegan told Earl that the ladies were concerned and wanted to help the growing number of hungry people in the community. She expressed that they had an idea that people shopping in Weingarten's, and other food stores, would be willing to donate food to help feed the hungry children and adults in

Houston. From that initial meeting, sitting around the agency's round conference table, the idea for the End Hunger Network was born. Someone suggested that if they had a steel barrel placed in every participating store we could promote the idea to have the shoppers drop a non-perishable food item inside that would be distributed to various food pantries. They all agreed it sounded like a good idea, but Barbara warned that all promotions in Weingarten's last only 30 days and are soon replaced. Earl popped up with his thought that if we do this a little differently, and use Red Barrels, and appeal to the conscience of the general public it might last longer than just one month.

No reason to belabor this subject as we now know that this program has morphed into the Houston Food Bank which today is one of the largest services to the poor and the hungry in the nation. Though those four wonderful and idealistic ladies have passed on - GDL&W worked tirelessly over many years to see this successful program grow. Gerry Hailer, copywriter and Mike Hulsey our broadcast producer were instrumental in producing many of the public service TV spots that would win all kinds of recognition, and helped fill the Red Barrels to brimming. Very few can ever forget the 30-second commercial using the most prominent restaurant chefs in Houston trying to sing and dance to the special End Hunger song written for this, which turned out to be a most hilarious TV spot. It got public recognition and food donations just soared. Many a kid didn't go to bed hungry because of the clowning chefs.

GDL&W worked for the Sisters of Charity of the Incarnate Word. Earl and the Sisters would travel from one of their 18 hospitals to another. He and his wife Natalie were adopted by the Sisters and were constantly invited to the Mother House whenever the Sisters had a celebration or party. One day the nun who was the Mother Superior called him into her office which was in St. Joseph's Hospital.

"Earl, we have learned to trust and respect you. It will no longer be required that two Sisters must travel with you on your hospital visits. One Sister and you have our permission to go wherever your work demands. Thank you for what you are doing and may God Bless You."

During the long tenure with the Sisters of Charity, Earl helped raise millions of dollars to further their good work by promoting the Pin Oak Horse Show which attracted thousands of people who generously supported their blessed works.

Both Earl and Natalie served the American Heart Association's Houston chapter for over twenty years. They received the highest awards for their and GDL&W's contributions to successful promotions in educating the public about heart disease, plus providing the needed help in fund raising. Earl was named honoree of the Heart Ball which is the American Heart Association's most successful fund raising effort annually. He also started the "Heart and Soul" 10K fun run which raised a minimum of $100,000 a year over a period of ten years, while also serving on the original Houston Marathon committee where he was responsible for introducing the 'run for your favorite charity' which has developed into an important element of Houston's biggest sporting event.

As a result of Earl's, and GDL&W's involvement with the Heart Association three organizations came to ask for help.

The American Cancer, The American Lung and the American Heart Association joined together to launch the "Smoke Free Class of 2,000." The plan was to teach young school children the dangers of smoking during the 1980's so that when they got into middle and high school they would be aware of the dangers to their lungs and heart which could possibly lead to cancer and other serious illnesses. He was the perfect one to go into schools and preach this lesson as he never smoked, drank liquor or even had a cup of coffee during his life which was amazing to all of us knowing he served in the Navy, was exposed to heavy drug abusers in his advertising career, and the temptations during an active social and business life.

What Earl proudly told us all, when he and Natalie went to visit in Louisville, Kentucky, with his son and family over the Christmas Holidays they were going into a public museum and in the front lobby was one of the GDL&W posters we had done for the "Smoke Free" campaign. Our word does get around, is what he would preach to the troops.

There are so many public service campaigns Earl would lead us into that it's hard to enumerate all of them. We worked for the March-Of-Dimes, the Institute for Rehabilitation, the Council of Social and Health Behavior, the Episcopal Church, Temple Emanu El, and whomever else would come knocking on our door that represented a worthy cause to help the hungry, homeless, mentally, or physically wounded, the alcoholic or drug abusers, etc.

Because of our wide client base we could involve our financial institutions, home builders, and food and beverage purveyors, plus a variety of retailers to sponsor many of these worthwhile efforts. It may not have put money in our till, but when you worked at GDL&W you could take pride in knowing your efforts and unique talents were helping thousands of other citizens no matter their religious persuasion or color of their skin.

Another detail about Earl is that he never took a ton of money out of the agency even when we were rocking ahead and had 185 employees, and making a handsome profit. I don't think his salary, including the annual bonus ever exceeded $150,000 a year when we were well aware that other much smaller advertising agencies principals took home considerably more money. He did have the agency pick-up the tabs for his many worldwide meetings and conferences for the AAAI and Young Presidents Organizations which we considered an investment in new business. He never abused that privilege by buying anything personal for himself, Natalie or the home. Every expense was documented as a true business cost. When he ran the numerous foot races around the country and in foreign lands Earl paid his own way, and never complained. He only drove Chrysler and Jeep products because we represented the local dealers' association, until he read that a new automobile was being introduced called the Delorean with wing-like doors on an all aluminum body. I imagine it was his desire to be an innovator that he placed a $1,000 deposit to get the first model to be delivered into the Houston area. It turned out to be a horrible mistake, not only for Earl but for the majority of Delorean buyers as the car didn't perform like expected, but it did get attention. His Texas license plate was "AD-MAN 1."

Earl was one of the very first ad executives to put in a liberal pension system for each qualified employee. GDL&W also introduced a profit sharing program which made Harry Paster of the American Advertising Association come back to Houston each time to squabble with Earl over his newest employee incentive innovation that he was ruining the business. "You need to squirrel the money away for the rainy day all ad agencies eventually face," Harry would admonish. Earl would smile and say, "Thanks for the visit, Harry, and have a nice trip home. Let us worry about the rainy day."

The only incentive program we ever dropped was when Earl came home from a California meeting and suggested we should install an Employee Stock Option Plan. In short time we found that it works best for a manufacturing company that needs to raise huge amounts of money for equipment and inventory so we dropped it.

Now seeing how Earl was dismissed out-the-agency door without even receiving the usual watch for his more than numerous contributions to the company he must be glad the profit sharing and pension program he was responsible for initiating are paying off for him, and the many other employees who worked and toiled at GDL&W.

No one can take away the numerous awards he earned during his long and illustrious career. I think he must be proudest that he was the first advertising agency member in Houston to be elected into the Southwest Advertising Hall of Fame. Well deserved recognition for my friend and leader – Earl Littman.

Before concluding, I have two more thoughts. As long as Earl was running the shop we never had a trophy case which we could have filled many times over. Every other ad agency had their medals, awards, plaques and trophies proudly on display for their visitors to be impressed at their prowess in the business. Earl thought he would rather have an old fashioned cash register on display in our conference room to remind both our staff and visitors nothing happens until we sell the products or services we advertise for our clients. Funny that one prospect, who later signed up with GDL&W, expressed Earl's sentiment that you see the display of awards in every agency, so there's nothing to differentiate one from another.

Weeks after we earned the Texaco business and our people had gotten more familiar with their teams, we asked the question that was haunting our minds, "Why did you select GDL&W from all the agencies you reviewed and visited?"

The answer was just what Earl's intuition had conjured, "We were narrowing our search down to a Texas-based agency, and had a choice of two different shops. Both were equally qualified. One spent all their time talking and showing examples about a famous woman's cosmetic they represented, and you guys told us that you would bend over backwards to do whatever we needed. WE ARE TEXACO! You made the choice easy."

Good luck, Earl, and thanks for being you."

GDL&W Is Out of My Life from Today On.

It feels like an unhappy divorce after close to a successful 40 year long marriage, and your partners turned on you to never darken their door again. What are you going to do? You just turned 65, yet you don't feel ready to retire. Without something to challenge you daily, and meet crisis after crisis, you know you will shrivel up like yesterday's thrown away newspaper. Should you become a consultant and chase after small new businesses again? Been there and done that, so what's the incentive, what's to be gained except more gray hairs and additional worry wrinkles. One day you are sitting on top of the mountain and now the mountain feels like a fresh dug early grave.

It's my last day here and I am packing up my office belongings. Everyone apparently is avoiding me because they are either relieved to see me go, or can't believe what has happened any more than I can, and they're too embarrassed to come in and wish me glad tidings.

Just then the phone suddenly rings. I stop packing some me-

mento and answer, "Earl Littman. May I help you?" A female voice I don't recognize says, "Mr. Littman, I am Dawn Mathis with the Drug Enforcement Administration, and we would like to see you as soon as possible."

A bewildered Earl can only mutter; "Excuse me Ma'am, but are you sure you have the right person? I have never had an illegal drug in my life. The only drug I take daily is a baby aspirin to protect my heart."

The cold response is, "Can we see you today?"

This must be serious, so I ask where their office is located, and she gives me an address of an unmarked office building less than a quarter mile from my home. "I will be there in 30 minutes, Miss Mathis."

I hop into my car with a million questions running through my mind. No, it can't be because of my kids. Was one of our employees caught using, or selling? Did someone make a horrible mistake and have me confused with some druggie? This is unreal. Why me? Don't I have enough on my mind right now? Maybe the account executive we fired a year ago for using drugs is trying to get revenge. Here's the building, I better park the car, and get ready for this unknown ordeal.

This building looks like it's seen better days and there is no identification on it other than the address. I open the entrance door and appear calm. A uniformed officer jumps out at me and I am no longer calm, cool or collected. "Yes, why are you here?" he accusingly questions. "Agent Mathis asked me to come over."

"O.K. Stay right here. Don't move. I will go up and get her. Don't leave."

Off he goes and gets on the elevator, and I am frozen in place. If shivering inwardly is moving then I am in deep trouble until the elevator door reopens and an attractive black lady comes striding over to where I am fixed in place. She's wearing a country-wide smile, and pleasantly greets me with, "So glad you were able to come here Mr. Littman. Thank you. Please join me upstairs."

That was my introduction to going to work with the Justice Department and the D.E.A. for the next exciting seven years.

Dawn Mathis walked me into a conference room where there was a petite Hispanic-looking brunette waiting to also greet me. We were introduced and Special Agent Yanina McDonaugh was to be my mentor as I was briefed what the ladies were inviting me to perform for the D.E.A. I couldn't help but keep sneaking stares at Yanina as she reminded me of a little doll that Madame Alexander would have conjured into a best seller.

The two ladies explained that the Outdoor Billboard Company in Houston had offered the D.E.A. one free public service billboard, and they didn't know what to say or how to get the artwork produced.

Could I please help? This was much easier than going to jail for a lifetime for doing something I never did, so I jumped at the escape. "No problem, ladies. Glad to be of help."

I believe they still thought I was the head-honcho of GDL&W,

but I wasn't going to argue with the D.E.A. I was ready, willing and capable of doing this assignment, and actually glad to be of help as it was a way of diversion of what I thought were my personal troubles.

Got the art and the billboard posted in no time and the ladies meantime introduced me to the Special Agent in charge and all the other key members of the agency. Within no time at all I was invited to create an anti-drug campaign which was a challenge as I knew zero, nada, nothing, about illegal substances. I mean I was a duck out of water but the Houston Region D.E.A. apparently had total confidence that I had special talents that they lacked and welcomed me with open arms. Special Agent Yanina McDonaugh was assigned to teach me the basic ropes.

If you are wondering as I did how a Latino lady had the last name of McDonaugh I soon learned she was married to a Special Agent who was in-charge of the shooting range. There was to be no fooling around with Yanina, and even if I, or anyone else tried, she could flatten you out before anyone might lay a hand on her. Sweet as candy on the outside, but tough as a caged tiger when attacked.

We would spend hours together in the commercial airports looking like passengers about to catch a plane as she instructed me in what to look for in possible drug smugglers. In restaurants she repeated instructions as to what we would do if there was danger. We attended dances in schools, rave parties and in bars to observe what the crazies were doing as they were abusing everything from marijuana to crack.

Yanina would walk me through apartment complexes to explain where the drugs were usually hidden along with the cache of guns, and who the runners might be that moved the money from buyer to seller.

This was a learning education to which you don't earn a cap and gown.

Then Dawn Mathis said we were going to Washington to meet with the high command and learn more about the duties the D.E.A. was responsible for performing both clandestine and publicly. I felt like I was once again in the Navy as I was right at home in D.C. going through basic training.

On my return to Houston I had to enlist in the University of Houston's same classes that they were giving to people that wanted to become licensed drug counselors. That's where I met John Cleveland, the instructor, who took a special interest in me and we became fast friends. Like most of the students, John was also a former alcoholic or druggie that had totally changed their lifestyle and was determined to try to assist others who had fallen by the wayside. I must admit I was impressed by everyone I met that had turned their clock forward to live a normal, productive life while helping others struggling to overcome their physical and mental battles with alcohol and drugs. Good for all of them!

My "handlers" Dawn and Yanina must have thought I was ready to be thrown into the Coliseum to battle with the lions.

"Earl, we would like you to try to educate young people about not using drugs. Are you willing to take on this important assignment?"

GDL&W IS OUT OF MY LIFE FROM TODAY ON.

They were taken aback when I said, "Not if I have to follow the D.E.A. protocol of starting in junior high school by showing a display of drugs, and then giving a scientific explanation of their harm."

At the Drug Enforcement Administration you don't say 'No'. The ladies were taken aback at my audacity to want to break the government rules they were trained to enforce even if it meant sacrificing your life.

"Tell us 'Why', Earl."

"I don't admire Adolph Hitler, but I learned that he changed a peaceful loving German nation into a war machine based on hatred by taking the youngest children and twisting their impressionable minds to believe and follow his horrendous doctrines. I will do what you asked, but you must allow me to do it my way."

Two startled ladies responded by saying they needed to report to the Special Agent in Charge to try to get his approval. When Mr. Howard learned of what I was suggesting he quickly said there is no way he could bend the rules, but he liked me and wanted to help. The D.E.A. would support my program, but not be able to fund my efforts, however he suggested that Special Agent McDonaugh assist me in soliciting grants if she could spare some time, and that Dawn Mathis more or less supervise my efforts to see that I stay within the bounds of the D.E.A. requirements.

It sounded good to me. So I asked Yanina if she would like to assist me in making a call on a potential donor for a grant. In practically no time, she and I were visiting with a gentleman I did not know, but had the reputation of being philanthropic for law enforcement causes. His office was in one of the Greenway Plaza buildings of which I was totally familiar as this giant commercial project was one of GDL&W's clients that I had acquired. Ken Schnitzer who developed the project was both friend and fellow Y.P.O. member.

No great surprise that when you walk into anyone's office with a beautiful Special Agent from the D.E.A. who is dressed in full uniform with gun at her side that you are welcomed. We stated our case to the tycoon with the deep pockets and he asked to be excused for a few minutes. He soon came back into his office and offered us a big smile with a generous check for $10,000 which launched my "Drugs Kill" campaign.

I thought how easy this will be to raise all the money we will need until I soon learned that Special Agent Yanina was being transferred to Puerto Rico to chase drug runners. Without her uniformed presence it became not only a challenge, but practically an impossibility. I became just another peddler with my hand out.

Next on my plan was to develop a logo and theme, and mentally create a business plan to execute my program to teach youngsters the horrible results of abusing any form of drugs including caffeine and alcohol. Since I followed that life style I felt comfortable within my own skin to go out and preach the gospel, "Don't Do Drugs".

The logo we developed was the picture of a pistol with a drop of blood red liquid coming out the barrel. The slogan was "Drugs

Kill...careers, families and neighborhoods". I was now ready to meet with an acquaintance that was the Houston Independent School District Board chairman. Laurie listened intently to what I was proposing, looked me in the eye, and said, "Earl, if we let you talk about drugs to our Kindergarten children as you are proposing, the parents will come unglued. We have enough problems on our plate than to cause a riot of irate mothers and dads. Thanks, but no thanks."

While walking away I thought that if I ever have the opportunity to talk with those youngsters their parents would someday thank me for possibly saving their lives.

I left the H.I.S.D. headquarters determined to not take "no" for an answer. My advertising agency background had taught me that if I couldn't get Zale's, the largest jewelers in the country, then what's to stop me from going after Gordon's Jewelers, the next largest company? I did, and Gordon's became one of our sterling accounts.

Just south of Houston was a rapidly growing area called Sugar Land which had the second largest enrollment of public school children. I called the head of the Ft. Bend Independent School District to setup an appointment. He granted me an interview in which I quickly explained my proposed program.

This time I didn't get a "No way, Jose" but an invitation to meet with their Supervisor of drug enforcement. Off I trotted to this man's office who listened to what I had to offer.

"Here's what we will do. You can talk to one Kindergarten class. I will have three Kindergarten teachers present, and the moment any one objects to what you are saying, out you go, and that's final. The end! Do you understand?"

The day arrived, not soon enough. I made my presentation which never was meant to be a speech; just a friendly grandfather play acting, singing, and dancing and asking questions of those absolutely adorable boys and girls.

"Have any of you ever seen anybody you know smoking cigarettes? Please raise your hands." Every little arm shoots skyward with their hands waving wildly to grab my attention.

"My Mommy smokes." "Mine too." "Daddy smokes fat cigars." "My baby sitter smokes." "Grandma smokes and my big sister does too." The chorus went on with each kid trying to outshout the other.

I quickly calmed them down while reaching into my pocket to slowly take out a fake cigarette. I deliberately start to place the phony cigarette to my lips causing total silence in the room where not a breath could be heard. Every eye is glued on me. No one moves.

After taking two long drags on the cigarette the tip lights up in a glowing red and smoke comes snaking out in a curling stream like a choo-choo train is puffing billows of smoke in the classroom. Their eyes widen in disbelief. I smile in satisfaction as I admiringly look at the cigarette. I pause. Then violently start coughing. Coughing loudly. Louder! My face is twisted as I grab my stomach, bend over and I suddenly fall to the floor with my feet kicking wildly, and I'm groaning.

Every kid in the classroom meantime has jumped to their feet to get a look at me turning cartwheels on the floor. In horror they are yelling "Poppa Earl. Poppa Earl." I quickly jump to my feet while smiling broadly to assure them I am O.K. and was simply acting. The next few minutes I calmly explained that smoking anything with nicotine, such as cigarettes, a pipe or a cigar, will get into your lungs and when they get filled, it can cause all kinds of sicknesses. To assure them, I add that it may not happen to everyone or work every time, but why take any chances? It's a risk not worth taking.

"Every boy and girl like you knows to never do anything silly or dangerous. Nicotine is a drug and all smart boys and girls DON'T DO DRUGS."

As the class is now over I hurry to the exit, and as each child leaves I look each one in the eye, and while smiling broadly repeat, "Don't Do Drugs." I gently place in each little hand a gift to remind them of the message taught and hopefully message learned. Meanwhile I am concerned and wondering what would be the reaction by the three kindergarten teachers that were assigned to monitor my initial presentation? Did I flunk my first Kindergarten test?

"Mr. Littman, that was wonderful. Thank you. When can you come to my school? I was concerned beforehand as to how you might handle this, but please come meet with our kids. They will love this."

"I am going to tell the Supervisor that we want you to talk to our school as soon as possible."

That started me on my acting career in each of the then 31 elementary schools in Ft. Bend which kept adding more schools as the growing population continued expanding rapidly. Every new school grade I introduced a more advanced illegal drug and tried to demonstrate the harm it may cause. Never scolding. Never preaching. Only providing knowledge packaged in fun and entertainment. Unlike some other substance abuse programs I would never dare to show the actual drug, or tell how it was administered. As my kids advanced to the next new grade I would repeat teaching that any of these illicit substances can cause devastating damage to their careers, their families and to the neighborhood in which they lived. My role was to try to make it fun to laugh while learning and absorbing about the harm and danger in experimenting, trying or using any of these banned substances. The goal was to try to implant in their young impressionable minds that "DRUGS KILL…DON'T DO DRUGS."

Talk is cheap, so Natalie and I early into the program decided we would offer incentives to try to help spur each of the students to stay drug free until they entered college. We offered a grant of $1,000 to each drug free student applying for a college education. Every 60 days as long as they remained enrolled in the "Drugs Kill" prevention campaign we mailed them a gift which might be our especially designed posters to hang in their bedrooms to remind them daily that "Drugs Kill." The posters featured local sports and entertainment stars that the kids would relate to like the young man from Sugar Land who won a Gold Medal in the Olympics. We invited this handsome young athlete to speak to an auditorium filled in every seat with high school students. The first question one of the young ladies in the audience asked was "Steve, are you married?"

Another popular poster featured a famous black female tennis national champion from Houston. There were over 4,300 young boys and girls that were enrolled in the program which kept Natalie and I busy looking for new incentives to design or buy, to pack, address and mail every other month during the seven years our original kindergarten classes were advancing annually into becoming seniors in elementary school. We depleted the funds from our profit sharing, our IRA accounts, and took out a Home Equity Loan to be able to continue serving our kids while I was doing my song and dance routine in the schools.

It was a daily task I thoroughly enjoyed. I would speak to three schools five days a week. My routine evolved into talking with two schools in the morning and one in the afternoon. More often than not I would talk to a local group of business people attending a Business/Commerce, Rotary or Lion's club luncheon, and maybe once or twice a week in the evenings address a Parent Teacher's meeting, or a group of parents involved in supporting athletic, cultural, or social clubs in which their sons and daughters were participating. I never thought of this being a task, but simply a labor of love though I frequently got lost on those dark streets in strange neighborhoods, and Natalie would be worrying at home as to what is taking me so long. I usually sneaked into a Dairy Queen while traveling from school to school, or to meeting after meetings.

I found I wasn't only teaching, but I was learning.

The first class each day was at the start of the school day, and usually would be held in the school lunchroom which also served as the auditorium when the tables and chairs were placed on the side of the room. Most frequently, each morning, there would be a table or two set up in the corner where some youngsters were being fed a free breakfast. Every once in awhile I would sit down to chat with these kids, and as long as I live, I will never forget this conversation with one youngster. I quietly asked him, "How come you don't have breakfast at home with your family?"

He turned to me, and innocently said, "Today's not my turn."

This is America. Houston, Texas, where money flows like oil and a little guy is forced to miss a simple breakfast because his family can't afford to feed him. I never asked the circumstances, but how must all those kids getting a free breakfast feel while their school mates are beginning to enter school and pass by their table. (Thank you Lord that none of my children ever had to miss a meal.) As young as all those elementary kids were, I witnessed the wall of lasting discrimination that we well-intended citizens were creating. Today is our turn to make things better.

It didn't take long for other school districts in Texas to call and ask me to present the 'Don't Do Drugs' campaign not only to elementary schools, but also junior high and the senior high schools. I was invited to Plano when they discovered a drug problem in high school, as far West as San Antonio; East to the Beaumont, Orange, and the East Texas counties bordering Louisiana.

I wrote songs, "I don't wanna marijuana, I don't need to smoke that weed,…" and, would get a great thrill seeing school busses load up with high school kids singing the lyrics as loud as possible. Some were hip-hop tunes about not doing drugs, and I would ask a couple of kids to come-up in front of the class and we would jive around together while having a blast. The drug counselors in each school became my best friends, but what really turned me on was when I would arrive at a school there would be an immediate response with all the kids whispering and shouting "Poppa Earl is here." The hugs around my legs from so many little ones made me feel important, and the looks I would receive from some kids who obviously needed a father figure who would tell them how much I loved them was more than worth all the preparation and effort for each class.

Believe me when I say that these weren't only students in school, but they were my kids…my own thousands of children who loved me and I worshiped them.

As expected there were some happenings that would shake me up like a malted milk. There was an elementary school almost in the shadow of Texas Southern University and as I am going through my usual prancing, dancing, and yakking about the dangers of certain drugs, I see two young boys in the back row paying no attention at all. They keep talking to one another. Yawning. Gazing at the ceiling, and definitely tuning me out. That was quite unusual because in the hundreds of other classes there was never a time that every child wasn't totally engaged in listening and participating.

What's wrong? Have I lost it?

The moment the class was over I confronted the teacher, "Miss, did you notice the two boys in the back row that didn't pay one bit of attention to what I was presenting?"

"Mr. Littman, I wouldn't worry. Those two are already in the drug scene."

"WHAT? What do you mean?"

"They're runners, and what cop in this neighborhood would dare arrest a 9 year old kid for delivering the drugs and picking up the money for the dealers?"

So, that's how two "babies" get hooked for a life of crime! Shameful.

Another incident happened after I finished what appeared to be a very successful series of talks in what would be considered a high school within a fairly prosperous area. I'm at home and just finished dinner I turned on the computer to read the incoming mail.

"Mr. Hot Shot, I'm the ecstacy dealer in this school and your crap is going to ruin my business. I betcha' you never even tried ecstacy. I'll make a special deal and sell you pills for 25 cents. I usually get paid a lot more. If you don't cut out your crap, you better watch out what we will do to you."

Next morning I rushed to the D.E.A.'s office and gave them a copy of the email and the name of the school. For the next few weeks I noticed Special Agents following me wherever I went, but I stayed equally alert. Time passed and I forgot the ecstacy dealer, but I had a haunting memory that I thought I knew who that young punk was who made that frightening threat.

The seven years went by quickly since that first Kindergarten test and the young men and ladies were going off to college or joining the military. Others might be looking for jobs as their initial step to climb the ladder of success. We awarded our first $1,000 grant to a young lady who was able to prove she followed our manta-DON'T DO DRUGS, and I bid farewell to my loyal friends at the D.E.A. and the many school drug counselors who constantly embraced and supported my efforts. A very special thanks to Judy Kajander at Dulles High School who would go out of her way to try to help many wayward girls. I know. I watched. I prayed with her to save their lives. She should have been born quintuplets to multiply her efforts.

What I really began to miss was hearing those young excited voices saying, "Poppa Earl, is here." You opened your hearts to me, and I pray my advice may have opened a path for you to follow a safe and healthy life style.

During those seven years at Christmas time the mailman flooded our home with sacks full of Christmas cards and many a photo from my kids, which I cherished and still treasure their memories.

Thank you, boys and girls for making my life much more meaningful. I hope you might have followed Poppa Earl's well-meaning advice because I do want you to know I love each of you as if you were my very own precious child.

Let's Get Off the Bus and Take Another Look

Those school days were different than some other drug-related things which were happening to this guy who wouldn't drink alcohol, and thought drugs were demons to be avoided at all costs.

One afternoon an attorney called to introduce himself, but he really didn't need to explain who he was because his fine reputation preceded him. He was recognized as an outstanding criminal trial lawyer. What he had to say was an unusual request.

"Mr. Littman, I am aware of your work with trying to educate students to 'Don't Do Drugs'. I have a totally different story to tell you. It's not about a young student who got hooked on drugs and is in deep trouble with the law. My client is a young mother with two little boys. She and her husband had recently gotten divorced and he left her with the mortgage on the house and the bills to pay on one car and a pick-up truck. Even though she had a pretty good job working in a mobile home sales office she was becoming desperate for money.

Her ex-sister-In-Law visited her and says, 'Honey, how would you like to make an easy and quick $18,000? Recently I met these two well-dressed gentlemen who just moved here from California where they hired young mothers like you to go to Europe and bring back something you will be asked deliver to them here in Houston. We don't ask what it is, but they swear nobody was ever arrested, and they do take care of the Custom Agents so there's nothing to worry about, and you are $18,000 richer without any darn taxes to pay. Do it honey, for the sake of the boys'."

The attorney continued.

"She met with the two gentlemen and is very impressed with their suave and gentlemanly behavior, so she agrees to do what they ask. They give her some money to go and buy some fancy clothes for herself and the boys so that she looks like a wealthy young wife of a prosperous businessman going to take a vacation in Paris for ten days. They give her the tickets and a fancy suitcase for her to carry over to France along with the paid for reservations at a nice, luxury hotel in the center of the city.

At the appointed day she goes to Bush Continental Airport and herds the youngsters through and off they go to Gay Paree. For the first week she spends every day sightseeing, Eiffel Tower and the usual tourist routine."

I listen intently trying out to figure what is happening. He goes on.

"All was peaceful and quiet when her phone rings, and an exuberant lady gets on the phone greeting my client as if they were long lost friends. 'Oh dear, I am so anxious to see you again. May I please come up to your room and see your darling little boys?'

She knocks on the door and my client lets her in. This stranger is carrying a duplicate of the suitcase that my client carried to Paris, except this is heavy. She is told to not open the locked suitcase and is given the key to be placed in a safe place and the lady leaves. My client gets ready to fly back to Houston. She and the boys go to the airport, check in without any problem and after the long flight arrive in Inter-continental Airport, and again no problem through Customs. The two gentlemen are waiting for her and they take the special suitcase, and promise to get back to her the next day. She and the kids go home. She resumes working at the mobile home office, but hasn't heard from the two gentleman that were supposed to give her the $18,000 pay off.

Within a short time a nice looking couple enters the show-room, and she assumes they are coming in to look at the mobile homes on display. They approach her desk to ask if they might sit down to talk to her.

'Of course, please do. May I offer you something to drink?'

The man looks at my client and asks 'Are you Mrs. Michelle Smith?' (not her real name)

'Yes, is there something you may need?'

'Mrs. Smith, we are with the F.B.I.' and they both show my client their badges, and ask to be shown to a private office where they would like to show my client something. The something turns out to be a complete dossier with photos of my client leaving Houston landing in Paris, entering her hotel, photos of the mystery woman carrying the suitcase, my client at the Paris airport, arriving in Houston, clearing Customs, meeting the two men that were waiting for her arrival and taking the suitcase that she was carrying.

'Mrs. Smith, the suitcase you were bringing to the U.S.A. was filled with ecstacy which is illegal. Please come with us. You are under arrest.'

Mr. Littman, I received a call from a distraught father telling me this story, and pleading I defend his daughter. This will really make you wonder. The father tells me that he is a former Texas Ranger. You know, the 'One riot-One Ranger famous legend', and he's mortified by what happened with his daughter, and the trap she fell into. I took the case, and to make a long story short, the Judge is about to send this lady to jail for a very long time. I am calling you, because I think you may be the best person to help keep her out of prison if you can get her to speak before schools telling her unusual story the judge may be more lenient. Will you do it?"

I don't know why, but I agreed and said, "Yes, when can I meet her?"

What the attorney had told me over the phone was the "Reader's Digest" version of the story. I now am about to meet and greet the real book. When I see this walking full-color cover girl I do not believe what I am now ogling. I had imagined I would be seeing some hardened old divorced woman who fell for a trap to pick-up some quick cash. Instead I am now looking face to face with a blonde that must have been the original casting mold from which they created Marilyn Monroe. She was the second most beautiful late-twenties woman, after my wife Natalie, that I had ever laid my eyes on.

Michelle didn't sound like a hardened gangster but a typical suburban mother who may not have gone to college, but was every day ordinary like thousands of ladies her age. Except she was absolutely stunning.

We hopped into my car and drove off to Klein where I had made an appointment to speak to the Klein Alternative High School. If you have never been to an Alternative School it's an experience in itself. Alternative schools are where incorrigible students are locked-up and attend classes. A young teacher in his early forties greeted us along with maybe 30 or 40 young men and women who are in his class. Both men and women students are each dressed in tan pants with a green tee-shirt bearing the Klein High School logo. They all have on brown high laced boots, and each walk to their desk, then stand at rigid attention until the instructor commands, "Sit down." In unison they follow his command and do as instructed with hardly a sound rippling through the class room.

The instructor walks to the steel class room door. He turns to me to say, "This door is locked and will remain locked for the next hour. No one will disturb you, but if they do we are monitoring this room. I will occasionally look through this unbreakable glass window to check your status and safety."

With this disturbing news he leaves and I can hear the key going into the lock on the other side of the heavy lock as he turns it. I realize I am locked in jail with a bunch of hoodlums.

I introduce Michelle and she explains she's a felon with which she yanks up one pants leg to display her monitor ankle bracelet. These aren't kids she's talking to. If you saw them on the street your guess might be that they are 20 to 30 years old. They were enraptured as she unfolded her story and told of her parole until receiving her jail sentence. No one moved. They listened intently, but it was hard to tell by their body language if they were buying her case.

My curiosity was killing me why these students, especially the young ladies, apparently liked these stark green cement block classrooms, the rigid discipline and total lack of freedom. I asked one girl, and this is what she straight out told me. "I like it here because I don't have the money to compete with the girls in regular school with their fancy clothes and expensive make-up. No snobs. We are all the same here."

Earl, wake up out of your fantasy land upbringing. Michelle and I were ready to escape from this dungeon as each student thanked us for coming to visit with them and sincerely wished Michelle good luck. She came through her baptism of fire and I was relieved to get back out into the open free air.

After a few more presentations to other high schools within Houston we were on our way to the Piney Woods in east Texas. If I make a mistake and drive into Louisiana she would have broken the rules of her parole, and nothing would save her.

The next high school is a school that was long past its ribbon cutting and opening day. A large school with a large student body, every seat in the auditorium was packed. The teachers, men and women, were standing in the outer aisles with their backs to the room walls. The principal introduced us, and I, in-turn, introduced Michelle who now was a confident presenter that could stride to the front of the stage and turn on an endowed smile before uttering her first words. The audience was captured.

As she lifted her pant leg to show the ankle bracelet, the students glanced at one another with a stare of disbelief and horror. How could such an unassuming, beautiful blonde with long flowing hair get involved in such a criminal act? As Michelle went on and related her story with all the details and how it has changed her two little boys, I scoped the audience for their reaction. The kids were staring straight ahead while absorbing everything she was saying like little sponges. It moved me to see every teacher, man and woman, wiping the tears from their eyes as each one could imagine themselves being in Michelle's early predicament of practically being broke, and then lured and hooked to try to get out of her sinking, stinking ship.

The students were allowed to ask questions. They must have ranged from 14 to 18 years of age.

"How many pounds of ecstacy were in the suitcase?" Michelle quoted what the F.B. I. had told her. Within seconds one youngster blurts out the exact money value on the street of the loot Michelle was carrying. A big 'WOW' came thundering through the room. Soon, we were on the road for our long drive back to Houston.

Every school where Michelle spoke the principal would write letters of recommendation asking the judge to keep her out of prison and let her continue talking to the students and the faculty about how easy it is to be recruited and how tough are the consequences.

During this long period both Natalie and I tried to make Michelle's life just a little bit more comfortable. She wasn't able to get or hold a job for very long. She went to work as a cashier in a neighborhood supermarket and when they learned she was a felon they canned her. This unfortunate experience happened time and time again. When Christmas came around Natalie and I loaded our car with every kind of toy the two boys would hope Santa would deliver, and we included a smoked turkey with all the trimmings. We both found her to be a sweet young mother who had dug herself into an unfathomable hole with no rope to climb out. All that time I kept wondering what kind of crazy guy had she married that would ever want to let go of her with a divorce, and leaving his family in a financial bottomless pit.

The end to this chapter in my life is comparable to Beethoven's unfinished symphony. We heard from the attorney that the judge placed her on parole and she didn't have to serve prison time. But Michele vanished mysteriously from our lives, like a fallen leaf blown off a tree to land somewhere unknown.

Choice or Chance

Mrs. Michelle Smith (not her real name) had made a decision of choice. We all know that Santa Claus doesn't come in a free trip on a magic sled whisking you to and from France. Those imaginary reindeers are a suitcase filled with pills that won't cure your headaches for the rest of your prison days. You should have awoke from your dreams, Michelle, and not risked taking the wild ride chance to pocket $18,000 promised by the suave, suede shoe swindlers.

Contrast Michelle's experience with my young grandson Collin Likover. He's now 18 and a senior in high school about to go off to college at SMU in Dallas.

December 6, 1995, my daughter Bonnie gives birth to a healthy little boy, which is her fourth son. It's a time for rejoicing that baby Collin has come into being with ten little toes and ten little fingers, and all is right with the world. He's cute and normal and as the weeks pass by he responds with his first smile, acknowledging people and words spoken. The housekeeper asked: "Donde esta la luna?" Little Collin would point his chubby finger to the moon, and a proud Grandfather exclaimed, "Collin is a genius!"

Months went by and Collin is around twenty four months old. As I am jogging with his mom, my daughter Bonnie, and I turn to her, and say between breaths, "Bon, I think maybe Collin can't hear very well. When I talk to him now he totally ignores what I am saying."

"You are wrong, Dad. He's perfectly fine!" was the indignant response in a tone which meant 'mind your own business'.

It wasn't too long after that we learned that my prognosis was confirmed. Collin had unexpectedly, and unaccountably, lost the hearing in both ears. One was discovered to be worse than the other. The sad medical diagnosis was that he was seriously hard of hearing. The cause…nobody could guess.

Was he bitten by some bug, had he caught a cold, a virus, an infection? Had he taken some medicine for a cold? There was no sure answer, but the news was damaging and disheartening. "A healthy, perfectly cute, normal baby…whatever happened?"

If you ever had the pleasure of meeting and knowing our daughter Bonnie then you will not be surprised at her actions and response. She was determined from that moment on that Collin will learn to lead a normal life. He won't sign. He will hear. He will be like his older brothers –perfectly normal, regular boys doing whatever young kids might do. Off she goes with Collin under tow to California where they both enroll and live in the John Tracy School for Deaf Children. John was the son of the more-than-famous Spencer Tracy one of America's favorite movie stars. An intensive month goes by when Bonnie and Collin return to Houston where Bonnie immediately enrolls Collin into The Center for Hearing and Speech.

The dedicated miracle men and women working there helped to transform that little tot into someone that with the aid of very special hearing aids, can listen to what is being said, and be able to pronounce words exactly as he is being repetitively told hour-after-hour, day-after-day. Collin was about three years of age when he started to work daily with the audiologists from early morning through the late afternoons with the exception of Sundays when he was able to be a little boy again.

Each year The Center would hold their annual fund raising dinner in the River Oaks Country Club, and they would invite a celebrity TV announcer Tom Koch to act as Master of Ceremony. From the time Collin was probably six years old he had an assistant Master of Ceremony – Tom.

Tom would give a brief history of Collin's hearing disability, and then ask Collin some questions about The Center, and Collin would deliver a perfectly understandable response that was also funny. The audience responded by standing on their feet, clapping their hands like trained seals and donating money. This act went on for a good number of years until it came to the point that it was almost unbelievable that this youngster was practically deaf.

It wasn't always easy for Collin to go through the elementary and middle school grades. Children can be the worst type of "bullies" when it comes to picking on other kids who may have severe disabilities and problems, but the teachers at The

Fay School did more than their best to shield Collin from any undue disturbances. They took pride in his accomplishments. One year there was a city-wide contest for who could write the best description of themselves, and Collin was chosen the winner. The School took pride. His family took pride. His classmates and friends took pride in this remarkable honor when Collin may have been 10 years old.

When Natalie and I were sitting in this huge auditorium, and the prizes were being awarded to the winning student entries, the presenter announced Collin's name and then read his entry in its entirety to an attentive audience. I can't remember what Collin had expressed word-for-word about himself, but the essence was, "I may not be able to hear what others may be saying about me, but inside my heart I feel like a red rose blossoming with sunshine."

Early on Collin participated in playing football and baseball in the Spring Branch League games. He was always at either guard or tackle as he would never be "off-sides" since he couldn't hear the signals. But, he only moved when he saw the ball was actually snapped to the quarterback. I am not going to make any claim that he was a super-star, but he held his own and made many friends from the teams he played. Mostly he made an admirer from his proud Grandfather who tried to watch him playing as often as possible.

He graduated from the Fay Lower Schools and now entered into Kinkaid Middle School.

Collin didn't look like one tough hombre athlete. He was of very average height. No, probably a little shorter, and lots rounder. He didn't run very fast. Correct that statement. He didn't run- he trotted. What he did have was guts and desire. He went out for football and Lacrosse...two of the toughest games to play.

The coaches must have been laughing up their sleeves to see this unfit kid trying out for their teams, plus he can't hear normally. 'Oh well, I'll give him a chance and he will drop out after the first one-or two hard practices. That way his parents can't complain to me.'

Collin played for four years on both the football and Lacrosse varsity teams while also working as part of Kinkaid's theatre stage crew, and writing an arts and entertainment column for the school newspaper. He practiced as hard as any of the super athletes on both teams no matter the weather conditions of hot, sweltering Texas summers or rain drenching afternoons extending into the dark of evenings. Collin was either a defensive tackle or guard which meant he would be playing against an opponent either twice his size or towering above him. I could only watch while biting my fingernails, but he generally held his own. Again he would never be called for being 'offside' and I would wonder if the kid on the opposite line would be using foul threats, and not knowing that Collin, with his helmet hugging his head, never heard a word.

He didn't play as often as I would have liked, but I understand that high school coaches have their jobs on the line of every game, and want to win each time as they too need to feed their families. The coaches are more concerned with running up the score than seeing that every player is on the field sharing equal time so Collin would sit on the bench gathering splinters rather than being out on the field regularly. I can't forget one game when Collin made a play on the opposing quarterback and the broadcast announcer blared out, "Tackle by Collin Likover!"

Every Kinkaid mother and father in the stands stood up shouting and ringing their cowboy bells as loud as the Bells of St. Mary for Collin. They knew the difference between their sons and what Collin had overcome, and wanted everyone to share in their joy and appreciation for my GRANDson.

Kinkaid's football team in their senior year won the Private School Championship and left the final game in Ft. Worth with an 11 to 0 record. No boy was happier than Collin, and my chest swelled with pride to see him sitting on the ground with the football squad and the cheerleaders smiling, and him embracing the trophy.

While sweaty and in his uniform Collin never missed coming over to me after each game to say, "Thanks for coming to watch me play."

What is the importance of this story?

Collin and both his parents made a choice. The odds were all against him when they first learned his hearing was almost nil, but they decided to work to overcome his handicap. The choice wasn't an easy one. It's taken years of work and investments in time and money to give Collin the opportunity to try to make something of himself and his future.

Many years from now, maybe 10, 20 or more, Collin's former teammates may be facing hard times, but I would like to think that they will remember that kid who wore those funny looking hearing aids, and went from a chubby-boy body into a tall, athletic built young man that overcame all odds to compete on the same field to become the best, and undefeated team in the league.

Young ladies, I understand that when you see a young handsome man who might be handicapped like Collin Likover, your brain also remembers he too has a mind, heart and soul. Maybe you mark him off as a potential boy friend or future marriage prospect. If you are as smart and brilliant, as I am assuming you are, then believe in the rose within your heart, that the two of you can live an undefeatable life together. In today's world there are many a wounded warrior, either physically or mentally handicapped, who deserve your love and care to live a lifetime of bliss in shared togetherness.

As for the readers who have been plodding through these pages with me, there's a lesson for all of us to follow. Every day we are fortunate to get out of bed, we are faced with choices as simple as what to eat for breakfast or as complex as your life's work. It's up to each individual to weigh the consequences. Is what you are about to undertake morally correct or can it end with you being in the early care of the funeral undertaker? Have you made the choice to drag your feet across the sands of doing something wrong, harmful to either an individual or society? In the long run, it's wiser to go undefeated because you took time to think and act as an unblemished member of what is a world's champion team of human beings.

We all can't win the Heisman Trophy, but there's nothing wrong in being dedicated to being the best we can be every hour of our lifetimes.

Makes No Difference

Since we are off the bus with the chance to contemplate other happenings which may have made a difference, I would like to share some advice my son Michael had offered me when he learned I was going to attempt to write a book. Mike is in the advertising business in Louisville where he's responsible for being the rain maker for Doe Anderson, an old and extremely well regarded advertising agency.

When Natalie and I first arrived in Houston we literally knew no one. No friends. No relatives. Two young people with two little girls who had to scratch and claw our way into a new society. Texas was on the opposite end of the see-saw from Pittsburgh and New York, and trying to level the field was our challenge. In both of those cities we had a legion of friends, but like birds of a feather we flocked together automatically to other Jewish families.

Not that there wasn't a Jewish population in Houston, but it was relatively small, and I felt that it's time for us to broaden our sights to become real Texans. That didn't mean wearing boots and a cowboy hat every day, but climb the fence and get into everyone's corral, no matter their religious, political persuasion, or skin color. We didn't consider ourselves better or worse or different than any other person we would meet, but wanted to see if we could share similar values and goals. Particularly if you were a patriotic American we would be brothers and sisters bound together like Siamese twins.

I was determined to not discriminate against anyone, and not cause anyone to discriminate against me. Being Caucasian is a recognized asset as my skin color was automatically accepted by most of the other white business people. Even though one of my war combat team once said that my face was the map of Jerusalem, I figured not too many people had visited that city so why let that be a hurdle. Just go out and attack the world as if it's my oyster.

Not all, but the majority of Houston's major businesses were in the oil and gas business. Since I had no prior exposure or experience in that field I would first concentrate on those companies marketing to the consumer. I didn't worry or care who owned or operated those manufacturing companies or retailers they were going to be my field of battle to conquer.

In the first year of Abbott and Earl with only one initial client Consolidated General Products, I had captured a total of 11 advertising clients. American Hat Co. was owned by Mr. Silver who happened to be Jewish, and Binswanger Glass Co. was also owned by a Jewish family in Philadelphia, with their regional offices operated under a Jewish gentleman's supervision, Mr. Herman. Their numerous retail stores and managers were Christian. My small but growing agency was a mixed-bag. I don't think any of them cared where I went to a Temple, Church, or Mosque. They were more interested in my being able to produce measureable sales.

And, as we grew the business and became more involved in the Houston community, we were able to prove successfully that we belonged here and were enjoying some measure of acceptance by some of the most influential companies such as the major banks, the light company and the largest department store, plus the fast growing Pizza Hut chain headquartered in Kansas. Our tentacles were spreading not only in the world of business, but equally in social circles. When the Alley Theatre, under their tireless leader Nina Vance, was undergoing a fund drive to raise enough money to attain a Ford Foundation matching grant, the Board hired us to help. This illustrious Board consisted of practically everyone of importance in Houston, or they knew every other person that carried the big sticks in our community. Most all of the Board members not only were our agency's biggest supporters, but also became my best friends. Today they all have passed on, yet many of their family members remain good friends. One good thing led to another, and if businesses wanted the best and biggest independent advertising agency in Houston they gave us the opportunity to "pitch" their business.

Where we really struck the mother lode was in extending our personal friendships far beyond our business. It's difficult to pinpoint what may have led to a legion of dear friends, but two examples stand out. GDL&W had gotten our tentacles into the Hotel Corporation of America when their management based in Boston decided to build the Hotel America in downtown Houston. We were selected to represent this plum account. Hotel America had a national advertising agency whose principal came down to Houston to interview us and see what this hick agency is capable of doing. During his visit he turned to me to ask, "Why aren't you a member of Y.P.O.?"

"Huh, what's Y.P.O.?" I inquired. He explained that, "The Young Presidents Organization was an international association of successful business people who were under the age of forty. If you are interested I will send you an application."

Being accepted in December 1965 opened wide the door to making lasting friends that were the wheeler and dealers not only in Houston, but around the world. I could spend many pages listing the friends we made, and the places Natalie and I visited, toured, danced, learned, were entertained, and thoroughly enjoyed every glorious moment. It was the time of our lives in which we bonded, and worked with like folks on all sort of committees. It was also the nucleus of forming a Houston based book club which met once a month for over twenty years. We have lived through deaths, divorces, second marriages, numerous births, graduations, grand children, great grandchildren, business changes, successes, problems, but best of all, a uniting of true and loyal friends. Only yesterday Natalie had lunch with four of the "girls" simply to keep their friendship renewed and alive. Two of the ladies were now living in assisted living facilities, yet these ninety some things were like young sorority sisters exchanging the latest gossip and sharing in the good fortunes of their various family members.

Our long years in Y.P.O. are some of the golden pages in the diary of our lives.

Maybe you are wondering why I haven't mentioned some of the people in our book club, or maybe not knowing that my small accomplishments fade in comparison to such giants as Gerald Hines, Jack Blanton*, Ben Love, Mac Wetmore, Craig Rowley, Gerald Pope, Bob Hervey, etc. All of these guys were not only smart but they picked the most beautiful and talented woman as their brides.

I told you how exceptional Natalie was, and still is. When the book club was first started and the ladies all got to know Natalie much deeper than her exuberant surface they once called me aside to ask, "Which private schools did Natalie attend? She's so utterly sophisticated and world wise. Was she a Vassar grad?" They weren't being catty, but were admiringly posing the question. I think they were actually taken aback when I explained her schooling was in public schools and from a city college. I honestly believe they admire Natalie, this Jewish friend from the Bronx, till this day.

There's no reason to claim we were pioneers in breaking the unspoken barriers of religious discrimination as many other Jewish tribesmen had assimilated into the Houston business and social community due to their unique accomplishments and accumulated wealth. Natalie and I were just two struggling immigrants from the North that were welcomed with wide open arms by Texans of every faith and nationality for which we can only say, "God Bless You All."

The other place we made numerous friends, too many to mention, was our membership in the Affiliated Advertising Association International. The comradeship of people all working in the same vineyard in non-competing cities led to many alliances other than just helping in the same business profession. I was invited to serve on the Board of our Tampa affiliate, and had the honor to visit many of the agencies as well as meeting their staffs. There were a few times I had the opportunity to speak to their local advertising or public relations clubs. Many of the agencies and there principals are long gone, but their memories from the bottom of our hearts still linger on.

Long live our kinships.

*BULLETIN: Jack Blanton died today 12/29/2013

*Blanton Bulletin

There is no way to account for what has just occurred. I just finished the last sentence, "their memories from the bottom of our hearts still linger on" regarding so many of dearest friends... when I get a call from my oldest daughter Erica Humphrey. "Dad, I have sad news. I just heard that Jack Blanton died."

My heart stopped still.

It can't be a coincidence that I had only minutes ago included Jack in these memoirs. God must be telegraphing me a message that my best friend (thousands of others must feel the same way about Jack) was being welcomed to sit next to God's throne as the two of them hold hands to make all the glory of heaven a better place.

This heart-breaking news brought a rush of fond memories over the past 40, or more years, in which the Blantons and Littmans shared many a bundle of experiences together. It all started when we first got into the Young President's Organization. Who can ever explain how two young couples from completely different backgrounds would simply bond together like a magnet attracts steel?

Laura Lee and Natalie formed a sister-to-sister love-ship. They could anticipate one another's thoughts and laugh together like little girls in a playground. I could never hold a candle to Jack's brilliance that would light up the world...both figuratively and literally. He was a champion tennis player, an oil baron, a great philanthropist, a pillar of society and leader of every worth-while cause in Texas as well as the U.S.A. But, you would never know it as he was unassuming, never boastful, always quiet and a wonderful example of being a devoted family man. The local newspapers recognized Jack's input on all society and ran a front page story along with a deep and thoughtful editorial which as thorough as the coverage was, could not hold enough space to enumerate all the good this kind man did in his 86 years.

Natalie and I travelled across the world with Jack and Laura Lee while attending many a Y.P.O. meeting where we would learn, laugh and light-foot across a dance floor as two happy couples. There is too much to tell about the fun and joy we shared, so I will try to narrow it down to two simple examples. I mentioned that Jack was a champion tennis player which is a most modest description. His trophies can fill a wing of The Smithsonian. Whenever the four of us would play a game of tennis together, Jack would instruct Laura Lee to stand next to the net as close as possible to the outside base line, and he would sweetly say "Honey, don't move." If either Natalie or I hit a ball to their side of the court we would hear Jack say, "Don't move. I've got it." And, he always did. And, he always won. He was a born competitor.

With all his medals and honors you would never know it from Jack. He never boasted, or bragged which is a lesson I well should have learned.

One time I had the privilege of introducing him to give a talk to a large audience waiting to hang onto his every word of wisdom. Jack began by introducing his wife who was sitting among the crowd. "Laura Lee, if I had known the joys we would be sharing during our marriage, I wouldn't have walked down the aisle. I would have run!" Every woman listening to this remark must have wished 'why hadn't I met a real man like Jack Blanton'.

Natalie and I have just returned from the service celebrating the life of Jack Sawtelle Blanton. The gigantic Sanctuary of St. Luke's United Methodist Church was filled seat-to-seat with people of every color, every income bracket, every religion and dignitaries of every political position in the city, state and union.

The sanctuary was still beautifully decorated with the Christmas enhancements; the choir wore scarlet red gowns with white lace, and the altar flowers caught my eye because of their simplistic but significant design. It was a lovely setting. Tom Pace, the Reverend, and like everyone else in the audience, was Jack's friend. He spoke knowledgeably that Jack had a style and passion that built bridges among people of every status, and he acknowledged that Jack was a gift of God. Everyone there had already experienced these virtues about their departed friend. Reverend Pace, went on to relate that Jack had called him one morning to invite him to come to his office for lunch where they would discuss church business.

"Jack told me he would order turkey sandwiches. Would I prefer mayonnaise or mustard?"

The Reverend then asked a question, "Can you imagine me, who was going to place an order to Jack Blanton?" Everyone laughed knowing the pinnacle of importance Jack Blanton holds in the community, and in their own hearts.

You and I have probably attended many a funeral service where the glowing description of the deceased far exceeded their personality or accomplishments. In this service there was not a word of exaggeration or twisting of the truth. Whatever praise which was uttered was modest in comparison to the significant accomplishments and deeds of our dear, departed friend and brother-in-life…

JACK SAWTELLE BLANTON.

Fare well dear lost friend until we meet again. Please, Jack, just once let me win one tennis game.

Latest Diary Entry

Today is December 24th, 2013 –the cusp of Christmas Eve.

Only last weekend a fellow octogenarian, Welcome Wilson, a highly decorated former Marine and prominent community leader, came over to me in The Houstonian gym to ask if I had any plans for this coming holiday week. "Sure do. On Tuesday I'm headed to New Orleans to have an affair."

A puzzled look crossed my friends face, and he asked, "Who's catering it?"

Just a few days earlier, Saturday the 21st was Natalie's and my 65th wedding anniversary. Pretty remarkable accomplishment in today's world where too many of our friends have passed away, or divorces became too common to end their marriages prematurely. Greed and instant gratification may have substituted for keeping the marriage vows to love, honor and obey –forever. When Natalie and I repeated those few sacred words we inscribed them in our minds, hearts and souls. They were lastingly planted in both our bodies knowing we would be obliged to carefully nurse them to grow from strength to strength.

Time has taught us that lasting marriage vows are a promise of love and fidelity which are easily pledged, but sometimes are challenged to keep and remain faithful. Nobody has ever promised that life is guaranteed to be easy, or if you break the rules you can return for a full refund. A successful business career, or marriage, and bringing up children is bound to have hurdles and challenges thrown at you which you learn to overcome. Failure is not an option in sports, work and especially marriage. I find it difficult to believe that most marriages of any length don't have an occasional spat, an argument, or a devastating disagreement. This may happen more than once, or twice, but my advice, for whatever it may be worth, is to take a deep breath, pause, and don't continue to aggravate the situation. You will only make the situation to slide downhill from bad to worse.

Get off the roller coaster and really think. Is this quarrel worth ending a romantic love affair? Because you may disagree at that moment in time does not mean the world will stop spinning and you can simply get off and instantly you will find paradise. Stop fooling yourself! The grass always seems greener on the other side of the fence, but the other green grass too can turn brown and die unless it is tended with continuous care and concern.

Remember, Earl, be a man! Nobody is perfect. The pursuit of happiness is my order to recapture the pleasure and joy of two people always being in love.

'Forget and forgive' is my chosen path to regain harmony, so embrace one another rather than destroy. What a blessing!

Even if I may continue to disagree with whatever may have created the argument it is better to simply and sincerely say, "I am sorry. I will try to not make that mistake again. That is a promise I will keep, so help me God." Then swear to yourself, and really mean it, to try to not repeat that grievous error again.

Forever.

I apologize for preaching, but sharing my experience over these past 65 years is worth telling if it will help guide others to realize that just because you put a ring on your finger doesn't mean that you can run rings around each other.

Wedding anniversaries are like candles on a cake. The flame glows brilliantly only to end after a brief life. I have looked at these anniversaries as being more than giving just another expensive or material gift that is only worn on special occasions, or mostly lies in a box or drawer hidden from sight. Every fifth anniversary I have tried to create a lasting memory that both my wife and I, along with our family, can remember as a lesson learned to never be forgotten that a marriage is a love affair never to be abandoned.

One year we hosted a party at our home, and as the guests all were enjoying a picnic on the lawn, an airplane flew by trailing a banner which read, "Our marriage was made in heaven." I have had outdoor billboards placed strategically around Houston which read, "It's wonderful being married to the girl I love for 15 years."

Would you believe that Natalie drove past those billboards and they never caught her eye? She was too intent on watching traffic so I had to ask her to get in my car and I pointed out to her where the signs were placed on the streets she travels daily.

One of the most memorable celebrations was on our 50th anniversary. The whole immediate family of our three children, their spouses and all of their kids, moved into a gated community on the outskirts of Las Cabo San Lucas. We all occupied separate homes which were right on the beach where the sapphire blue waters kissed the shore of the Sea of Cortez. The grandchildren spent the days on the beach romping around in the sand while I jogged from one golf course to another taking in all the local scenery from the small stores to the grand hotels. In the evenings a chef we had hired would prepare an absolutely delectable Mexican feast fit to feed Santa Anna's army.

December 21st, the evening of our anniversary, we drove our caravan of cars to a designated church perched high on a hill top. Imagine a pure white stucco Mexican church bathed in the glow of white flood lights with its old bell tower pointing like a traffic sign to the heavens with stars blinking there silver welcome. Hand in hand, Natalie and I climbed our way up a winding path lined with bountiful red bract bougainvillea to enter into the church through huge wooden doors hanging heavily on antique black hinges.

Inside every pew was filled with our family and friends. After greeting each person with hugs and kisses Natalie and I renewed our marriage vows. At the end of the full replica of our 1948 wedding I once again stomped on the glass cup to hear the repeated wishes of Mazal Tov (Good Luck). The photographer asked the immediate family to gather around the pulpit for a photo of lasting memory.

Grandsons, God bless them, couldn't pose for a picture without crossing their eyes, sticking out their tongues or distorting their faces into wet mops. So much for those pictures that remain hidden from everyone's viewing who would be wondering if all those boys had gotten the Mexican tourista.

As we are approaching our 65th wedding anniversary wondering what sort of surprise I can pull off without giving Natalie a clue. She hadn't been feeling too well and said she would not like to go north where the weather might be cold and disagree with her arthritis, so together we decided we would go to New Orleans. It was taking a chance that the weather would cooperate and not get too cold or wet in late December.

The Royal Sonesta in the French quarter was one of two hotels in New Orleans that our ad agency had helped open and represented over a good number of years. The Royal Sonesta sits right on Bourbon Street which is the scene of all the action, both lurid as well as fun, in the very heart of the French Quarter. Fine restaurants share space with strip joints, bars, novelty and art shops to create a magnet for tourists as well as native Louisianans. New Orleans is also home of the World War 2 Museum, along with many cultural and sport facilities such as the Super Dome that hosts college and professional football games.

I was aware that the Sonesta had balconies overlooking Bourbon Street so my choice of where to stay was relatively easy even with the multiple choices of lodging facilities in the Big

Easy. I contacted my friend, Don Brown who had worked at GDL&W for a good number of years. When the agency was sold, he left to form his own shop named Brownchild. Don did an admirable job in building his agency along with his partner. One of their stellar clients was Palais Royal which was a clothing store chain that GDL&W had represented for a good number of years, Don actually improved the image we had created which was a compliment to his talents, and possibly to the lessons learned at GDL&W.

Don more recently left the agency he had founded and helped build, to pursue his dream to open a travel agency. I called Don and told him about my confidential plan to celebrate our anniversary in a most unusual way. He immediately began negotiating with the hotel to acquire three rooms, and after repeated tries worked out a very accommodating room rate, however the hotel would not assign a room facing Bourbon Street with a balcony as they claimed it was too early to tie-up those prime rooms that would be used by the Rajin' Cajun L.S.U. football fans coming into town to play Tulane on the Saturday night of our anniversary.

I panicked, but decided to try my luck with the head of the catering department, and the Director of Guest Relations. Initially my repeated emails and phone calls were not able to resolve the issues. Then I finally made contact with an Event Planner group in New Orleans and revealed my unusual plans for the celebration over the phone to Nicole of Signature Events. When I explained what I was proposing, the young lady said she told her associates and some of the ladies broke out in tears. No, they weren't upset, but thought the idea was very romantic and wondered why their boyfriends or husbands never did anything romantically original. I told Nicole I wanted a band and she offered to contact the U.S. Navy jazz band. I told Nicole I wanted an "angel" dressed in white flowing gown with a gold-colored belt, angel wings and a halo over her head. And, could we try to get the Victory Belles who were carbon copies of the famous Andrew Sisters to sing some of the popular 1948, '49 and '50 love songs? In case you may not know, the Andrew Sisters were three young ladies who sang songs appropriate for the World War 2 years for the troops and general public. They were tall, statuesque ladies who captured the hearts of all Americans and became as popular as Beyonce is today.

In short order, the Navy Band said they would love to participate, but rules prohibited them from entertaining at private parties. We decided to switch to a local musical trio. Nicole said she would go to a costume shop and she would wear the angel costume during the event. She soon reported that the costume shop does not rent the expensive costume to anyone other than a model they employ as the costume is form fitted and too glamorous to let anyone else wear it. I said, "O.K." but was wondering how that might work? Nicole was able to get the three Victory Belles to agree to perform. I was not aware that there are actually 15 Victory Belles that form 5 different teams of 3 ladies each that entertain not only in the WW 2 Museum, but at many special events across the country.

Meanwhile I wrote the copy for 20 different 18" X 24" flash cards which enumerated the history of my falling in love with Natalie when she was a mature lady of 15 and I was a gangling teenager all of 16 years. The flash cards were to be shown by the angel during our little performance to be held across the street from our hotel room overlooking Bourbon Street. Each card recounted a special event in our lives from the day I first spotted Natalie at summer camp and instantly fell in love with her, and at 16 decided she was the girl I would marry. Each sequential card related when Erica married Ronnie; Bonnie married Larry; and Michael married Mary, followed by our grandson Brent being born to Erica and Ron Humphrey; Clay, Kyle, Lee and Collin being born to Bonnie and Larry Likover; and Ryan and Robert being born to Mary and Michael Littman; Brent marrying Stephanie; Clay marrying Jennifer; with Stephanie giving birth to our first great grandson Nolan, and after that string of eight boys Stephanie breaks the mold by delivering our first great granddaughter, Melanie. The last "flash card" had a very current full color photo of Natalie and me printed with "Natalie and Earl – Two in a Million." I also ordered 50 silver colored helium filled balloons to be given to the folks on Bourbon Street that may gather around out of curiosity to see what all this hoopla was about.

Everything was now planned and pre-set for the big event. Everyone was sworn not to mention a word to Natalie as it was to be kept secret from her, and traitor Edwin Snowden, the leaker of our monitoring potential terrorists. On Tuesday, our very good friends Audrey and Ray Maislin drove into Houston from their home in Austin, and along with Natalie and me we fully stuffed my 2013 silver Jeep Grand Cherokee with our luggage and overcoats from floor to ceiling in the back compartment. I cannot look out the back window, and have to push hard to be able to finally close the rear trunk door. We are off to New Orleans following Highway 10 through Beaumont, Lake Charles, Lafayette, and Baton Rouge, down to New Orleans.

The weather is cooperating all the way as it's cold but clear with blue skies. We stop at a Cracker Barrel to get a bite to eat for lunch, and make one more stop to fill the car with gas while we all use the restroom. So far, it's pretty uneventful, as the roads in Texas were smooth as glass, whereas Louisiana needs a little attention to eliminate the repetitive bumps that keep reminding us we are not in New Orleans yet. The landscape consists of acre after acre of rice fields, interspersed with oil field equipment, and one billboard after another announcing the availability of Cajun food, or how to win a fortune at the next gambling casino. These gambling places which line the roads more often than lamp posts try to lure you in like fishes biting on a baited hook by promising you will get rich quick.

While I am driving, my mind is wandering and I keep wondering how they ever built this elevated road over miles and miles of swamp land. There surely are alligators in these waters idling below the speed limit on the highway above, but I am not tempted to take a closer look.

Up ahead we see the skyline of New Orleans and we approach the maze of narrow only one-car wide streets that we need to navigate to get to our destination on Bourbon Street - the Royal Sonesta Hotel. We park the car and the bellman fills his trolley to meet us at our rooms.

Raymond and I approach the Registration desk and confusion needs to be undone. Finally they agree that I will check into the original room until Saturday when we can move into the room facing Bourbon with the balcony. After more gentle haggling and persuasion, the manager joins the reservation clerk and agrees to change all three rooms to be adjacent to one another and have balconies overlooking the future scene of our celebration scheduled to take place in five nights. We agree to pay a bit more for the rooms after they discount the price by 40%, and we then go upstairs to unpack.

By now, it's time for dinner and we all admit we are starving, as if we had walked from Houston to the French Quarter. Without restaurant reservations we decided to take pot-luck and walk a few blocks to see what may be available. It's around 7 p.m. now, but no matter what time of day or night, Bourbon Street is a jungle path replica of Broadway in New York as it is always packed with people. The difference here is that 9 out of 10 people are walking with either a beer or hard liquor in hand, and are dressed, or practically undressed, in the wildest, different set of clothes. Some have their faces painted, and their tattoos cover their head to toes. Guys strolling hand in hand with one another. Women on high heels that make them skyscraper tall though they are actually 4 foot 6 inches. Hair color may be anything that a dye can bleach, with beards that can touch the floor. Mainly they are drunk or sleeping off the drugs as they lay across the brick covered sidewalks.

Some kids are doing a street tap dance hoping someone may give them a few cents. There is a mish-mash of musicians also trying to make the passersby open their wallets. It's a zoo within a circus of people crushing together as they blow cigarette smoke in one another's faces. Look closely at those faces. Many are expressionless as if drugs have transformed them to be walking robots. Others are smiling from ear to ear as the alcohol has them thinking they are King of the Hill. There are college kids laughing, and girls eyeing every guy, and there are hustlers trying to entice people into the bars with girls wearing only their skimpy underwear standing in the doorways of the cabarets promising to strip out of whatever they are wearing which hides practically nothing.

The five of us are squeezing our way through the maddening crowds. We get to the corner of Bienville and on the opposite side of the street I spot Arnaud's Restaurant which is a place Natalie and I ate at a zillion years back during a previous visit to Sin City. I fight my way across the street to go inside the restaurant and I'm met by a haughty young man.

"If we are not dressed too fancily, as we have been travelling, can we get a table for five?" After sneering down at me he reluctantly nods agreement so I signal the other four to join me.

We are shown to our white cloth covered table, presented the menus and asked for our drink order. When I ask for lemonade and explain that both Natalie and I don't drink alcohol the waiter's eyes roll, his eyebrows raise in an arc, and he apparently sees that he won't be getting as large a tip if we don't pad our bill with abundant amounts of expensive liquor. He becomes a bit more relieved when our other three dinner companions Seena, Audrey and Ray order something from the bar. The meal is quite delicious. I started with a seafood gumbo as my private plan was to try this dish in each of the restaurants to compare the differences of how the different chefs prepares their soup in comparison to the restaurants we frequent in Houston. A pleasant surprise was a trio consisting of a slumped over alto sax player, a football sized banjo player and an elderly black base fiddler were entertaining the diners. They were playing a mixture of sentimental ballads and local jazz music and doing it quite expertly. The felt hat wearing sax player also had a lovely voice and belted out a number of tunes which I personally enjoyed. Then the trio left their corner spot in the restaurant and would visit each table to play any requested songs.

After hearing repeated requests for playing "When the saints come marching in," I left my seat and approached the sax player who was obviously the leader to ask him to come to our table and play some tunes as we were in town to celebrate our wedding anniversary.

"Which one?" he asked. I responded; "Our 65th." He looked me straight in my eyes and cleverly made a flattering statement, "No way!" By purposefully shaking his head slowly from side-to-side he indicated that I looked too young to be married that length of time. He instantly became my immediate best friend for life.

Then the trio came to our table and he took one look at Natalie and said, "You're much too young and pretty to be married 65 years." Suddenly he turned to the diners in the room to make the un-called for announcement that Natalie and Earl were celebrating our 65th wedding anniversary. Nobody seemed to give a hoot, and kept on eating whatever was on their plates. The trio asked what are our favorite songs for them to play, and my mind went totally blank, and I couldn't come up with any suggestion. It must have been the lemonade I was drinking. They played a few lovely songs. I slipped them a $20 bill, and we left Arnaud's with a belly full of Creole dishes and creamy rich desserts that kept me tossing with stomach pains all night long.

It Must Be Tuesday

Because I had trouble sleeping, I would get up out of bed and peek through the window drapes to look down on Bourbon Street. No matter the hour the drunks were weaving down the street, and there never was a let up in the mass of people walking up and down the crowd packed street amidst the lady dressed as Santa Claus who rode a fire engine red bicycle wagon that played loud music to make sure nobody slept in any of the hotels or inns along the pavement of broken dreams. Bourbon Street is a street that never sleeps as Frank Sinatra would sing about New York City which is half way across America. Yet, I'm thinking it's the thundering noise billowing on Bourbon Street that keeps those New Yorkers awake at night.

It's now Wednesday morning and after grabbing a bite to eat I am having cardiac arrest as the breakfast bill is close to $100. Oh well, it's New Orleans and we are here to relax and have fun. So, why is my gray hair suddenly turning chalk white?

The five of us agree to follow my pre-conceived plan that we MUST visit the World War 2 Museum. I had already made arrangements with the beautiful redhead Lauren Bevis, who is the Donor Relations Manager, to meet us there at 10 a.m. She's ready and waiting when Ray and Audrey, Seena, Natalie and Earl arrive only to be greeted by a number of other WW 2 veterans who graciously host all the visitors.

Both Ray who is an Air Force veteran and I are given the special treatment reserved for those who served in the war which the Museum commemorates. Lauren guides us into the first exhibit which is a film presentation hosted and produced by Tom Hanks. This is no ordinary film like I have ever seen before. It's an experience.

On the stage there's an old Philco type wooden case radio that announces the declaration of war when the screen opens up with silhouettes of ordinary citizens crossing the stage to enlist in the armed forces. It quickly progresses to the battles in Europe and as the bullets begin to fly and the bombs blast the floor, when the seat you are sitting in shakes, rattles and rolls as if you were the target being shot. The scenes are as real as if you were engaged in the battles and the simulated snow actually falls on you to create the illusion of your fighting during the bitter cold weather. Your comrades in arms are falling like the snow while the medics try their best to heal the wounded.

This is my second time to witness this film, and I don't know how the others in the theater react, but I can't keep the tears from falling across my cheeks as I find myself engaged in similar missions attempting to save the limbs or life of a combat warrior. Unfortunately not always successfully to my never-forgetting regret.

When the nose of the American fighter plane leans directly into the faces of the audience, and the artillery is being fired at you with enemy fighter planes attacking, your seat shakes as fast as your racing heart beats that you honestly think you are engaged in being blown out of the sky and dropped to your death on the earth below.

Of course, this film has a happy ending with the fall of Germany, and then Japan; yet, one can never forget the horrible cost of lives and property on both sides engaged in the war. Your eyes pop open wide in horror at seeing the release of the Holocaust victims turned from human beings into scarcely living skeletons. There is no tragedy worse than our fallen heroes whose blood spread across too many lands for the Allies to regain peace across the world.

I won't describe all the exhibits as I truly recommend that you make it your duty to visit this remarkable museum filled with exhibits of every type depicting the tools of war. Be sure that you also enter the U.S. Submarine which will take you on a simulated tour where you are made to feel you are part of the brave crew launching torpedoes against Japanese ships in the pacific. Then BOOM! Your sub has been hit by a mine, and you and your crewmates swiftly go down to the unforgiving bottom of the sea. Miraculously, a limited few lucky sailors escape using their Momson Lung which allows the survivors to breathe as they rise from the depths of an unforgiving ocean that has swallowed their fellow crew members.

I must admit that most visitors looking into the open rear doors of a khaki brown military ambulance might just glance in and walk away. Nothing too unexpected, a few backpacks, miscellaneous gear topped with a hospital corpsman's helmet resting at a slight angle. Again a rush of memories flooded my mind. This helmet had an oval of a white circle up front and repeated on both sides with a bold red cross in the middle to identify to foe and friend that a medic was wearing this identification. By international law medics, on both warring sides, were to be protected from harm. It was illegal to shoot or harm them and they were not to engage in battle as they were there to perform humanitarian efforts in caring for the wounded. Do you think a Japanese soldier who was commanded to sacrifice his life for his Emperor by killing the enemy would stop at not shooting or bayoneting a corpsman? They knew that for every corpsman they could eliminate they were also probably killing or downing another ten or twelve troops who might be saved to fight against them again. In combat all medics were prime targets for the enemy! When I looked at that lonely helmet sitting in the rear of the ambulance all I could think of was that 68 years ago I would rub the sand and water of the beaches on which we secretly stole ashore to use the mud to hide the red crosses that were bulls-eye targets for Japanese bullets. I already told you I am no hero, but I also am no shmoe. Better to play it safe than be sorry.

Statistically more airmen were killed, however, percentage-wise due to their fewer numbers, more medics unfortunately died during World War 2.

The majestic buildings containing the artifacts of the "war to end all wars" are surrounded with sidewalks paved with blood red bricks, on which are described the names and ranks of those who served in any and all branches of the U.S. military. Natalie years ago signed on as a Charter Member of the World War 2

Museum in my honor, and we have continued to try to support this magnificent museum which exemplifies the significance of the size, scope and importance of World War 2.

There must be thousands of bricks honoring those men and women who courageously served. Trying to find "your" brick is like searching for the needle in a huge haystack, but nevertheless as you read each brick you understand that you are looking at some Soldier, Marine, Sailor, Airman, or member of the Coast Guard who served with honor for our country, and we owe each one our respect and gratitude for the sacrifice they have made for every American.

My brick is in front of the Victory Garden in section marked NG in the first row, and is the fifth brick which is engraved, "EARL LITTMAN – U.S. NAVY – COMMANDER IN CHIEF – BACK OUR VETS". I thought wouldn't it be nice if when someone stepped on my brick the Star Spangled banner would automatically play, and at night the brick would light up and shoot red, white and blue rockets off to the stars above.

This year when the Museum's Annual Dues came ready for payment our daughter Bonnie and her husband Larry, generously donated the fee in honor of our 65th wedding anniversary. Thank you both for understanding what is dear to our hearts.

We bid goodbye to our sweet hostess Lauren Bevis and the large number of volunteer veterans, and went back to the hotel with fond memories of a day well spent.

Mess Call

What is New Orleans famous for? The food and enjoying every morsel. Off we go to Mr. B's which is maybe just two streets away down Bienville St. We are quickly seated; order our meals with Audrey, Ray, and sister-in-law Seena, who all have some wine, and Natalie imbibing an iced tea with a slice of lemon, and me going all the way with the tall lemonade.

Naturally, we engage our waiter to ask about the Brennan family that owns this Mr. B's restaurant. He explains that there are a number of Brennans who each own a wide number of restaurants not only in New Orleans, but also in other places including the famous Brennan's in Houston. What was fascinating and most interesting was when he explained that this restaurant was under water during Hurricane Katrina, and was closed for two years while being renovated keeping the old charm, yet was updated with some new fixtures and appointments. He proudly stated that the Brennan owner paid the full staff of long time employees their salaries, and kept their benefits in force during that long period of time.

The food not only tasted good, but learning of the generous benefactor of this establishment made this meal something special and much more than memorable. Thank you, Mr. B.

Next morning we have decided to take the recommendation of the hotel's concierge to take a bus tour of the city. Audrey, Ray and Seena want to first go to Café Dumonde to have coffee and beignets. All five of us take a leisurely stroll from the hotel down to the Riverside area walking past numerous antique and art galleries. I can't wait for the opportunity to spend more time examining their wares shop-by-shop.

Just before we arrive at the Café Dumonde we stop to pur-chase the bus tour tickets, and in "get-'em-while-you-got-'em" style the two ladies selling the tickets try to persuade us to "up-grade" our tickets to two days of tours, plus offering not only other incentives, but additional things we NEED to do and see while in New Orleans. "You won't want to miss this!!" "Thanks but no thanks. When does the bus leave on the tour?"

Both Maislins and Seena go into the Café to load up on beig-nets, while Natalie and I cross the street to have an American style breakfast, without the fried dough blanketed in sugar beig-nets. Within 25 minutes Raymond leaves the Café Dumonde with a big smile on his mouth smothered in flakes of sugar, and his polo shirt sprinkled heavily with white sugar crystals. Since it's just a few days before Christmas he appropriately is Frosty the Snowman.

Then we board the two level yellow and red bus, and slowly climb the steel staircase to sit on the upper deck. With each of us being over 80 years slowly is our natural choice of pace. The weather is delightful, so, except for the slight wind messing up our hairdos, we are sitting on top of the French Quarter world.

Our tour guide is a native of this city and shares a wealth of information about the history of each area as we go from one significant place after another. No surprise when he points out that booze is the number one source of revenue in New Orleans. There's one pit stop at the Louis Armstrong Park and Visitor Center. I was fascinated by the railroad displays and musical memorabilia and was tempted to buy some items, but I remembered how filled to the rims our car was with luggage, so I bravely resisted the temptation. However, when the bus stopped near the Victory Garden of the WW 2 Museum, the tour guide proclaimed, "These sidewalks contain the bricks with the names and ranks of our fallen heroes." All five of us shouted in unison, "Not true." The bricks commemorate anyone that served honorably. "Earl's brick is right down there. We think that he is here as living proof he is still alive."

Thanks guys. I needed that affirmation.

The born salesman tour director apologized for his error, but I am not certain he will change his spiel on future rides. Audrey and Ray got off at Harrah's Casino to let Audrey gamble big time. We later learned, after gambling over two hours, she won $7.15 at the penny slot machines. Natalie was tired and took a taxi back to the hotel, while Seena and I decided to walk back on Juliett Street to look inside the art galleries. That wasn't a walk, but a hike to get back to the Royal Sonesta. Seena doesn't favor contemporary art, but prefers the more traditional styles of paintings and sculptures. My taste is more eclectic and almost anything well done, or innovative, is more than acceptable to me. I believe we both enjoyed tramping and looking at the wide variety of art we found from one place to another. The architecture from ultra-modern to up-dating the old warehouses and buildings to display these painting, sculptures, furnishings was almost as interesting as the items they housed.

We both hadn't eaten since our early breakfasts and Seena was not only getting tired, but thirsty.

"Earl, aren't you tired?" I lied, "No, it's just my arthritis in the right hip which is slightly painful, but I am feeling great."

Just in time, we came to a "Smoothy King" and I got in line to place our order. There was a lady standing to the side and immediately Seena recognized her as the person who sold us the bus tour tickets much earlier in the day. They struck up a conversation, and I was afraid the bus tour lady would wrestle Seena into grabbing a new special discount on something more for us to do in the French Quarter. We escaped unharmed and rescued from dying of thirst while quickly quenching down the chocolate smoothies.

Strike Out on Bourbon Street

Tonight was our night to go to Commanders Palace which is a well recognized establishment known for its fine food. All five of us squeezed into a cramped taxi with Seena and me crawling over seats to sit in the back row, and repeating our acrobatic act when we arrived at the restaurant. The maitre'd started to lead us up the stairs to the second floor when both Audrey and Natalie rejected that idea, so we were ushered to a table near the entrance into the main dining area.

A young, blonde whose hair fell across one side of her face greeted us and said her name was Emily.

"Where are you from Emily?"

"Oh, Oshkosh, by gosh. You're a Wisconsin girl...where they make the luggage."

"Where did you go to school, Emily, and what did you study?"

"What, you studied food archeology...what brings you here then?"

Briefly, Emily said she was interested in the culture of foods across the centuries in many different countries. She had travelled to many places around the world to actually experience unique food preparations. There aren't too many places she could put this experience to work so she took a job at Commanders Palace where she could serve the best of alcoholic spirits and cuisine. Emily was amazing.

When Ray ordered a special wine she would counter with a knowledgeable question about the variety and characteristics of each type. Audrey and Seena each asked about another alcoholic drink and Emily would provide both questions and answers for them to make an informed choice. I listened and was impressed with Emily' unique knowledge. Never before have I ever witnessed anyone serving drinks being so intelligent about every choice of alcoholic beverage.

She was equally wise about the full choice of dinner items. Never did she act condescending if we had little or no understanding of what her description of each item contained. Emily would rank a number 10 among all the food waiters I have experienced working in the best restaurants. After a full meal which was a delight to the palette, Emily disappeared to be replaced by Cody from whom we ordered the wide variety of delectable desserts. I am a dessert freak and frankly could skip the appetizers, soups, salads, entrees for a good dessert, especially if it's chocolate. Tonight was the crème de menthe of a treasure chest of choices. Not necessarily a cream with a mint flavor, but my choice of dessert came in the form of an Eiffel

Tower tall parfait to die for. In a huge glass they packed the best of everything too delicious to describe. All I can say is that I used my spoon to clean the glass so that they wouldn't have to use a dishwasher to get it sparkling again.

Why did Cody replace Emily? When we asked, we learned that it was Commanders Palace's way of training their newest servers as to how to properly conduct themselves with their clientele. No wonder this restaurant is packed every night with happy patrons and enjoys such an impeccable reputation. They practice attention to every detail to try to make the dining experience 100% perfect.

We taxi back to Bourbon Street where I try to wipe the smile of content from my face and attempt to fall asleep in peace and comfort. Impossible! The noise on Bourbon Street every hour can raise the hair on the dead. Our room is right across from the Music Park where the band tries raising the noise level higher than the rowdy home team crowds at an NFL football game.

Peeking through the window drapes I can't help but wonder what is going on inside Rick's Cabaret, directly across our room, which is a strip joint where my sleepy eyes remain glued and wide open to the guys mostly, with an occasional woman in tow, disappear inside and apparently never leave. Two doors down are two similar joints so there always is intrigue going on to stimulate my imagination, but not enough to make me have the guts to participate. What can you do with a born again chicken?

Alright, without disturbing Natalie who is already in dream

heaven, I slip into my jeans and put on a sweater and go onto the balcony with a pock-marked moon overhead , and look down at the herd of people crowding the way through Bourbon/Beer street either making out or trying to. At 86, I don't crave wild sex, but admittedly I think about it since I'm not yet in a padded wood box. I sneak into the bathroom, turn on the light and stare into the mirror. Clint Eastwood just made my day. His latest photos don't make me look any worse than he does. We both have a network of face wrinkles and his baggy eyes don't look much better than the trunk sized swollen peepers I tote around on my face. I decide that I am going to take a test 'down the street of dreams' just as if I were buying a new car.

Down the hotel elevator I go, and the very first things I see in the lobby are two promiscuously dressed women walking my way. Their blouses are cut so low that I can tell the color of their toe nail polish. They are obviously ladies of the night on the prowl. I stare at them and they walk by without even a glance in my direction. No problem. Out the hotel lobby doors I go making sure I am walking as upright as the sentries guarding the Tomb of the Unknown Soldier in Washington, D.C., and no shuffling of my feet like my peer group is prone to do. It's my futile attempt to look maybe twenty years younger…only fooling myself.

I mangle my way through one person after another as I search the faces of every woman whether they are alone or with someone else. Not one ever peeks at me as I keep hoping for that come hither look which I see in all the Cyalis TV ads. Does every girl over eighteen have a built in radar screen who sees me and automatically reads a sign hanging over my shoulders which tells, "Not available. Married for 65 years?" Do they carry an x-ray machine that can read my wallet to indicate I have credit cards, but very little cash because there's not much more in my meager bank account? Just because I removed my wedding band is that white band around my finger a signal to look the other way or straight ahead without any signal of recognition?

Oh well, I don't know about these other folks but I have walked half a block and I am tired. It's better to go back upstairs and climb back in bed. However, all is not lost. I think back to a time not too long back when I am sitting on my bike in the early morning spinning class when a young lady saddles up to me and whispers softly, "Earl, you're the sexiest man in this room." I break into my most charming, self-satisfied smile and feel my chest swelling with pride when I look around to realize I am the one and ONLY guy in this harem of bicycling women.

I decide to take the pledge to resign from thinking I am America's sexiest man. However, Earl, take solace. It's never too late to try for the world's title.

Dying to Meet You

It's a new day. We take my car out of the expensive nightly storage at the hotel and head for our own tour of the city. Tulane University is a must see as Seena's son Bob graduated from there. Her niece is now graduating from high school and has received her acceptance to Tulane so we need to check it out, along with the neighboring La Salle University.

I'll admit I am a Houstonian at heart and couldn't imagine that either of these two campuses could compare to Rice University with its beautiful mixture of old and new buildings forming a precious jewel in the center of the bustling and busy city We drove by the shot gun houses in some of the poorer sections as well as the block wide mansions in the Garden Center of town. The Street Car named Desire crossed our path as we toured along St. Charles, and worked our way along Magazine Street which is crowded with stores like a Turkish bazaar.

Up ahead was a Texas institution--Whole Foods, so we stopped to get some refreshments and I found a different brand of power bar that actually tasted pretty good. Back into the car to look at the various Christian cemeteries with the unusual tombs raised above ground and grass growing on the Mausoleum roofs. In contrast we came across a lone Jewish cemetery with the grave markers and monuments at ground level. I have been wondering ever since why the difference?

My fascination with Louisiana cemeteries can be readily explained. While attending a Y.P.O. seminar at Harvard University I met a most unusual gentleman. He was portly to say the least, and I decided to strike up a conversation with this stranger which became the start of a twenty or more year business relationship. "Pardon me, but my name is Earl." "I'm E.J. Ourso from Donaldsonville, Louisiana."

"Pleasure to meet you, E.J. Mind if I ask you what you do in Donaldsonville?"

"Well Earl, I make a million dollars a month a nickel at time."

"E.J., you must be kidding. How can anyone do that?"

"I sell funeral insurance to people all over the state, and we collect payments every week with 5 cents at a time from thousands and thousands of folks. It all adds up. I also own and operate the finest funeral homes in New Orleans and in many other Parishes."

That simple conversation led to our representing Security Industrial Insurance for all their advertising over many wonderful and successful years. This became a mutual love affair between E.J. and myself. Who says opposites don't attract? I am lean as any marathoner, and Ourso is round as a turnip. He's a staunch

Catholic and I am a Jew. He's as rich as any Rockefeller I know, and I am Rockpoor in comparison. E.J. loves to eat his Cajun diet, and I have a power bar and Zero Coke for lunch. E.J. drinks whatever comes with the meal or without it, and I limit myself to lemonade, Diet Coke or Pero – a coffee substitute.

Almost without fail, once-a-month I, along with Rich Witmer, would fly into either Baton Rouge or New Orleans, rent a car and drive to Donaldsonville. At the risk of hurting some locals' feelings, my impression of Donalsonville was a sleepy Louisiana town surrounded by sugar growing farms (close-by a gigantic chemical plant), that may have seen better days. 'Downtown' was a ghost of its former self. There was a department store that looked tired, a corner bank that even a thief wouldn't give it a second look, and a series of stores from a bye-gone era.

Security Industrial Insurance Co. occupied an abandoned bank building smack in the middle of store row. This bank building, even in its glory days, couldn't have been any beauty. The only toilet facilities were a row of outhouses in the back yard. Inside was still as quaint as a log cabin. There was nothing fancy. And modern meant an old typewriter. What it did make was money, and lots of it.

The monthly company meeting was held in the old school a few streets away. All the sales managers would gather to hear E.J. give them "heck-and-thunder" to produce more sales. They were berated to do better, make more calls, close more sales, and don't dare fall behind on the weekly nickel collections.

Orson Welles, was an E.J. look alike, but could have taken acting lessons from him. Ourso was usually a tyrant demeaning anyone and everyone who didn't meet his standards for monthly production. There was no one who could escape man or woman if he was displeased. What really upset both Rich and I was how he would berate and mistreat some of his black employees that may not have reached their monthly goal.

"Boy, get up and sing a song!" The poor guy, who was forced to depend on his weekly pay check would have to get up before the group, with trembling voice, sang some whatever-you-want-to call-it song, and then sat down slumped in his chair.

I am embarrassed till this day that I didn't have the gumption to get-up and walk out on this unnerving display, but greed for the commissions we earned, outweighed courage. A mistake for which I humbly regret.

If the Security group as a whole met the monthly goals, they were served a steak with all the trimmings for lunch. Should they fail to meet the sales target then all they got to eat was a cold frankfurter from the school lunch room.

E.J. must have believed that power starts at the top, and cracking a strong whip is what motivates the horses to pull the wagon faster. This was the only side of E.J. Ourso which was in total contrast to his daily personality. Makes you wonder if all of us have a mean streak hidden inside of us just waiting to come out into the open to wreck havoc and misery on others. Better we should lock that devil up and throw away the key.

The real E.J. Ourso was kind and understanding who generously supported his church, his community, his university, and legion of friends. Rich and I would always be invited to share lunch with E.J. usually at his home that was a very short walk from the office. The house was probably the largest in Donaldsonville that I ever saw. The kitchen was the biggest room, and the giant pots and pans were lovingly filled with food which Mrs. Ourso slaved over to prepare from scratch to heaping plate. She was a charming lady with a smile as broad as E.J.'s belly, which was really big from eating all those saucy-rich Cajun meals.

Twice a year the Oursos would invite Natalie and me to their home whenever they were holding parties which were more like Kingly feasts that must have had the breweries throughout Louisiana working overtime. The shrimp fleet of boats was emptied as their catch was fried, boiled, broiled, and smothered in every seasoned type of spicy sauce that has ever been conjured to tear up your unsuspecting stomach.

E.J. also had an apartment on the ground floor of one of the classy high-rises in New Orleans. Whenever I was invited to visit we would go to any of the finest restaurants. No reservations ever needed.

"Welcome back, Mr. Ourso. So nice to see you. We are delighted to show you to your table." The owner knew he had just earned the restaurants profit for the day, and possibly of the week. Great food was E.J.'s passion.

What was E.J.'s pride and joy was to show me his gorgeous funeral homes that were beautifully built and elegantly furnished where he never spared any of his nickels to make them outstanding showplaces of comfort for his clients and their grieving families.

When GDL&W changed ownership I sadly lost contact with E.J. and Security Industrial. My fault. However, I wasn't too surprised to later learn that Louisiana State University named their Business School after E. J., whose given name was Eucharist Jesus Ourso.

God has made certain that Eucharist Jesus will rest in peace.

What a Beautiful Day

Whoa! Let there be no confusion about E. J. and his empire. I should have warned you that I tend to scramble wherever my mind wanders. You may have come to the conclusion that I am no author, but just a very ordinary guy putting his common sense thoughts down for whomever wants to see that maybe this puzzle holds something of interest.

Where we were last is returning from Commanders Palace after dining out Thursday evening. We all get up early, around 10 a.m. on this overcast Friday as its vacation time in New Orleans and we meander around the corner to have breakfast. If you ever want to have a breakfast surprise that will make your mouth water and create desire for more, I suggest you order French toast made New Orleans style. However, heed this warning; one plate will be more than enough for two, if you are eating without me. There's no adequate way to describe this scrumptious taste except to use that tired old phrase, "it's like dying and going to heaven." Boy, did I land there in a hurry after finishing off my yummy in the tummy share, and more. Thank you Natalie for letting me steal your plate clean!

Natalie and Audrey hurried off to the beauty parlor, and I decided I was going on a walking tour of the nearby antique and art shops. Earlier I had noticed in the corner of one of the store windows a piece of glass sculpture by Willkimson which was quite similar to a piece we had bought while in Aspen in 1996.

Ours sits on a black round pedestal which is chest high that is located in our front entrance hall. Almost every visitor remarks how unusually handsome and capturing are the carved man and woman facing each other as if they are about to kiss. The piece in the store had three faces and a large clear glass wing protruding off the side.

I went into the store being curious as to how much this display piece might cost. A lady approached me and I posed the question which prompted her to look in a big black catalogue. She quoted $11,700. After I explained the piece I already owned she asked if I knew the name so she could compare what its value might be today. For the life of me I could not remember the name, but I did think we had paid someplace between $1,500 and $3,000 which might have increased in value to two or three times the original price of 17 years ago. The lady kindly showed me around the gallery and pointed out her favorite pieces of art, and we had a long, friendly discussion about the various artists the gallery represented.

Then she asked what I was doing in New Orleans, and figuring she couldn't tell Natalie, I explained my secret plans for surprising her with the anniversary celebration. She looked at me with a tear in her eyes and gave me a warm hug as her way of expressing admiration for what I was planning.

I continued in and out of the shops. Some things were of little interest, while others challenged my pocketbook which was more than empty due to the expenses involved in arranging for the forthcoming big celebration event.

In the far back corner of one gallery was a rather small but most interesting painting of a bald eagle's head in front of a waving American flag. The light bulb went on in my head and I thought it would make a patriotic cover for the book I was attempting to write.

The price was reasonable to actually consider buying the painting. I wanted to learn more about the artist, and found he was a prolific young man whose works were climbing in value. This particular piece of art which I was interested in was being used as the logo for a chain of banks headquartered in Kentucky. The light bulb went dark as I immediately recognized this painting would be an infringement should I use it for a commercial purpose.

A few more stores and I open the door to enter into a very interesting, and large showroom selling antique furniture, art and sculptures. I am browsing around when a young sales lady starts a conversation. Soon as she learns I am an out-of-town visitor, "Have you been to the World War 2 Museum as yet?" I respond and say I am a WW 2 veteran. "Oh, my Dad served in the Navy" and that opened up a long discussion. I immediately found her description of her father as an image and replica of my life. We could have been twins. It was an amazing coincidence, and I would really have loved to have more time to meet this gentleman. Before I could say goodbye, this young lady wrapped her arms around me with a great big hug and a warm thank you for my military service and her best wishes for a Happy Anniversary for me and my wife.

Not bad for one afternoon…two hugs without spending a dime.

Guess what? It's time to go to dinner. This time the hotel concierge has made reservations at, where else but, The Bourbon House which is just three short blocks away, naturally on the corner of Bourbon Street. Not even enough effort to work-up a big appetite, but we have learned to manage. As we enter we pass a big and crowded oyster bar to reach our table in this cavernous large, but handsome room. One more great meal and Ray is in seventh heaven eating a large platter of three or more different fish specialties. Meanwhile, everyone else is oohing and aahing over their delectable meal. We feel like we won the Lotto with one better dinner followed after another –Arnaud's, Mr. B's, Commanders Palace and now The Bourbon House.

The waiter brings out the desert and hands me a white platter holding my chocolate cake that has "Happy 65th Anniversary to Natalie and Earl" inscribed in chocolate around the plate. The hotel concierge had tipped off the chef to provide this welcome surprise. I lifted my lemonade and we all clinked glasses in a toast.

Tomorrow is Saturday, the 21st, and the day of the big surprise. That evening I simply tell Natalie that I have ordered some hors d'oeuvres we will serve in our room, along with the bottle of champagne we had brought from home. Seena, Audrey and Raymond along with Lauren Bevis, and her boyfriend Nate were to join us. I explained that I invited Lauren as I believe we owed her for being so nice and hospitable to us every time we visit the Museum. Natalie nods affirmatively, and I also inform her that I have asked a videographer to come and record the cocktail reception so that we can share this champagne celebration with our children.

With a hidden sigh of relief I can see Natalie has no idea of what will happen next.

I hand her a gift wrapped large package which I had hidden in our luggage that she tears open. It's a gold framed full color photograph of the two of us which was taken within the last week while we were both attending an ADL luncheon honoring past chairmen. During that luncheon I was asked to make some very brief remarks which resulted in someone saying to me, "You are THE PREACHER of PATRIOTISM."

Driving home thinking about that innocent remark, I was inspired that I should start to write this book to share my innermost thoughts about the remarkable changes and notable differences between the time the troops returned home after World War 2, and what I am observing currently which is forming today's history.

My children, grandchildren, great grandchildren need to know and understand why my thinking may have been formed and selectively hammered into a totally different way of looking at the world with its myriad perspectives and both frightening as well as enlightening changes.

I am not that egotistical to think I am totally right. But, I do feel it's my parental obligation, to share what is tattooed into my heart and soul after being fortunate to have lived this long, and observed the world we all must absorb and lovingly adopt as our own.

Stormy Weather

Natalie is fairly tired and is getting ready to retire, so I make up some excuse and go down to talk with the head lady from the hotel's catering department to tell her I would like to have a flower arrangement at the next night's dinner table. She agrees and says let me see how she can take care of that request without spending any additional money. Sounds O.K. to me.

I next meet with Katherine who has been my right arm at the hotel in seeing to all the details.

"Katherine, I am concerned that Natalie won't be able to read the flash cards because it gets too dark outside at 6:30 p.m. Can the hotel provide a spotlight?" She says that's not possible, but she will talk with Terence at Signature Events. I am thinking how will I be able to get to Home Depot to buy a spotlight without Natalie asking why I need to go there?

Meanwhile the concierge has checked the weather forecast which is predicting a heavy rain downpour over Houston which is heading to New Orleans, and the rain will be accompanied by windstorms and a possible tornado that is expected to arrive precisely when our Bourbon street shebang is scheduled.

Katherine and I head huddle to try to figure an alternative plan. We go to the Courtyard which is beautiful during the daytime because of the lovely trees and flower plantings, but it too is wide open to the skies, and certainly doesn't have the excitement or people traffic of Bourbon Street.

Another night of guaranteed tossing and turning worrying about a long time plan going astray. In the Navy that was the responsibility of the officers. Now the guy in charge is a basket case in pajamas trying to catch a wink of sleep.

Planning a surprise for Natalie to celebrate the consummation of our 65 years of being man and wife has been challenging. The immediate hurdle to avoid, or overcome, is the forecasted thunderous rainstorms heading down Highway 10 from Houston directly toward New Orleans threatening to drown out our anniversary party celebration.

Since early morning on this Saturday the dark clouds gloomily were lurking overhead as an ominous jury about to announce the sentence of hours confined to solitary horrors of countless hours of rain. Every peek-a-boo there was a brief sign of the sun fighting its way to send a pinpoint of light through the towering wall of dark clouds, only to fade back to a dark curtain about to close down our parade.

Around 5 p.m., a half hour before the waiters were about to cart in the trays of chicken salad wrapped in lettuce and the other canapés to our room, I stepped out to the balcony to do another sky check.

Immediately to my left the balcony was overflowing with a boisterous, wolf howling group of Rajin Cajin red polo-shirted men and women hooping-it up before heading out to the 8 p.m. football game in the Super Dome between their beloved L.S.U. team that was about to clash with the local team from Tulane.

These gregarious folks, mainly from Baton Rouge, along with a small scattering of Texas alumni, were having one great time by lubricating their bodies with ample doses of alcohol to get into the proper school spirit of rooting and tooting for L.S.U. The guys were leaning dangerously over the balcony rail trying to lasso every pretty lady down on the street below with strings of colorful Mardi Gras beads. If they hit their target they would be rewarded with a smile and a cheer leader wave which was enough incentive to down another drink.

There I am standing like a man from Mars having landed in the wrong place since I am wearing a pinstriped dark blue suit with a gray polka dotted tie busily looking like a Cape Cod lighthouse searching the horizon for any signs of dooming rain.

"Whatcha' up to, man?" came out of a familiar Texas drawl. I quietly explained my concerns over the predicted rain, and why. This gentleman, a room neighbor, was obviously the leader of the howling mob scene, and he impressively told one friend after another who passed on the message like Western Union carriers until everyone gathered around congratulating me.

When they learned I was a former Navy man one guy disappeared momentarily into their room, and came out to present me with a very special string of Mardi Gras type beads of blue and white with a Navy flag and a small battleship. Very unusual and most appreciated. I soon learned the man with whom I first spoke was from Houston and lived off North 610 down a few miles from where I reside off South 610. He introduced me to his wife and then to his outstandingly handsome son who had just graduated from L.S.U., and was busily looking for a job in a similar business to his dad who manufactures oil field valves which he successfully sells all over the world. Small world – happening unexpectedly on a balcony overlooking Bourbon Street.

Every one of those Rajin Cajins couldn't be any more friendlier and happier to be vicariously sharing our anniversary celebration. The men, their wives, girl and boyfriends, young and old, as they were leaving for the game gave me the thumbs-up and smiled their good luck wishes. It must have charmed the heavens above for the dark clouds disappeared as night began to fall on a heaven blessed, rain less Bourbon Street.

Hooray and Hallelujah!

Pop the Cork

What follows are Natalie's own very personal thoughts and her recount of what happened that magical night of December 21, 2013. She describes her feelings and reactions as the show was about to open on the theatre of my street of dreams, hopes and silent prayers.

"There I was busily ensconced in our hotel room waiting on Earl to finish dressing so that I could don the party clothes I had brought along for the celebration. Earl had informed me earlier that everyone would come to our room for cocktails. I meanwhile was hurriedly trying to tidy up a bit and hide whatever extraneous possessions were sitting around like Earl's two U.S. Navy caps standing guard on top of the desk. Truthfully, I was thinking of nothing more than the toast I was planning to offer while we would be sipping the Dom Perignon champagne that we had carefully toted from home. I was determined to preempt Earl, and anyone else who might steal my thunder when we raised our glasses. I was hardly paying any attention to my groom who I then realized was dressed and looking mighty handsome. He jolted me out of my deliberations with, "You only have 30 minutes to finish looking beautiful."

In my own mind I had conjured up a few good lines to address to the boy of my dreams, and the man I've been lucky to love and share my life with as I quietly reminisced. The rest would come to me, but all I needed to do was transform myself into the magnificent Cinderella at the ball.

I tried the best I knew how, and it wasn't long before the waiter was rolling the hors d'oeuvres into the room and placing the array on top of the credenza with the iced champagne. Also, in came our 2 guests from the Museum – sweet Lauren dressed in a most becoming bright red dress along with Nate her charming beau. Then came sister Seena with our two dear friends Audrey and Ray.

Oh yes, Earl had in an offhand manner, informed me that a video photographer would be filming the cocktail party just so that we might share some photos with our family when we got home. Much to my amazement, he also had delivered beautiful silver balloons imprinted with both our names and "TWO IN A MILLION" that lent a festive party air to our hotel room.

As I visited and imbibed with our guests, I did get to make the first toast to my mate as well as to my sister who had served as my bridesmaid, lo those 65 years ago, and to our friends who have been at our side on many an occasion. I was trying not to be too self-conscious while appearing to be totally relaxed. At that time I wasn't aware that Earl and Seena had stepped out onto the balcony until I heard their call pleading for me to come and see the commotion on Bourbon Street.

My first reaction was 'why is my sister yelling for me to come see the latest drunken body lying inert on the street below our room?' But when I could see that she was obviously more than excited over the happenings, I walked onto the balcony to look down into a sea of happy people. What was about to take place was happening right in front of my bewildered eyes.

It was dark, but directly across the narrow street, I could make out a bright light spotlighting an Angel perched high on a white platform, surrounded by a trio of musicians, many-many more balloons held by 3 cute lassies, all dressed uniformly.

The Angel began turning large placards, one by one, with each unfolding the story of our journey together. "1943 it started in Camp Brookwood, Glen Spey, N.Y." continuing to encompass the births of our three children, weddings, births of our grand children, and great grandchildren and ending with a recent color photo of Earl and me imprinted with "TWO IN A MILLION."

I was too caught up with the Angel flashing the placards in rotation to even begin to fall apart or break into tears. I watched the crowd of hundreds of people, looking at us, applauding, and not making one sound on Bourbon Street, other than repeating over-and-over "Happy Anniversary" as the music played on.

At this point I was so overwhelmed with this unexpected "happening" that, even though the pit of my stomach was reacting, on the surface I remained intact. One thought was racing through my mind: how could Earl have pulled this surprise off, and how had I been so oblivious and naive to what had taken place in our home prior to this week? This was the $64 million question I asked myself.

I could hardly wait to wrap my arms around him and offer one resounding kiss, for taking what was a week of celebration and turning it into the most amazing single event in our married history!

All throughout our 65 years of being together, plus the previous five while dating, I have known Earl's capability of astounding me at many a celebration with planes flying over our home in foggy nights bearing signs of love, billboards lined up on streets and avenues that I regularly traversed, and me, a person intent on doing one task at a time, blissfully driving by without seeing a one, only to be congratulated by friends and neighbors relating their reaction to the love messages.

I never focus on what the next anniversary will bring, or if the hand of Earl the magician, might somehow wave a few wands and create another breath taking moment. All I can think of is how blessed I have been to have latched onto Earl at the ripe old age of 15, and been smart enough to hold on for dear life!

I would be remiss if I didn't further recount December 21, 2013. The evening just began with that fabulous Bourbon Street introduction. It continued from fantastic to better than! As our group of seven left our room and walked into the Courtyard of the Royal Sonesta Hotel which was on our way to the Revolution Dining Room, we were stopped by the three young ladies who had been standing next to the Angel. They introduced themselves as the Victory Belles and asked us all to sit down in an abundant tree and flower area, so that they could entertain us. Earl and I were seated on a park bench while holding each others' hands.

Their three voices blended in harmony which was beautiful and enchanting. They sang while also doing some play acting and dancing to the songs of the late 40's and 50's and by then I was in a total trance. I could have held onto Earl's hand and sat there all evening, but for the fact, that our food awaited us.

After bidding the Belles goodbye we were a stone's throw from the restaurant where we were warmly welcomed and shown to our table. The white cloth was sprinkled with tiny silver stars surrounding a low floral arrangement sitting in the center. Beautiful surroundings, wonderful meal replete with a three-tiered red, white and blue layered cake, and proudly standing on the top was a miniature bride and groom. The icing decoration was patriotic stripes of red, white and blue which was a sure sign that Earl must have had a hand in designing this anniversary tribute. Too lovely to cut, yes, but we were all anxious to partake so we dug right in to our heart's delight. Dieting can wait until we devour every morsel.

From 5:30 p.m. to 11 p.m. I feel certain the video photographer amassed enough film for us to share with all of our family and friends near and far. I'm sure that this time Earl outdid himself, and we will all have many more remarkable memories to cherish.

With good fortune and good health I am looking forward to celebrating Earl's and my 66th wedding anniversary with God willing and his blessings."

THE WIZARD OF COMMON CENTS

Thank you, dear Natalie, for sharing this remembrance through your photographic recall of every precious detail of an evening filled with joy. However, you didn't report that I didn't drink the champagne. I only dipped my finger tip into the glass and took a quick lick with my mouth. Your presence alone was enough to make me deliriously happy.

Natalie forgot to mention that when we were getting into the elevator to go down to the lobby a man also came inside. He looked at the balloons I was carrying, and said, "You must be the Earl of the Two In A Million. Earl, how's it feel to live a million years, old man?" Good question.

Whoever has been blessed has not had the good fortune of being married to Natalie, my best friend and partner from the time we were literally children. How lucky was I to look across a summer camp campus, and see the most beautiful girl in the world. As young as I might have been I quickly and wisely knew that Natalie (BooBoo) would be my wife. A decision I have never regretted and have been able to beam with pride and joy at her every step by my side.

In these turbulent times we have witnessed that too few couples ever find a marriage blessed by the Gods like ours.

Disappointments and Heart Breaks.

Too few of us are ever immune.

During those earlier busy and sometimes hectic days my wife had one unfortunate miscarriage, and at age 70 she was diagnosed with breast cancer from which she is now considered a survivor. However, we believe that the long and arduous treatments left her with serious other problems of body aches and pains combined with mental anguish which she bravely fights each day. Abundant medicines and massages do very little to relieve the constant pains, but she always puts on the best face to meet the world with a coast-to-coast wide smile. She is the personified real Angel before and after our anniversary celebration.

I love her more each day.

Time to Climb Back on the Bus

We all love someone during our lives. I wanted to share how Natalie and I celebrated a special gift of being blessed with a 65 year marriage made in heaven. That is a rare celebration indeed.

To remind you, I was unceremoniously shown the exit door at GDL&W. Then I lucked out by doing my best to teach young boys and girls the evils of abusing illegal drugs including the gate opener marijuana. Some people would like to throw a fit and would like to give me a "sucker punch" for my so-called ancient idea that marijuana kills. I've heard from many that have told me they tried it when they were younger and it never hurt. Look at them now. Doing great and prosperous with success. Happy as a lark, with your head buried in the sand.

Fortunate for those innocents, but may I suggest you think of your friends and associates who blew their careers by indulging in drugs, and may have lost their license to practice medicine or the law, or cut the rungs of their ladders short as they tried climbing to the top of their business. You don't have to look far to see the abusers filling the rehabilitation facilities, crowding the jail cells across America, lying prematurely below the earth or sleeping on the cold and unwelcoming streets.

While working with the D.E.A. I was indoctrinated by true, and undisputable scientific evidence how a simple drug such as marijuana will alter your mind and damage your brain cells. As the money grabbing dealers would hook their unsuspecting users by adding even more dangerous substances into what kept them in their fancy cars and gold neckpieces - misguided folks were buying their message that it's a safe medical cure for their ailments. In my personal opinion, it's just another way for some profiteers to line their pockets while they are doing their best to dumb down America along with the politicians bent on cutting the funding of education.

If you are a parent then you have a responsibility to teach your children what is right from wrong. "Honey, don't touch that flame it's hot and will burn you!" "Son, look both ways before you run into the street. A car or truck could kill you if you aren't careful." "Stop. Never swallow that. It's poison and you could die."

Mom, Dad, what is wrong in trying to make your son or daughter understand that there are some things they must avoid, as they can get hurt and poison their well being for the rest of their lives? I have seen young teen girls trading their bodies for a drag of marijuana. The tattooed arms of too many boys hide the needle marks of drugs.

If you love your kids then practice prevention by talking and mentoring them to counter the pressure they will be subjected to from money grubbers who only see your dear child as a mooch they can ring dry to fill their dirty cash registers. An ounce of prevention can stop a freight load of harm, shame and disaster for those who are tempted to fall by the wayside which can bring them - their families and careers - into an uncalled for, off-the-rails, train wreck.

Be both coach and parent to your kids. It won't hurt, but it can help. My son Mike has lovingly told me that he was brought up on "don't do this, and don't do that" which helped make him the grown man whom both his Mom and Dad are so very proud. Take a well deserved bow, Mike!

Along with our two girls, Erica and Bonnie, the three children are our proudest creations and have been a true blessing in our lives along with their families. For the next two years after ending my career as Poppa Earl attempting to mentor the thousands of young people, I continued being involved with working with the adult victims of alcohol and drug abuse. I can't claim to be an expert, but in a few short years I was exposed to every type of alcoholic and drug abuser, and all the available treatments. It was a learning experience for which I am most grateful as it definitely helped me understand many of the causes of addiction and the possible treatments to attempt to restore a successful life. There were failures, and there were returns on the investment by both provider and the user. I observed and learned from both, and feel I am the better for this experience even after watching some of the users lose their families, careers and often their lives. It has helped me to better relate to those men and women military veterans facing those same daunting problems.

I can't account why, or how, or what has led me down this twisted professional career path, but I am beginning to believe there is a reason.

Long before we were exposed to watching television only on a relatively large screen in our homes or places of entertainment, I felt there must be a better way to influence the sale of products at retail especially since the days of the small mom and pop retail store were quickly vanishing and being replaced by the big box store without the personal interchange between clerk and customer. I put my mind to thinking what might substitute for a sales clerk who can instruct, inform and SELL a prospective buyer in a retail store directly at the brand's point-of-product display. I applied for a patent and created P.O.P. ShelfAds® which are a combination of full color and audio TV screen with text messages that play automatically only in the presence of an interested shopper. They must be wireless so that they can fit anywhere the brand/product is displayed-on the shelf, on the freezer door or floor stack displays. I raised the start-up money primarily from trusting friends and family and personally digging into our own pocketbook and tried to introduce this unique, new advertising media. I soon learned that just as Philo Farnsworth who originally invented television and never could get it to be successfully utilized commercially, that it isn't always easy being the pioneer.

Philo Farnsworth, the boy genius, died being a drunk and penniless. My goal is to avoid that fate, and it has led me in a totally different direction. By this time I was entering the mid-eighties and began thinking about whether there is a legacy that I can leave which might be more meaningful than dollars or awards hiding walls in our home.

It didn't take long to put two-and-two together. Why do I believe I may be endowed with special gifts of experience that can be channeled where they can do the most good? For all these years I had never attended any military affairs, functions or meetings as I was too busy building a business and working with numerous charitable organizations. Admittedly the only spare time I spent was with my immediate family taking the girls to their various activities, and helping my son in his chosen sports, or getting away on a Sunday afternoon to a baseball or professional football game. In the early years our vacations were combined with business conferences or meetings, and as we grew older we would take advantage of weekends and holidays at our country farm, and then later as the years went by our now grown children would invite us to their out-of-town homes to spend some quality time together.

Did I want to sit at home just reading or watching the political news to only get upset at how things weren't working out like I envisioned they should? There were two wars going on and I, along with countless others, would rarely give it a thought. Every once in awhile I would see a young man or woman wearing a military uniform and I would thank them for their service, then walk away saying to myself, is that all I can do, just say thanks and never give it another thought? I can't account for why lightening struck and awoke me from my deep slumber and shouted in my practically deaf ear, "Earl, baby! You have been blessed with a unique life and honed skills that can make a difference. Do it while you are still able and capable before the clock of life may soon be still."

I rolled up my sleeves and went to work by researching the PROBLEMS of the veterans which all the politicians constantly yak their heads about, and do very little except talk and make unkept promises. I dare not, cannot, and will not criticize any of those sterling non-profit charities which work diligently to serve our veterans and their families. I do recognize that with all their efforts and hard work there is so much more they are capable of achieving if they only had larger financial resources at their disposal. In the blink of an eye I decided that I should take on the role of being the horsepower to raise money these excellent organizations require to provide more help and assistance to those in need. My mind was made up that I could help raise the money without conflicting with any of their fund-raising efforts such as their acquiring grants, philanthropic donations or conducting money-raising events. That was not to be my effort. I was going to do something unique, innovative and totally different than any other charity. It had to be original, yet be significant and complimentary to veterans and acceptable to the entire nation. Some people, when I first mentioned my fund raising idea, said it was brilliant! As heart-warming and ego satisfying as that remark might be I can only agree when we see that it works, and meets or exceeds our ambitious goals.

There was one thing which was gnawing at my soul and tearing my thoughts apart. That was the fake charities claiming to help the veterans while their sole purpose was to make those fraudulent thieves rich. They appealed to the kindness of thousands of generous people and instead of a dime going to worthwhile charities they would get innocent food companies, and clothing manufacturers to donate their products in the name of the crooked, charlatan operators. When this fraud was exposed on national TV, I instantly made the decision that I was going to stop that criminal activity and created "BACK-OUR-VETS – The Arsenal of Hope" for our troops, vets and their families.

THE WIZARD OF COMMON CENTS

My purpose in life, at 86 years young, became a crusade to raise $1 billion annually by using WE-THE-POWER-OF-THE-PEOPLE to voluntary donate just 2 cents on top of the consumer's retail purchases.

Some would ask, "Why just two cents when it's easier to get larger donations?" Good question; but you can be dirt poor or filthy rich and you won't miss two cents. I didn't want to place any hurdles on these Free Enterprise donations, and no one would be discriminated against if they were Democrats, Republicans or Independents. Your skin color or ethnic background nor your religious or sexual persuasion wouldn't matter. It isn't a tax, but it was designed to be a grass roots, voluntary contribution with an open door to every American who wants to participate as frequently as they prefer to put in their common 2 cents to BACK-OUR-VETS.

Why is it relevant to have my history and my story of my life? It doesn't appear to be relevant, nor is it in any sequential order? Reflect for a moment how my friend E.J. Ourso raised millions of dollars by collecting nickels weekly from people throughout Louisiana. That experience led me to believe we can do even better by enlisting an army of patriotic contributors across America donating 2 cents when they shopped to BACK-OUR-VETS.

I was determined to be sure that 100% of every dollar raised through the consumer donations are going directly to provide care and counseling to our needy men and women veterans. Never again would any American veteran, their family or survivors be homeless, hungry or lack medical care and concern for their welfare.

This was my time to hone and homogenize my lifetime acquired skills by applying them to a new setting – a noble cause to BACK-OUR-VETS, the ARSENAL OF HOPE for our vets and their beloved families.

Now, it's time for a reality check. Without any key retailers acting as collection points throughout every hamlet, town and city throughout the country we can't collect the common 2 cents donations. So, I diligently emailed, wrote and called the top 25 supermarket chains including the biggest discount clubs, the leading 15 fast food restaurants, the 4 biggest drug retailers, the largest home improvement, department, electronic, auto supply, clothing, house-wares, hardware, sporting goods, toy, hobby, book and beverage stores, plus many of the smaller independent stores such as floor and rug, dry cleaner and jewelry. I thought I left no stone unturned, but I was either ignored or turned down cold-flat.

Oh where, oh where have the open-minded Mr. Vincent Riggio's of American Tobacco disappeared? Are they all hiding behind their "gate keepers" to keep opportunity away from knocking on their doors?

The excuses I heard were down-right frustrating.

"We donate money in huge amounts to support our veterans."

Who are you kidding? Those donations are a small, relatively insignificant amount of your profits, and are tax deductible!

"We hire hundreds, thousand, multi-thousands of veterans."

Good for you, but are they paid low minimum wages for un-skilled jobs with limited, or any, benefits such as health plans, profit-sharing or pensions?

"We always support veterans in our local communities."

Good work, but veterans are everywhere and our program serves the needs of veterans wherever they are living in every community including where your stores are located. The courageous veteran serving in some foreign land was fighting to protect every American without regard to where anyone lived in our country.

Please don't get me wrong. I do immensely appreciate and embrace the efforts these stores and businesses are making on their own - BUT – they can do much more by enlisting the voluntary help of their shoppers to add just 2 cents on top of their total purchase whether it's on a $5 cup of coffee, or $55 on groceries, or $555 for clothing. It all adds up, yet it doesn't cost the retailer anything more than the clerk at the register punching in the total customer purchase, punching in the sales tax or the coupon discounts, plus punching in the 2 cent donation. Just as the retailer pay their vendors, at the end of each month they send the total of the accumulated 2 cent donations to BACK-OUR-VETS, Inc.

We, in turn, distribute 100% of those funds to the various vetted charities which directly serve the needy veteran community.

Benjamin Franklin once said, "To make a loyal friend, don't lend him a book; borrow one from him."

Simply, get the other person involved. America's retailers can learn from this simple philosophy by encouraging their customers to participate daily in a noble and patriotic cause that will create long and lasting customer loyalty.

To-date, the retailer attitude may be discouraging, but I am not quitting. I don't intend to pull a Philo Farnsworth and turn to drink and death. Instead, I will follow Bruce Barton of the Advertising Hall of Fame who said, "Nothing splendid has ever been achieved except by those who dared believe that something inside of them was superior to circumstances."

I decided that I would bring my message to the people through the media to enlist a "grass root" Army of true American patriots who are willing to fight for the 65 million living troops, veterans and their military families. What makes me absolutely positive that there is an innate spirit of patriotism for America is the experience of watching 70,000+ men and women standing on their feet in respect, and clapping their hands off while veteran heroes are being introduced to the crowd at a Sunday football game while in Reliant Stadium in Houston.

Paid advertising is expensive and I sorely wish I could afford to get the BACK-OUR-VET message out to the general public repeatedly, so I have to rely on the generosity of the media by allowing me to appear on the nation's broadcast media or have the story told in print. I attended a Publicity Summit in N.Y.C. where I fortunately met 50 to 100 representatives of different media sources.

Within just a few very short weeks I was invited to be interviewed on three radio stations from California to the East

Coast, and I did an hour radio show with a decorated Host who served as a medic in the Army. As a former Navy medic, we related very well to one another, much to the benefit of his radio listeners. I also was the radio guest of a woman Host whom I had the pleasure of meeting while we both attended the P.R. Summit in New York City. During our air time I pleasantly discovered that my Host's father and father in law had both served in the army in World War 2. Her daughter had served in recent years in Korea and Colorado. I met other media reps who also said, "We want you on our program," but I am patiently waiting for them, and countless others, to allow me to meet their loyal broadcast audiences to educate them to the PROBLEMS our veterans and troops face which we can SOLVE with our unique 2 cent common cents SOLUTION.

This may sound redundant to you, but our President, our politicians, our media and even our citizens all talk about the serious problems our veterans and troops experience, yet no one has offered a positive, simple common cents solution.

What are we as individual citizens, or collectively as a nation, doing to help the HUNGRY; the HOMELESS; the WOUNDED physically and mentally; the alcohol and drug ADDICTED; the TRANSITION into civilian life; PROVIDING new education and employment skills; finding gainful JOBS; PREVENTING family abuse and divorces?

Without sounding too egotistical, I believe I have the SOLUTION to all the veterans' problems, even including a positive answer to the current news informing us that there were 50,000 cases of sexual abuse reported in the military this past year.

Will we continue to turn our backs on the 22 suicides a day by our troops and veterans?

Shameful when there are answers available if we would only take advantage of the professional knowledge which exists, and have the funds to provide the skilled, expert care. If, and when, we can accomplish our noble goals we will also be relieving the burdensome load the Veteran's Administration faces. The internecine delays which our veterans face in attaining their benefits which have been promised and continue to be delayed or denied is a national disgrace.

Admittedly, from the lack of any encouraging response from our government, national and local officials, nor from the important retailers my loving wife, family members and dear well meaning friends suggest I should give up and go do something which doesn't take 12 hours a day, seven days a week and has created dark bags under my eyes bigger than those jumbo beach bags ladies carry around.

There continues to be a fire in my belly which is burning a path to eventual success.

Earlier I had mentioned how upset I got to learn about the fraud and deception of some unscrupulous people who were milking the public under the cloud of their helping the veterans. I tried to avoid having unsuspecting shoppers adding their two cents to their bills thinking every penny would be used to BACK-OUR-VETS while some crooked retailer was actually going to pad their own pockets. It was then that I decided to consider converting the wireless technology of the P.O.P. ShelfAds® to be used to identify an authorized participating retailer.

Each retailer who agrees to act as an authorized collection point to collect their customers 2 cent donations will sign a three year lease to acquire an nTRANSads display which will be installed at each entrance to their stores. These floor displays will be 6' tall and be lifelike full color photographs of either a uniformed member of the Air Force, Marines, Sailors or Soldiers. Across the chest of the military representative pictured on the display will be our wireless electronic video and text message unit that will automatically greet each shopper entering the store with a short message, such as "Welcome. Please BACK-OUR-VETS by signaling the cashier at check-out that you are voluntarily adding a 2 cent donation on top of your total purchase. Thank you!" The glasses free 3D video is our exclusive to actually demonstrate the two finger Victory/Peace sign as an example of how simple it is to let the cashier learn of the customer's 2 cent voluntary donation.

It may be interesting to learn that each nTRANSads display will be installed, operated and maintained by a veteran who will be trained, and skilled in this technology. Depending on the geography as to how close each participating store might be we anticipate that one man or woman vet can service 3 units per day, or a total of 60 per month. When we meet our goal of having 150,000 locations we believe we will have created 2,500 good paying new jobs for veterans. Each quarter the lifelike displays of the various military representatives will be rotated to different locations to keep the image looking fresh, different and new to the shoppers. We plan to provide some sort of reminder at the check-out register to BACK-OUR-VETS.

The lease cost which is paid by the retailer to our planned non-profit 501 (c) (3) is tax deductible. The monthly lease (based on current cost quotes) is just $125 per month, which is the equivalent of $4.16 a day, or approximately 17 cents an hour for a 24 hour day to greet each shopper. Every time the electronic display is automatically triggered when a customer comes through the entrance it is recorded, and this information is available to the retailer for important marketing information (number of shoppers, date and time of entrance to compare against sales numbers and offers to compare against prior days, weather and special incentives).

This privileged information also allows us to be able to measure the number of triggers against the number of donation transactions to be able to review any possible incidents of cheating by either a cashier or the retailer. Remember, our goal is to see that every cent goes to servicing the vets and their families through the sterling organizations which have been thoroughly investigated and vetted by us as well as charity watchdog groups.

Currently we have a list of 26 qualified non-profit organizations we plan to support, and that list will be available to qualified interested parties. During our investigation we were shocked to learn that some of the best publicized organizations serving veterans were spending too much of their funds on paying absurd compensation to their executives and in operating their money raising activities. Our preference is to support those organizations that keep their expense ratio down, or below, 15% of their total annual income. Any non-profit not on our approved list will be welcomed to apply if they can meet our stringent requirements. We are well aware of individual cases that have been turned down by the Veterans Administration for some reason or another, and we are not ever going to be that hard-hearted not to see that deserving individuals may need financial help.

You have every right to ask, "If this is such a noble cause, and you believe you have developed a brilliant solution to answer the veteran's problems – where does this crusade of yours stand?"

I must humbly answer, "To date I am a disappointed total failure."

I may have lost the battle of pleading on bended knee with retailers of every size…some of which are led by former graduates of West Point and the Naval Academy who have served their country (you know who you are) that I was depending on to lead the charge.

The initial battle may have been lost, but with determination we can and will win this war to BACK-OUR-VETS.

I am not ready to surrender and hoist the white flag.

We may simply need to change our plan of attack. Let's consider some new strategies to gain victory.

These might be considered "What ifs."

- *The President of the U.S.A. determines to make BACK-OUR-VETS a priority project and uses the bully pulpit to enlist the help of the retail community and the general public to use their common 2 cents.

- Either one of the two major parties adopt this plan, or amend it, to help their candidates gain political offices from local races to the White House.

- Governor's in 50 individual states see the opportunity to not only help their veterans, but to stimulate a sense of pride and unity within their communities.

- National veteran organization's such as the American Legion or the Veterans of Foreign Wars take on this role in addition to their already successful fund raising programs. It's a positive way to recruit new members that are younger than their current base.

- The major sports leagues of baseball, basketball, football and soccer not only salute veteran heroes during their games, but get into the field of real battle and support our troops, veterans and their families by funding and promoting BACK-OUR VETS.

- It's a wide open opportunity for a major national advertiser to use their advertising/marketing/promotion dollars to BACK-OUR-VETS and win the loyal support of all 65 million family members of our military, and the thousands of other Americans that are willing and happy to lend their support. Use your "Brain Sells" by being original that is certain to capture business. Mr. Advertiser, you and I know the importance of differentiating your brand against your competitors. You are investing millions, and in some cases billions of dollars, to outshout, outsmart, outspend your competitors. Invest 10% of your U.S.A. budget to become the voice and champion of our veterans. You will win the Medal of Honor from your customers, your investors and your shareholders, plus the pride of all your associates knowing their work has helped make America a better country because we left no veteran and their beloved family behind.

- You and I have seen the millions of dollars wealthy people give to candidates running for office in the hope to buy their support for the things which they advocate. Some more than generous individuals have pledged to donate substantial parts of their fortunes to worthwhile charities. Form a special group of maybe a dozen of you that will be a special task force to each donate 18% of your wealth to BACK-OUR- VETS. It won't hurt any of you, but it sure will help many a veteran lying in bed nursing the wounds of war.

To those to whom much is given, much is rightfully expected. We live in a global, golden age of opportunity. Think, dream and do BIG!

- There are so many different associations advocating for the businesses which they represent. Think out-of-the-box and see what tremendous good you can gain when you adopt BACK-OUR-VETS to support, and every member shares equally in the benefits and good will you create. Maybe it's primarily small businesses like independent dry cleaners, or possibly small restaurants, or convenience stores that can't afford big advertising campaigns to compete with the big box stores. Together you can steal the big guys thunder when you become the BACK-OUR-VETS sponsor.

- Possibly there is a relatively small, but eager organization that currently is involved with helping the veteran community, and would want to grow to a national presence. I would gladly pass on the baton knowing that you have fought in the trenches and your team can win this championship race.

These are only my top-of-the-mind ideas. I welcome any, and all suggestions, including paying the retailer 5% for handling the collections of the donations. If someone isn't concerned with using the nTRANSads to try to eliminate fraud, or not interested in collecting the research information at retail, I promise to listen and decide together the best path to take for success over the many years before us.

America – you are too smart to let the enemy of a defeatist attitude, or to hide behind false camouflage to not join together to win this battle for the men and women who have given their time, limbs and lives to sacrifice for you to afford the guaranty of life, liberty and pursuit of happiness.

I must make this abundantly clear. I intend to resign from my position as Commander-in-Chief of the non-profit BACK-OUR-VETS, Inc. should there appear to be a conflict of interest, as I am the 100% owner of the patent, and have approximately a 22% ownership of P.O.P. Broadcasting, Inc. that can contract with a manufacturer of the electronic displays. I would be happy to turn the leadership role of BACK-OUR- VETS to a professional manager experienced with non-profits that has a breath taking vision for the future, and who has hopefully honorably served in the U.S. military. If the law allows it would be my honor to actively serve on the Board of BACK-OUR-VETS, Inc.

THE WIZARD OF COMMON CENTS

With my 87th birthday staring me in the face (Jan. 29 2014) I knew that only God knows my fate. My life may not have always been perfect, but I have been blessed. No one knows when the ever ticking clock of time will soon run out, but I do believe that now is the only time we possess to live, love and toil with a will to change the world for the better.

While making this confession, I must admit that I have some regrets for making mistakes in my long career. As I carefully look back on it, I was staying too busy and overly devoted to my business or the causes I cherished to take ample time out to develop more than a few carefully chosen lifetime friends.

To my many acquaintances across this wide and wonderful world I want each of you to know and understand I will always remember your kind and thoughtful help and guidance to someone who never said "thank you" often enough in appreciation for your helping hand. Having come from a generation where boys never learned to type, and the new fangled technology of blogging, social media and creating websites is beyond my limited scope of knowledge. You know who you are that have rescued my futile Neanderthal efforts time and time again. I can only say you have been my lifesaver when I sorely needed rescue from drowning in perilous waters way over my head.

Be a Billionaire

Haven't you ever thought what would it be like to be a billionaire? Well podnuh', stop thinking because today, starting right now you can Join the Billionaires Club.

It's easy and let me show you how. Step up to the nearest mirror; put a smile on your face; raise your right arm and repeat after me: " I, (your name) am an American citizen and I solemnly swear to voluntarily add two cents to my total retail purchases to BACK-OUR-VETS."

Congratulations! You are now a proud member of the Billionaires Club and by so doing what you have pledged and promised your repetitive 2 cent donations, combined with your fellow members across America, will total more than $1B annually with every penny going to the non-profit charity organizations that daily serve those military men and women that have courageously served this nation we all cherish and love.

Figures don't lie. Here is how the money grows 2 cents at a

time. It all adds up, so please follow this simple COMMON CENTS arithmetic.

The average cashier in a supermarket will do over 1,000 transactions in a day. Assume each shopper voluntarily added 2 cents on top of their total bill that is $20 daily. Over 350 days in the year this $20 has grown into $7,000. With 150,000 cashiers throughout the U.S.A. participating YOU just helped raise $1,050,000,000.

Good for you and every Billionaires Club member. It's better to give than receive especially when you know that your pennies are going to reduce and solve the problems of many of the needy troops, veterans and their families that are struggling.

I promise you won't miss those pennies no matter how often you give at the grocery store, the gas pump, in the department store, grabbing some fast food or sitting at a bar.

Sounds too easy? Or too difficult?

There are over 30,000 supermarkets and thousands more grocery stores that represent over one-third of our Gross National Products. If they each average five cashiers per store we reach our goal of 150,000 cashier collection points.

Smoke dream, Earl? Not really. Not when I think of the thousands upon thousands of retail operations that the numbers will amaze you. I can almost bet that you didn't know that Subway operates 40,8555 restaurants in 105 countries, Auto Zone has over 5,000 USA locations, CVS operates 7,600 pharmacies, Staples has 2,000 locations and Starbucks alone has 11,000 stores. This limited number of chains probably represent over 50,000 cashiers who if they were participating by collecting the 2 cent contributions they would add another $350,000,000 - $500,000,000 to BACK-OUR-VETS. That's no small change to sneeze at. Rather we can all say "God Bless."

Imagine, for example that McDonald's restaurants has over 34,000 stores worldwide and serves 70 million customers daily. According to their annual report the U.S.A. represents approximately 32% of revenue. Using that figure as a base let's assume that there are 11,000 McDonald's in the U.S.A. serving 22,400,000 customers DAILY. If every day each customer added their 2 cents to the meal we would raise $448,000 and over one year this one chain would help raise $156,800,000 to BACK-OUR-VETS. Unbelievable, but certainly possible!

It doesn't sound easy to you. I get that, but we all started crawling before we learned to walk. Once enough of you join the Billionaires Club and make your loud and clear voices be heard where you shop and buy, then the Gibraltar size retailers will crumble and we will no longer be stumbling on our way to success. In this land of the free we have the right to choose and shop where we know by putting in our two cents it is making sense for the common good of every man and woman who wore a military uniform. Be a hero in your own community and let your voices be heard and America will smile all the way to the bank of good will and good deeds.

I believe your taxes may go down because this money will help relieve the burden of our funding the over-whelmed Veteran Administration as the non-profits which these funds are supporting will be able to lift many of those responsibilities.

Who are the vetted, non-profit top charities, each with a sterling reputation of helping veterans and their families in their times of need? They each have passed muster with charity watchdog groups such as Charity Watch and Charity Navigator by getting the most out of every dollar given on behalf of American heroes.

The American Legion
Organizes commemorative events in volunteer veteran support activities and volunteer assistance at Veterans Administration hospitals and clinics. It lobbies' on behalf of veterans benefits such as pensions and the Veterans Affairs hospital system.

The Armed Services YMCA
Provides free, specialized programs and support services to military members and their families, with a particular focus on junior-enlisted men and women.

Fisher House Foundation
Donates "comfort homes" built at major military and VA medical centers, to serve as a home away from home for military families visiting a loved one during hospitalization and treatment.

Folds of Honor Foundation
Focused on providing secondary-school scholarships for the children and spouses of Gulf War era service members killed or severely wounded in combat.

Gary Sinise Foundation
Champions the causes of veterans, first responders, their families, and those in need by providing fundraising, financial and

organizational support for a broad array of groups including Building for America's Bravest, The Stephen Siller Tunnel to Towers Foundation, Snowball Express and Hope For The Warriors

Homes for Our Troops
Assists severely injured veterans and their immediate families by raising donations of money, building materials, and professional labor and coordinating the construction of specialized homes to give wounded warriors maximum freedom and independence.

Hope for the Warriors
Dedicated to enhancing the quality of life for post-9/11 service members, their families, and families of the fallen who have sustained physical and psychological wounds in the line of duty. Services include care, coordination, family support, reintegration services, community outreach, and outdoor adventures.

Injured Marine Super Fi Fund
Offers rapid financial support, family counseling, specialized and adaptive housing, transportation and equipment, and education aid for injured and critically ill post 9/11 members of the U.S. armed forces and their families.

Intrepid Fallen Heroes Fund
Originally founded as an aid organization for the widows and orphans of those lost or killed in action, the IFHF has expanded to provide financial aid in the form of "Family Grants" and scholarships for severely wounded veterans and their families.

Iraq and Afghanistan Veterans of America
An organization of more than 200,000 member veterans and supporters that provides healthcare, employment, education, and community services for Gulf War-era service members.

Marine Corps Scholarship Foundation
Founded 50 years ago the MCSF is the oldest and largest provider of scholarships to children of Marines and Navy Corpsmen, with a focus on those who had a parent killed or wounded in combat.

National Military Family Association
Provides military families with counseling and services to help with uniquely military lifestyle matters of deployment, spouse education, separation, moving, and more.

Navy-Marine Corps Relief Society
Since 1904, the NMCRS has provided need-based financial and educational assistance to Navy service members and their family members and survivors.

The Navy SEAL Foundation
Provides family services, financial support, educational programs, and activities for both active and veteran U.S. Navy SEALS, special warfare combatant-craft crewmen, Naval special warfare support personnel, and their spouses and their children.

Operation Homefront
Provides emergency financial and other assistance to the families of U.S. service members and wounded warriors.

Our Military Kids

Financial grants for children of deployed National Guard and military reserve personnel as well as the children of wounded warriors in all branches of services. The money can be used to pay for sports, fine arts, camps, and tutoring programs that nurture and sustain children while a parent is away on assignment or recovering from injury.

Puppies Behind Bars

Teaches prison inmates to care for and train service dogs who are then given free of charge to severely disabled U.S. war veterans to help them with their basic daily activities. To date about 40 service dogs have been paired with wounded warriors as a result of the program, which also serves as a positive form of counseling for the participating inmates in six prisons.

Special Operations Warrior Foundation

Provides scholarships and family counseling to the children of special operations personnel who die in the line of duty, and immediate financial assistance to severely wounded special operations personnel and their families.

The Soldiers Project

A collaborative of professional mental health therapists, psychologists, and psychiatrists who offer free counseling services in a private setting for at-risk veterans and their family members in several metropolitan areas nationwide.

USO

Since 1941, the USO has supported the troops by providing morale, welfare, and recreation-type services to America's men and women in uniform serving throughout the world.

Veterans of Foreign Wars
Currently has 1.5 million members belonging to 7,644 posts, covering all 50 states, and is the largest American organization of combat veterans. Provides a variety of positive awareness programs including Free Call Days to service members deployed abroad.

Wounded Warrior Project
Dedicated to raising awareness of the plight of injured service members, while directing programs and services to meet their needs. Their motto is: "The greatest casualty is being forgotten."

By regularly putting in your 2 cents to any and all of these charitable organizations can make a world of difference in the life of a returning war hero or a veteran who has honorably served OUR country. BACK-OUR-VETS serves as the united fund which collects the combined COMMON CENTS and distributes it fairly and equitably among these noted charities to perform their common good. This makes COMMON SENSE to this humble American PREACHER FOR PATRIOTISM.

There are several other pro-veteran laudable organizations that do noble work and Back-Our-Vets is open to their requests for support, however we will investigate every cause and refuse to support any charlatan individual or group. Don't expect one cent if you are violating your faith in God and sacred trust for our men and women who deserve a hero's hug and help from every true-blue American.

Together, all 300+ million U.S.A. citizens can be rich as BIL-LIONAIRES because within their hearts is a rose which can shine bright with a golden warmth of caring and concern for their fellow brothers and sisters who have each made our lives safer and more secure.

Your 2 cent voluntary daily contributions open-up America's purse strings to life, liberty and happiness. Let's do it – you heart-rich Billionaire member!

To My Immediate Family.

The Likovers, Humphreys, and Littmans all shed a river of tears when our beautiful grandchild Kyle passed away on his eight birthday despite all the herculean efforts to correct his heart birth defect.

He may have been small in stature, but Kyle was a wealth of talent, and had a giant personality. My heart has born a deep cavity ever since he left all of us, and his memory is what reminds us to make each day count to be the best we can deliver to make this world a better place for every child, parent and human being.

If I Were King

Hasn't everyone ever thought what they would be able to do if they were King of this great big world?

Don't laugh, because some few people, due to the wonders of what they have accomplished, actually rule the world. Think of the Pope with his influence, or someone like Nelson Mandela who upon his death the world mourned. Not everyone can make a worldwide impact like these two individuals whose words and deeds explode like a nuclear bomb on our universal conscience.

Much earlier in this dissertation I related how all America opened wide their arms to the returning boys and girls who had within a few years matured into much wiser, hardened men and women from World War 2. Behind all the parades, the hearty pats on the back, the firm handshakes and cheerful smiles, even sailors kissing strange women on the streets, there still existed the despair of discrimination to people of different religions or skin color.

An aristocratic couple living in the White House also was celebrating our nation's magnificent contribution to the victory over vicious and malicious hatred and bigotry. President Franklin D. Roosevelt and his wife Eleanor, "the most influential woman of her time" knew that there was still a war over prejudice and racism to be won on our native soil.

Against fearful opposition, together the President and his partner created a modern America with a consequential destiny to UNITE the States to become the "Greatest Generation." To get a much greater understanding of the strife through four years of war, and the leadership thereafter, I suggest a best-selling book to read-- Doris Kearns Goodwin's best selling Pulitzer Prize for History book: "No Ordinary Times." The last paragraph from that illustrious book...

"Eleanor derived constant comfort (following the death of her husband) from a little verse sent to her by a friend. 'They are not dead who live in lives they leave behind. In those whom they have blessed they live life again.' Three simple lines she wrote, inspired her to make the rest of her life worthy of her husband's memory. As long as she continued to fight for his ideals, he would continue to live."

One of the Roosevelt's ideals which shaped my thinking along with the greater majority of Americans was, and I quote again from "No Ordinary Times"...

"The society of a few haves and a multitude of have-nots had been transformed. Because of the greatest – indeed, the only –redistribution of income downward in the nation's history, a middle-class country had emerged. Half of the American people – those at the lower end of the compensation scale –had doubled their income, while those in the top 20 percent had risen a little more than 50 percent. Those in the bottom half of earners had seen their share of the country's income increase by 16 percent while those at the top had lost 6 percent. As a result, social historian Geoffrey Perrett observed, "barriers to social and economic equality which had stood for decades were either much reduced or entirely overthrown."

If Rush Limbaugh and the likes of the conservative blogosphere/talk-show world, are reading this statement, I can hear them crying "Marxist!" just as they make claims to Pope Francis' core message of 'Jesus Gospel.' You can't get too much more radical than Jesus Himself who told the rich man to sell everything and give it to the poor.

Bill King of THE HOUSTON CHRONICLE posed an interesting question, "If Jesus came back today, would He recognize the U.S. as a country founded on his principles? Would He be marching in anti-abortion protests, trying to make them illegal or would he be ministering to young women with unwanted pregnancies to support them in keeping their babies?"

As Pope Francis has correctly stated, "Who am I to judge?"

I wouldn't dare compare myself in the content, or shoes, of Nelson Mandela, Martin Luther King, Franklin D. Roosevelt or the other giants of achieving social justice which both Moses and Jesus practiced and preached during their time on earth. But a nation which cherishes free speech gives all of us the opportunity to exchange error for truth. Partisan bickering and polarization in Washington should not deter us from examining and exclaiming different views. Ordinary citizens, such as you and me, need to understand and discuss both ordinary as well as complex issues. It takes our citizenry to make educated choices by deliberation on public matters which will affect all our lives. This may sound like heresy to some, but I believe that truth based on today's economy and political discourse override tradition and faith, to achieve levels of meaningful results.

Two people, equally learned, can read our Constitution and both disagree on the meaning and interpretation. The various decisions of the Supreme Court verify my claim, however what is in the best interests of the general social welfare is where I would hope we can be united on contentious issues, such as gun control.

After participating in World War 2 I vowed never to shoot at another human being. Clay pigeons won't harm anything. If others want to shoot deer I understand it is helping to control that ever expanding population. Jesus and Moses never spoke about guns, but handed us the Ten Commandments declaring Thou Shall Not Kill. Using cartridges filled with multiple bullets to destroy innocent children in schools or creating mass murders in public malls is beyond human acceptance. I would prefer to limit gun ownership to licensed citizens who are free from a history of crime, or recognized mental illness, and allow firearms for personal safety and for legal hunting purposes. Period!

Forget the conspiracy theories that our government wants to take away your firearms so they can control your lives. Show me the proof. I haven't seen one case where the Government of our United States of America is determined to take away our rights by the use of force. Be sensible and sensitive to every citizen feeling they are safe rather than fearing the senseless act of another crazy with an automatic weapon wielding multiple deaths and destruction of human lives.

May I please remind you of the sonnet which I wrote.

'Bullets are for battle. War is for peace. The Arsenal of Hope is a cartridge of love and caring to BACK-OUR-VETS.'

By now you must recognize I have the propensity to offer un-called for advice as well as asking disturbing questions.

Earlier I spoke of the problems too many of our returning troops and veterans face as they wake up each day to their aches and pains. Will we go about our daily lives forgetting how we treat the homeless, the hungry, the thirsty, the mentally and physically wounded, the naked, and the lonely, the victims of rape and those struggling with alcohol and drug addiction, the jobless, those fighting family abuse, the sick, those wanting to further their education, and will we continue to ignore the ris-ing rate of suicides among our returning men and women from Afghanistan?

Do we block out of our consciousness those in prison and con-tinue bashing homosexuals or rejoice in deporting 18 years olds of immigrant parents?

People, we have a lot on our plate in our effort to move Amer-ica from when we created the Greatest Generation, and then through self-centered bickering, and worshiping at the altar of greed and corruption - while practicing instant satisfaction -

that has put us on the very edge of America's death. Together, we MUST begin working to build the GRANDEST GENERATION this country, and the world, has ever seen. Despite what some nay-say-ers may comment, many of us no matter their religious beliefs, do firmly believe we have the duty and responsibility to remain our brother's keeper. Love and sharing is a command we can all adopt by being generous with our understanding that no one is immune from being in the other less fortunate person's shoes.

I must interrupt my thoughts as the clock is advancing to deliver in the New Year.

This is our year – the one to own- not a "No Year."

My best wishes to you for a Happy "Know" Year – as we make the best of every day throughout 2014.

Turn the Clock Forward

May I dare ask, are we going to move forward in 2014 or be content to continue to fall back?

Are we going to improve Obamacare, or waste time on political theatrics trying to tear it down? Social Security and Medicare faced these same hurdles when they were first being introduced because too many of us are unwilling to change and try something new which may prove so beneficial it becomes the very fabric of our lives… a safety net we can use to escape the unexpected calamity which may affect our way of living the rest of our years.

There's an unhappy faction in this great nation that is resolved to cut government "waste." Can't they understand that they are the major recipients of that so called waste when the majority of them depend on Social Security payments and depend on Medicare to help them through their sicknesses and ill health as we all grow older? Texans remember the Alamo, but every American must remember that every tax dollar comes out of our individual pockets which should turn us into becoming

Scrooge living with a big heart to remain our brothers and sisters keepers who need help when they urgently need our care and concern. No American should ever be left a life confined to a garbage can of suffering. That is not what makes us great. We attain glory and satisfaction where we become one big family concerned for one another no matter their circumstances.

Are we going to shore up the middle class, and create jobs, or give away more tax cuts to big corporations and the wealthiest Americans? No one despises waste in government AND big corporations more than I do. Do we reward those giant companies for not husbanding every dollar, or rewarding top executives for their mistakes and allowing them to pay huge bonuses or take golden parachutes as their reward for screwing-up? I can name more than one major bank or Wall Street tycoon who is laughing at us for being blind to their misdeeds. Why, when you and I pay our rightful taxes, is it alright for many a corporation to hide their profits overseas to avoid paying taxes, and in some cases earning tax refunds rather than paying their fare share?

We must demand a fairer, and simpler income tax method. Eliminate the mass confusion that even the tax experts need to hire more profound experts to figure the newest tax dodge. I don't claim to be an expert in these matters, but common sense would make us want to equal the playing field that everyone, and every business, must pay their rightful share with no unfair loop holes to be able to jump through. Every dollar earned by a U.S. citizen or company should be subject to a graduated income tax based on their earnings including hidden income from tips or gambling. I will let the financial guru's figure the minimum and maximum rates to provide the required annul funds to properly operate our national government. The only tax deductibles I think are necessary to stimulate the economy is to continue the deductions on home mortgages, plus I approve the charity deductions which support so many of our notable non-profits and cultural institutions. Depreciation and business losses are the cost of doing business and are the responsibility of the individuals or companies involved. No special treatment as far as I am concerned. Keep it simple – stupid!

When we eliminate the tax dodges we should be able to collect more money and therefore reduce the tax rates for all the payees across the country. Makes common sense to me, but the accountants and tax preparers will probably scream and holler louder than a rap singer. So what, we all need to do is our part to make this a stronger economy to be able to rebuild our infrastructure based on what is urgently needed rather than awarding pork such as building bridges to nowhere. No more favoring the rich at the expense of the welfare of the less endowed working class. That's not socialism. It's simple social justice.

Where I am not in favor of tying our economic hands behind our back is the investment in keeping our military the largest and best in the world. Unless we carry the biggest and most advanced technological club there will always be some tyrant or rogue nation wanting to take advantage of the weak and unprepared. Remember Pearl Harbor that found us fleet footed where we almost sank into the hands of our treacherous enemy. This doesn't mean we let the Pentagon and their suppliers run rough shod over our purchasing power. We must be scrupulous in our dealings as if every dollar was in our very own personal bank account…which is actually where the money to keep our military strong comes from, and let's not forget it!

I am adamant about not retaining, or continue adding yesterday's bows and arrows to our armament.

We must be dedicated to stay in front of the rest of the world in building the most modern and forefront equipment to keep Americans safe and protected. Which brings up another personal thought in protecting our security. As a former secret combat warrior sworn to never reveal our clandestine activities which were performed to win the war against our enemies I heard the shocking news that some pipsqueak ran to Russia to reveal the fact that we were monitoring Americans to weed out the threats of potential terrorists. My wife's knee jerk reaction was that he is a martyr for freedom of speech, while I screamed he is a TRAITOR. I would prefer to keep terrorists under the microscope of spying on their illicit activities by having some trusted agent listen to my innocent phone calls with my children or business associates.

If I haven't done anything wrong who cares who listens to my conversations which is just what we used to experience when our telephone calls were shared lines, and weren't private? If we trust someone to do the government's work and responsibility to try to ferret out those who will fly airplanes into our Twin Towers, or try to plant bombs in our subways, I am all for saving American lives. Let's not waste time arguing this principal. I am as liberal as anyone when it comes to defending and protecting social rights, but America comes first and always when it is a matter of keeping our country safe and secure from harm.

O.K. you caught me standing tall on my soapbox preaching for America which always brings me back to trying to come to the aid of the people who use the military equipment to defend our liberties. The machines and artillery are only as good as the officers and enlisted men who use them proficiently. How can we ever refuse to honor those brave men and women to the utmost of our abilities? We can't and we never should let them rot in our minds and pocketbooks.

Earlier I was suggesting how we might band together to BACK-OUR-VETS, but I have just begun, and want to cajole, coax and place a bee in the ear of some of our nation's leading advertisers. Don't sit on your fat assets ignoring the largest untapped niche market…bigger than the black or emerging brown market – the Red, White and Blue troops and veterans along with their families and other people directly involved with the military. They number 65 million strong which is one out of every five consumers of products and services.

I am talking to you Messrs. Coca-Cola or Pepsi; Proctor & Gamble or Unilever; Hershey or Nestle; General Mills or Kraft; Budweiser or Coors; and any and all major manufacturers of Consumer Products Goods. Call me today, and I will help you increase sales by a minimum of 3% with accurate measured results.

No more guessing which percentage of your advertising investment actually worked to lift sales.

Where do you get those sales increases? From your competitors- whose sales you have legally stolen - which means you have actually increased your market share by 6%. How? By adopting the orphan who is waiting for a sugar-daddy willing to invest 10% of their ad budgets to BACK-OUR-VETS. You will own the loyalty of 65 million shoppers, along with their friends and others, who want to donate their common 2 cents to insure no veteran will be forced to dive into a dump truck to find a scrap of food, or have to wait to be compensated for his exposure to Agent Orange, and is confined to living in a wheelchair with his hands so twisted that someone has to help feed him before his wheelchair transforms into an electric chair of sure death.

If you don't want to call me then insist that your advertising agency has the courage to face an old man who is willing to fight for his brothers and sisters in arms.

Don't think that I am letting you big food stores get off easy. You all have private labels that not only compete with the name brands, but other competitor store's private labels all offering lower prices. You too need to and can differentiate your private label brands by embracing the BACK-OUR-VETS campaign. It costs you less than peanuts because you can use your current media budget to incorporate the sponsorship message that will endear your customers.

When will you Messrs. Walmart, Krogers, Target, Kmart; Costco, Sam's; Walgreens, CVS; RiteAid; Safeway; Publix; H.E.B.; etc. start ringing my phone off the hook, or are you waiting for the next guy to prove he has gotten the jump on taking your customers away from ever darkening your store again?

Just because you are giving a few tax deductible bucks to veteran causes you shouldn't hide your generosity. Modesty is not becoming when you can set an example for others to also come out of the trenches in which they are hiding. Your investors and stockholders should know that you are leading the charge to BACK-OUR-VETS. The little old lady in Dubuqe will love you, and buy at your store, knowing that you have put your money where your mouth is. Simply it makes common cents!

Today is New Years Day. January 1st, 2014. A new beginning. A new blank page that we can fill with our fondest hopes and dreams coming true.

What I hope that we can forget and get over was last year's government shutdown. A near debt default. Record-breaking obstruction. Sequester actions that are continuing to obstruct progress. It's time to turn over a new leaf and stop the stone walling, and move America forward.

When an elected party leader, of either party, announces publicly that he/she has pledged to stop any proposed measure or recommendation by a President that was victoriously elected by the majority of the voters, in my humble opinion, that is considered treason. It's a resolve to not even consider compromise or to work for the good of all the people, all the time. It's childish, immature behavior and not worthy of respect or reelection.

Now, today as we start 2014, is the time for the resurrection of America to its former democratic rule of government to make progress rather than retrogress into the despair of becoming a third world nation of have nots – and do nothings.

Can we as thinking Americans ignore the lessons of history and forget our costly Civil War where too much blood covered our land, and families were torn apart like a broken string of pearls tumbling down a stairwell announcing another American died in vain. Are we too stubborn to not sit down and decide how to compromise for the good and welfare of We The People? Patrick Henry said:" "Give me liberty, or give me death." I would paraphrase that to say; Give me liberality (generosity or broad-mindedness) or give me death."

A New Year brings resolutions to keep, or make your best effort to attain positive personal and political results.

Let me start with the hungry amongst us. I pointed out the success of the End Hunger campaign that begun across the table in my ad agency's conference room, and how it has developed into a source of daily food for thousands. Many years back, I visited with the nation's largest supermarket chain to ask them to introduce the Red Barrel campaign in their stores. Their final response was that they do use Blue Barrels to collect non-perishable food for the needy during the holiday season. What happens to satisfy the hunger of stomachs crying for food between every meal of the year? There isn't a food store in this nation that shouldn't want to tap the generosity of their patrons to help feed their neighbors in need. Contact the Houston Food Bank to get the information of how they collect millions of tons of perishable and non-perishable foods, fruits and vegetable to insure that children, and adults don't go to bed with their bodies craving for just a morsel to starve off hunger. You profit by selling food, now resolve to help collect the food donations to keep your community well fed.

There are the homeless among us. Last time I checked more than 62 thousand were homeless veterans from the Iraq and Afghanistan wars with an alarming rise of these younger ex-service members.

The U.S. government determined that somewhere between 600,000 and 650,00Americans were homeless in 2012. Are you as surprised and shocked as mindless me? The one-night count methodology nationwide was disputed by some homeless advocates who estimated the number of the homeless population close to 3 million!

It's not easy to come-up with more opportunities to remedy the problems of homelessness in the United States, and I won't belabor the varied causes. I simply want to offer a common sense possible solution.

According to the American Religion Data Archive, in the year 2,000 there were 250,402 of what are called mainstream Congregations in the U.S., out of a total of 268,254 all told. The vast majority of these are Christian denominations. There are 3,727 Jewish congregations, and 1,209 Muslim congregations.

If the members of these various congregations practice what they believe, they may be acceptable to my "off-the-wall" suggestion to love thy neighbor. This idea I am proposing for consideration may conjure up thoughts of a hobo drifting from place to place to find somewhere to find comfort for a night.

Imagine along with me, that half of the quarter million religious Congregations in America participated in taking-in daily an average of 25 homeless people. 125,000 Congregations (small, large and mega-size) times 25 homeless men women and children would equal 3,125,000 human beings. That would be more than enough to totally eradicate our nation's homeless! I am not so foolish to think that will ever happen, or even a small number will consider taking on this responsibility in 2014, but we should act to reduce our homeless population. It shouldn't take too many dollars to purchase 25 foldable cots with the proper number of sheets, blankets and pillows per participating Congregation. The rules can be made quite simple for everyone to follow that the "guests" are responsible for setting up and storing the cots and the linens. Nothing, absolutely nothing will be allowed to be taken from the facility belonging to the Congregation or from another guest, and the rules would be strictly enforced. There will be no drinking of alcohol or smoking while inside the facility. No gambling or illegal substances allowed. Everyone will be accepted no matter their religious persuasion or skin color. No unbecoming conduct will be accepted and firearms are absolutely prohibited.

Maybe I am a cockeyed optimist, but I believe that just because someone is homeless by either choice or circumstances doesn't mean they are a thief. Some Congregations may choose to offer coffee, but that is their elective. It just makes common sense to make a meaningful measure to keep our fellow human beings off the streets. We all will sleep peacefully knowing we have tried our best to provide shelter and comfort to our fellow citizens. Which church, synagogue or mosque will be first to step-up and give this program an honest-to-goodness effort? I pray it is your Congregation.

Please allow me to depart from chronological order. I make no claim to be anything other than a businessman who spent the majority years of my life practicing advertising. Most businesses selling services or products to the consumers use adverting to help introduce and sell their wares. Good ads attract customers and build sales. Economic conditions throughout the country vary for many good reasons. In bad times it is not good sense to cut the advertising because you are cutting your nose to spite your face.

Why would some well meaning, but misguided people think our government is any different than a thriving business and want to cut necessary expenditures which create sorely needed jobs? Forcing a sequester only creates a stoppage of performing the necessities to regain the momentum of a slowed economy. It's a much wiser investment to create required jobs by improving the decaying streets and building the tired infrastructure. Fix the bridges. Tear down the street lights and place the wires underground where they won't be continuously damaged by floods, rain, snow, tornados or vehicles knocking them down. Avoiding unlit street lights or non-operating traffic signals is a wiser investment than creating a repetitive problem. Spend the money to alleviate auto traffic as we add more vehicles such as cars, trucks and busses to haul people and freight around. We not only need better and more roads, but we must improve our public transportation system. Invest in high speed rail to move our people to work faster, or to get to another long distance further and faster. Replace our horse-and buggy mentality with the most advanced technology which is safer and quicker. We can't stop the world of progress so jump aboard and lead the way. I am pleading to not let our schools or libraries crumble including investing in new facilities, and hiring more and better teachers. Of course, this all costs money, but if we don't continue to improve then there won't be any money left to even exist. We can't cut costs continually which results in lost jobs, which creates the domino effect of reduced taxes, that can only exasperate further unemployment with less and less taxes available to keep our economy from drowning in a sea of personal and government debt. Instead the sequester makes our government print more and more money which eventually loses its value until it becomes worthless. We will soon run out of paper on which to print unless we come to our senses.

I am not suggesting we go out and spend money recklessly, but if painting a mural inside a public building will improve its shabby appearance, and it has created jobs then let's do it. If widening a road will move more traffic safely then let's do it. If extending or adding more airport landing strips will improve traffic and safety let's do it. If including more bicycling and running paths will improve public health and safety then let's do it. If producing more products in America rather than shipping them overseas, and be willing to pay for the slightly higher labor cost which may be involved which creates more jobs then let's do it. I beg you to exchange the "no's" for a more positive and progressive approach by agreeing to say "yes, let's do it." That's the more common cents approach to add better and more jobs putting money back into the pockets of 'We The People' and the American economy. By now you have to realize that I am proud to love our military. I make no excuses for this patriotic behavior. However, as a free and independent civilian I am entitled, as well as you are, to be critical of what I consider offensive behavior. To name two things which I believe needs addressing from a broader viewpoint than being controlled within the military structure- the methods of controlling the appalling number of reported suicides, and sexual abuse needs to be openly examined. I do not want to attempt to interfere with the experts within the military as to how to perform their primary function which is to defend our country from aggressors. However, in the nature of mental health and justice under the laws there may be an opportunity for improvement to be examined and explored.

The Veterans Administration estimates 22 veterans per day commit suicide. I am not certain if that horrible figure is only for troops that have recently served or if it includes veterans from many years ago. We have been a nation at war for 10 years so admittedly these figures are a bit confusing, but nevertheless they are most disheartening to say the very least. It is interesting to learn that 50% of the suicides are by men and women that never served in combat.

The trauma of war and its aftermath can affect everyone who serves. Stress can be aggravated by being under the pressure of constantly staying prepared to enter combat, or missing normal family life, or possibly worrying about how to be able to transition into civilian life. It isn't quite as easy as we might think to lose your source of regular income, the provision of your clothes from head to foot, and a place to sleep and recreate. Reconnecting with those you love isn't as simple as taking a short business trip or a week's vacation. I am not certain if there is a quick and simple identifier to who is more prone to taking their lives. To the best of my knowledge there is no registry for veterans that are apparently capable of taking their own lives.

This does not mean we should both inside, and out of the military, not address this problem to make every effort to try to reduce this statistical and human question.

I do believe that in the greater population outside of the military there exists a wider number and variety of professionals capable of handling the mental causes that can lead to someone committing suicide. The military will probably balk at what they may consider outside interference. I personally witnessed this type of experience when I was on leave and suddenly was experiencing all kinds of stomach pains. My Mother ran to the phone and in panic called our family doctor to explain what was happening to me. He immediately advised that she must call the nearest Naval Hospital as the military prohibits providing medical care to someone in service by an outsider. I am not accusing the military of not having competent provisions for preventing suicides among the forces, but wouldn't it be nice to tap the very best, and widest, resources who work with the folks most likely to commit suicide?

It makes common sense to tap the knowledge and expertise of the highly skilled psychiatrists, psychologists, behavioral mental scientists, who spend all their professional time working and studying the causes of suicides, and how to prevent and stop them from happening. Such a group can be gathered who are dedicated solely to identifying the cause and prevention of mental health problems that typically result in a person taking their own lives. The screening and mental care of suspected military personnel could be assigned to this independent group. Any effort to save these troop and veteran lives is worth the time and the investment. Possibly a hospital or a University would be interested in taking on this role that could result in a critical benefit to the military as well as the general public.

I wish I had a 'eureka' moment that was the common sense solution to halting suicides, and eliminating sexual abuse in the military. I am proposing random ideas, but they may not be the final answers that are cast in concrete I would seek. What I am suggesting for the suicide problem by using outside experts to try to heal the mental wounds may be considered a parallel response to the prevalent sexual abuse running rampant throughout our military service organizations. All America was shocked to learn in the early part of 2013 that approximately 22,000 cases of women were being sexually abused by men within the military forces including a smaller percentage of men being attacked by other men. The news filled the airwaves incessantly as an incredulous nation learned that these cases ran rampant from the halls of West Point and the Naval Academy down to the hills of California across the country to the grass plains of Connecticut.

Much to the great credit of the military command they made a herculean effort to address this problem and opened wide this closed closet door hiding the behavior of shame. Cases were tried and punishments rendered that were enough to encourage other victims to step forward and report their individual attacks. Before 2013 came to an end the news reported 50,000 sexual abuse cases were filed as the victims began to feel that they may be able to get justice without being castigated. Progress is good and is more than welcomed, however it still created in my mind the question if there are many others in the military still afraid to bring their personal abuse problem before a military tribunal?

Businesses have their levels of responsibility and authority, but nothing comparable to the armed forces where rank is worn on the sleeve. Rank shouts authority, not to be questioned or challenged, especially where proof may be difficult to prove, particularly if you haven't earned your number of stripes.

My common sense solution is not too complicated unless you are hiding behind bars of silver and gold worn on your shoulders and cap. I would suggest the trials of sexual abuse be tried as they have currently been successful, and encouraged more of the abused to come forward with their cases. What troubles me is that there is little or no recourse if the victim feels they may have been discriminated against. Do they go back to duty bearing a scarlet letter on their forehead knowing they will be disgraced and tormented because they dared to challenge the commissioned abuser no matter what rank they may hold.

My suggestion would be that when the victim feels they have not received a justifiable verdict they have the right, and freedom, to bring the case before a civilian, secret Grand Jury knowing that if they are proved right the defendant, no matter their military rank, who is found guilty is automatically dishonorably discharged. I think that message would penetrate the minds of any and all who think since they are of any higher rank can take advantage sexually of anyone whose lives and actions they totally control. If you never served a day in any branch of the service you have no idea of the control and authority each stripe represents to anyone below. It works its magic to keep the military in command of their duties and responsibilities as they serve, but we cannot allow it to act as authorization to allow approved compliance of sexual abuse. I rest my case.

Love Letters

There's a small country town nestled between Galveston and Corpus Christi, Texas which sits on the shore of the Gulf of Mexico. It's very tiny population caters to fishermen and recreational boaters – the majority of which are primarily blue collar families bringing their RV's, or towing their boats on trailers to spend a few hours in the sun and on the waters. Most of the small businesses cater to providing the restaurant meals and bait and supplies these tourists require. No one would ever guess that this remote, quiet, laid-back place creates a miracle each year which should make every American proud to stand up and salute this unexpected patriotic extravaganza.

The humble residents and more influential folks maintaining their second homes in Port O'Connor and nearby surroundings annually invite 500, or more Wounded Warriors to fly, or be bussed into being their guests for a weekend of fun, fishing and feasting. Unless you are actually there it is hard to believe what practically are a few handfuls of people can accomplish to make life a little more enjoyable for our physically and mentally wounded heroes.

Excuse me for I know I am not capable of doing this scene justice by using my limited printed words to try to describe this masterpiece that Rembrandt couldn't capture its glory and pageantry and mostly the heart-warming love and thanks afforded our nation's warriors who have left their limbs and mental abilities lost somewhere in Iraq and Afghanistan.

Port O'Connor is lost in the fields of scrubby pastures where you might spot an occasional cow or two, and a lone oil well. There's only one two way road leading into P.O.C. which is also the only road out. If you need gas for your car you will find it at a convenience store which has grown pregnant to include a variety of grocery, sundries, beach, fishing, clothing and gear plus, a newly installed fast food service. This P.O.C. place ain't much to look at as it's no Miami Beach or Riviera, but they have a gold mine which is in the spirit and hearts of all.

O.K., I will get to the point, hoping you understand that magic is about to unfold.

Let's make believe for a moment you are one of the invited wounded warriors. Before you leave your hospital bed or room some place far from Port O'Connor you are given your special tee shirt, hat and identification. The wheelchair, or any other special needs, are packed and toted along. You are picked up and taken to an airport where you fly down to Victoria which is the closest town a plane of this size can land where you then are transferred to a bus. Now within 30 to 45 minutes you see highway signs stating you have just a few miles to get to your place of destination – Port O'Connor. What's this you are beginning to see in this desolate place on a hot summer day in Texas? Along the barbed wire fence designed to keep the stray cow from crossing onto the road are people. Not just one or two local families coming out to see where these yellow busses filled with hundreds of soldiers, marines, sailors and air force members might be headed, but there's a parade of what looks like thousands of moms, pops, kids of every size and age waving flags and saluting as you whiz by. Oh, my gosh, look at that bevy of Texas beauties! Where did all of these people come from to give such a loud and hearty welcome to blast above the noise of this caravan of busses?

Within half a mile the bus pulls into a parking area and out the window is a grassy meadow of what probably looks like an acre of land with every foot sprouting an American flag. The waving red, white, and blue welcomes you to step down and what is this amazing thing which makes your eyes pop-out in stark wonder?

Within a few feet you stand there looking up, and up to see an American eagle that is over 15 feet high, and its wings spanning left and right for what appears to be football field wide. This carving is made of sand which was trucked in by the carloads and lovingly sculptured by a few experts with the help of local people. There are the boots of fallen heroes and a rifle on one side accompanying the symbols of war and combat of every branch of service. One wall of sand works its way to the rear and the names of hundreds of fallen heroes from near and far are carefully chiseled into the wall of sand. On the opposite side, is another wall on which the name of everyone of the wounded warriors that were invited to this event has been carved. This sand castle of majestic glory makes you not only think of its creative beauty, but also of the people that generated hundreds of hours to take tiny grains of sand and hold it, mold it, and carefully carve it into a tribute to each of the 750 wounded warriors in attendance.

Hey guys, you are in Texas so come join in and treat yourself to a real down-home Texas barbecue with all the trimmins' you can eat, plus every type of beverage to drown your thirst with enough liquid to make you think you are a porpoise swimming in the nearby Intracoastal waterway. Come meet your host and hostess — the family which will take you into their home and treat you like long-lost kin. This is where you will sleep and rest from the time you arrived on Friday until you leave to go back on Sunday morning. Some of you will stay at the inns or other lodgings within the immediate area of P.O.C., but everyone will have a comfortable bed and all the requirements of a stay at the Waldorf Astoria.

It's Saturday morning and your host takes you and your buddies back to the central convention area for everyone to load up on a hearty breakfast because today is the day you have long been waiting for. You are going out fishing on private boats to small sized yachts. You are handed a giant bag full of goodies, drinks and a full meal and off you go down to the boats. Two of you are coming to my daughter's and her husband's home where you will spend the day cruising out into the bay, and fishing till your arms get tired from casting. I am along as part of the two man crew to try to assist which makes four of us. After exchanging greetings and handshakes we climb aboard and head for the open waters. Within minutes we are exchanging conversation as if we have been lifelong buddies. Both of you have been in Iraq where you tell us you were brought up on a farm, and know your way around fishing. Your wounds are well hidden by the clothing hiding the damage of the fragments when your truck was blown up from under you. Since you learned I was a medic in WW 2 you tell me how lucky you were to come out alive thanks to some brave medic who got to tend you as quickly as possible. My son-in-law Larry is a prominent orthopedic surgeon who is busily captaining the boat also makes some encouraging remarks, but we had promised we wouldn't spend too much time discussing the war and injuries. This was to be a fun adventure, and we were determined to live up to our promise.

The other warrior guest was quite different than our other loquacious guest. He wasn't quite as athletically built and obviously had difficulty climbing into the boat. I couldn't help but notice that guest number one, whom I will call Al simply to differentiate from guest number two, who we will name Juan. Al never left Juan alone. He stood close by his side and helped Juan with every step of the way. Please don't try to tell me we are not our brothers keeper when I was fascinated to see how he cared and watched over Juan. Al quietly told me that Juan was mentally disturbed as a result of his war duties, and we left it at that. Though I believe Juan may have been older than Al, it was Al who baited Juan's fish hook, and watched him hawk like that Juan was seated in a safe and totally comfortable bench out of harms' way, or from falling overboard. It was Al who would use the net to bring the fish which Juan had hooked into the boat, and clapping Juan on the shoulder for his catch. Al was Juan's anchor in a life of unspoken turmoil.

I didn't need to see much more to realize the importance this fishing outing meant to these guys confined to a hospital to try to heal their physical and mental wounds. Of course, we got back to shore and learned we didn't win the contest for the most or biggest fish caught. We did win the jackpot of helping two guys who have given so much for their country. God Bless them and all their fellow brothers and sisters in arms.

Now I wasn't there at the time, but since it was another wounded warrior who reported this story to me I believe every word is gospel. The guys had all gone back to the convention hall to have a fried chicken dinner that would make the Kentucky Colonel envious. Many of them were walking around the sand sculpture when one guy who was carefully studying the wall dedicated to the fallen heroes shouted out to his buddy. "Look! That's the name of the guy who was my best buddy in Iraq." There were two civilians standing close-by. A middle-aged man and a woman.

They turned to look at this warrior and said, "He is our son."

Three absolute strangers stood there united in tears and hugging each other in unspoken silence. I call this remarkable true story: LOVE LETTERS WRITTEN IN THE SAND.

I could go on and on describing the love and affection being bestowed on every one of those wonderful heroes by the generous people from Port O'Connor and the neighboring little towns that raised over $500,000, and somehow or another assembled a small fleet of boats to demonstrate they haven't forgotten, and they care about the men and women who have and continue to serve our nation.

Please join me in saluting the kind and generous people from P.O.C. – the Port Of Caring.

Games Lost

Contrast the previous account with what I will write about now, all of which relate to our attitudes toward veterans.

America rejoices and celebrates national holidays that honor our veterans such as Independence Day and Veteran's Day. It's generally hoopla and parades and hearing more politicians praising our troops and veterans to win votes and adoration. Can't they learn from the lesson in Port O'Connor that there is more to be gained by being directly involved with the men in uniform. It's nice to sponsor a fishing, hunting, biking, running, golfing, baseball, praying or other activity, but there's more to be acquired by hosting AND participating. Making friends, sharing meals, playing together just makes more sense without costing many more cents.

I mentioned earlier that on occasion a nice radio or TV host may invite me to share my thoughts on the veterans with them. I took it upon myself to contact one of the prime local TV station's to remind them I would be honored to talk about veterans on their Veterans Day show. We talked numerous times and exchanged emails. They declined my offer, stating they do not want to discuss the problems of our veterans and only want to thank them for their service.

It's like shaking hands and thanking vets for their service only to walk away blindly to their problems of being hungry, homeless or without a job. It's really not much different than our Congress throwing in the towel and not wanting to openly discuss how we can use common sense to solve our nation's problems. If you personally find you have cancer you can ignore the treatments and soon die. Or, you may be able to arrest the cancerous growth with the available treatments while scientists continue to search for a permanent cure, not just for yourself, but future generations as well. Just as my wife Natalie has discovered there may be long painful periods during this stretch of healing time, but you live in hope that some brilliant discovery will finally put to death not the patient, but the fatal killer itself.

Isn't that just what happened after President Roosevelt was struck down with polio and scientists leaped at the opportunity to find a cure to prevent this from happening. Today polio is no longer the monster which crippled our population.

Ignorance is not bliss. For a media to refuse to discuss the problems of multi- million Americans because it's too serious a subject to talk about while we are continuing to battle in Afghanistan is not only amazing to me, but do they think we are playing tiddly-winks with our men and women fighting overseas?

While I was attending the National Publicity Conference in

New York City I remember standing in a long line waiting to present my case for BACK-OUR-VETS to the producers of the number one morning TV show. Finally, I was first in-line and stepped forward with the biggest smile I could muster, and gave my two minute spiel. "No way. We only want fun and pleasant subjects like what is the latest hip-hop star up-to, or we love talking about Hollywood divorces or who is running-round the backs of their spouses." One more conscious step in dumbing down our ignorant masses.

It's not only Washington, D.C. that our people who are supposed to be representing us are covered up in their sleeping bags along with the lobbyists, ignoring the fact that we can't live in the past, or even the present, because the future is being launched every minute like a rocket ship headed to the moon and beyond. Woe is us unless we start using common sense to wake up out of our slumber to what is happening with our growing competitors around the world.

Talking about playing games this is one that has the mystery of keeping score being the unsolved problem of the century of my life which took place during the last few months of 2013.

Somehow I learned there was a national contest opened for small businesses (less than 50 people) that can compete to win a FREE 30 second TV spot during the forthcoming Super Bowl in January. To be able to have a free opportunity to present my BACK-OUR-VETS message to over 110, 000,000 viewers would be a God send. To actually be able to buy that same 30 second time on TV would cost me just $4 million of which I might be able to scrape together $40 as a down payment with 4 million years to pay the rest.

If I could pay that amount I would be able to earn lots of points to travel anywhere I wish, but who am I kidding?

What have I got to lose by trying to win the Big Game Little Business contest, so I made the decision to cross my fingers and enter knowing I may have little chance of winning? I got on the internet and carefully studied the rules which were plain as day. Amazingly, I discovered there was a printed opening which included non-profits to compete. That encouraging bit of information made me begin to believe BACK-OUR-VETS entry has as good a chance of winning, since the field was leveled, to compete against the profit oriented small businesses. Actually, I began to believe that maybe we had a better chance of winning that grand prize because we might be the sole entry honoring our countries veterans. After all, in many sporting events across the country they take time out to recognize a veteran or two, where in our Super Bowl 30 seconds we can bring attention to all 65 millions of the troop and veteran population, and show how each viewer can get involved by donating their common 2 cents. We might even open the eyes of some retailers when they would see for themselves the opportunity which BACK-OUR-VETS is offering. It's a win-win so go do it.

I sat right down and wrote the 600 character maximum entry describing BACK-OUR-VETS, and included the required photograph to be considered for Round 1. I chose to use the famous photograph of our Marines raising the American flag on Iwo Jima. I pressed "send" and off it went to the contest headquarters. The sponsor made it clear from the start that out of the expected 50,000 entries only 20 would be chosen for the first round. It was not only the written entry which would count, but how many emails would be registered supporting that particular company's entry. There I am with a company of one- just me, and my shadow, who is too unrecognizable to place a call. I got busy contacting and emailing everyone I could think of to vote once a day to BACK-OUR-VETS. I have no record, or could I know, if anyone was taking me seriously and actually voted to BACK-OUR-VETS. All I could do was to wait for that expected day to hear back that we were chosen to be one of the fortunate 20 businesses to be entered into Round 2.

There were $1,000 prizes being offered by the sponsor. This didn't capture my interest as I was motivated solely to get the veteran's plight known to the general public, and try to influence 300 million patriots to become involved in helping raise $1 billion dollars to BACK-OUR-VETS with 2 cents at a time. The $1,000 prize would be much more helpful to those struggling small businesses working to turn their dream into profits.

True to their word on the exact date they had promised to announce the 20 winners I received an email from the contest team notifying us that BACK-OUR-VETS had made the official entry into Round 2. I couldn't wait to share the great news with Natalie and my immediate friends and family. To top off my elation and joy, within hours I received another email from the Chairman of the sponsoring company congratulating BACK-OUR-VETS and wishing us continued good luck. We hadn't quite yet struck the jackpot, but at least we were in the running. Told once, and then confirmed by the number one honcho running the business, would never conjure up a future problem.

I was ready, willing, and capable of running the race, so I immediately began to follow the rules to become one of the four finalists to be welcomed into Round 3.

Each of the 20 competitors were asked to submit a 60 second, not a second over 60 seconds, video explaining our business and demonstrating our passion to succeed. We were also given 4 questions to answer within the amount of characters allowed. I didn't waste a minute putting my mind to the task, so I did what I thought I could possibly get accomplished the fastest and quickest which was to write out my considered answers to the four questions. After a few futile attempts I was satisfied with my explanations and put them aside while I took on the more complicated task of writing the script for the 60 second video, and trying to figure a way to get it produced without straining my already empty wallet. Putting my thoughts down on paper for the 60-second video was not as big a hurdle as I had contemplated. Hadn't I thought and been living with my idea, 24 hours daily, as to how to BACK-OUR-VETS?

Earl, just write it like I was talking to you if we were sitting across one another over a luncheon pizza.

The pieces fell quickly into place.

The first slice was to separate myself from the other competitors that were probably operating small stores or manufacturing a new product or launching a product. I decided I would ask the manager of the Houston Veteran's Cemetery if I could take a few steps in front of the entrance sign identifying the cemetery to explain to the audience that, "No, this isn't my place of business, or store, but it is my passion to keep every veteran from lying here prematurely..." From here, now that my brand was immediately differentiated from the other entre-preneurs, I could explain the problems, relay the solution to do-nate 2 cents, and ask to form a UNITED States of America to BACK-OUR-VETS. A production company which I couldn't recall ever using to produce our TV commercials during my ad agency career, generously (make that "magnanimously") vol-unteered to help once I explained the cause and purpose of the video. This lady, who I can never thank enough, opened her studio, and staff, to accomplish our mutual goal to produce a compelling video to win the votes of the judges.

This wasn't going to be easy as we were informed that the 8,000 employees of the giant company would be the judges to select the four finalists to enter Round 3. Once again, we were asked to support our entry with as many emails as possible to rein-force the importance of our business.

There were approximately two or three weeks to accomplish this herculean task, but I never could have anticipated what happened. On Friday night, my grandson Collin Likover and his Kinkaid High School team are playing a game at Kinkaid. As usual I got there early to plant myself on the 50 yard line, and I was sitting next to my daughter Bonnie who is Collin's Mom. Sometime during the game I said to Bon Bon, "I have a funny pain running from my left elbow down to my fingers which really is disturbing. Maybe I lifted weights this morn-ing incorrectly." I forgot it while watching Kinkaid run up the score for another win in their 10-game schedule. Next morn-ing I awake to find my arm red and swollen. I can't move my fingers as my hand looks more like a baseball catcher's glove. Natalie takes one look and says we are rushing to the hospital. The Emergency Room physician took one peek, and immediately admitted me into the hospital while I am protesting that I have a video which must be produced and only I can deliver the message. "That can wait! You have a severe staph infection which must be treated immediately." Nothing I can do about Doctor's orders except stew in bed.

I hear people complain about hospitals, the staff and the food. Nothing in my personal experience is further from the truth. I want to compliment everyone at Memorial City Hospital for their care and concern for my comfort. and return to good health. Not that I wasn't worried because I couldn't remember hitting my elbow, or being bitten by a spider, wasp, bee or any other harmful insect. What caused this malaise that had more medical pipes and tubes running into me than a West Texas oilfield? I kept pleading for me to have just an hour to leave to shoot the opening scene at the Veteran's Cemetery. I was given permission, but warned I must be back in bed within the two hours. Since I was wearing a suit jacket my bandaged left arm wasn't visible as I did my scene through gritted teeth. It began to rain so my worried chauffeur Natalie quickly rushed me back to my hospital room where I was reattached to the lifeline of antibiotics to drip slowly into my veins. The week was up and I was dismissed as I apparently seemed to be improving, but not before taking a new culture of my blood. It takes three days for the culture to be read which caused an emergency call from the doctors to hurry back to the hospital. The news was not good. The infection had advanced to being sepsis. Though it was years since being a hospital corpsman I remembered this was a poisoning caused by the absorption of pathogenic microorganisms into the blood. If not treated properly death can occur within 24 hours. How's that for good news when my mind was preoccupied with how can I finish the video in time to meet the contest deadline. I suggested to the doctors to let me get out of bed and simply shoot new antibiotics into my arm while I get the video done and shipped to meet the ever-coming-closer deadline.

"You are the craziest human being ever to be in our care. Do you think you're still in the Pacific fighting Japs? You are fighting for your very life. If you are out of the hospital and not being treated under Medicare, even if you are Bill Gates, you can't afford it. Lie down and be still."

I had no choice, but to die or go bankrupt, so I shut my big mouth and took my medicine in the arm like a good boy.

The nurse took a photo of me in my hospital gown, wearing my blue plastic hair covering, and being surrounded by all the paraphernalia that was keeping me breathing and alive. We sent it off to the contest team telling them of my plight, but we are still determined to complete the materials as requested, and on-time.

Miracles do happen, or my Christian friends would say that Jesus takes care of those who earned His help. Whatever, or whomever, was responsible, the next culture proved I was recovering since the inflamed bursa was surgically removed and the surrounding tissues were carefully rubbed, scrubbed and tubbed to be germ free. I was dismissed and had a drain left in my elbow which every afternoon for at least two weeks had to be reexamined to be sure it was releasing whatever junk was still in my arm. I quickly ran to the arms of Natalie, followed rapidly into the production film studio to complete the 60-second video and ship it off on time to the contest judges. Whew!

But, I still have got to get the voters organized once again to support our BACK-OUR-VETS entry. I did, and waited to hear the results from the sponsor if we had advanced to be one of the fortunate four in Round 3.

The telephone rings, I reach out and lift the receiver to my ear, when a business friend in New York calls to report, "Earl, I tried voting today for BACK-OUR-VETS, but you are NOT among the twenty contestants in Round 2." "John, you must have made a mistake. We have been notified by both the team in control, and again by the Chairman of the company sponsoring this contest that we are included in this round. Let me check for myself."

Sure enough, I thought I was about to die during the hospital stay, but it was nothing in comparison to verifying that we had been dropped without any notice from the sponsor. Nothing! Why? Who could figure? I began by calling and a young lady snottedly gave me no reason, or excuse. I gentlemanly tried to explain my history with giant corporations in handling their advertising, promotions and contests and understood the pitfalls. She suddenly changed and calmly said she would investigate this happening further and get back to me quickly. Now the fun begins as to who can pass the ball to someone else to avoid being the fall guy, or girl. I am frustrated so I finally gather up enough nerve to courageously call the man who sits behind the biggest throne at the top of the heap of executives. He surprisingly and willingly takes my call. He says he understands my questioning, and will ask the man in charge of veteran affairs to talk with me, but not before explaining that both he and the new gentleman I am about to meet are former officers from the military academies, and have served proudly over the years. I AM impressed, but still not knowing why we were dropped like a hot potato. No reason to keep belaboring my being tossed around from pillar to post until I finally get to visit by phone and emails with the number two guy. Still no explanation but obviously a planned program to not admit any mistake on their part. "Earl, we are getting close to the holiday season. Why don't we wait until after the New Year to discuss this further?" They must think I am addle, and don't know that by delaying there's no way we will ever have our 30 seconds of free time to deliver the BACK-OUR-VETS message during the fast arriving bowl game.

To give them a way out of trying to hide for cover I offered them an opportunity to run the B.O.V. 30-second spot in some key local markets such as Los Angeles, New York, Chicago and Houston to keep their cost down, yet allow us to reach the important retailers as well as the consumers. No response.

Would it have been so difficult to invite me to their offices to explain man-to-man what may have happened? Certainly they as business people should recognize the time and cost to prepare the materials for staying in the contest, and then to be kicked around more frequently than a soccer ball during a game was a bummer.

One of my long time friends in Houston runs one of the largest law firms with a Fortune magazine front page recognition of their repeated success in bringing giant corporations down to their knees. We spoke and as friend- to- friend he advised that we have a legitimate case, but it would take years before it could be settled as the defendant has all the gold in the world to keep delaying before paying. I stated earlier that the money was not my purpose in life. My goal was to BACK-OUR-VETS and get them the help and support they have earned. So, I licked my wounds and haven't had a good night's sleep ever since.

I keep tossing and turning trying to figure why their sudden turn of action by kicking us off the contest field. My mind and thoughts have examined every legitimate possibility, and I have come to one conclusion. Remember that I earlier pointed out that President Kennedy had spoken about forming the new Navy SEALS based on their standing on the shoulders of the World War 2 secret warriors.

I innocently assumed when folks asked what I did in the war was to simply say "I was a Navy SEAL medic" since few if any ever heard of the small clandestine group in which I served. Rightfully so, when a few real, live SEALS heard about this statement they literally blew their tops. "No one can claim they are a SEAL if they didn't go through B.U.D." They were right as B.U.D. didn't exist before 1961 so in their opinion I had no right to imply being a U.S. SEAL.

They used social media to defame me, and publicly announced that I was a fraud. I can't blame them as I totally respect every SEAL and meant absolutely no harm. I will admit I would dress as a clown if it meant I could help any veteran or member of the military. To my ever remembering regret I will confess to my non-intentional sin which MAY have been the reason BACK-OUR-VETS was shot dead by the contest firing squad. I don't really know for sure, but this unfortunate assertion has been an expensive conscious searing experience. We all make mistakes, but this was the skyscraper of errors.

May God forgive me and not seal my fate to never forget.

I can't leave this subject without pouring my innermost thoughts out about our nation's SEALS who stand as our country's spearhead against the Bin Laden's of this world. Each and every SEAL from their early inception through tomorrow's recruits send a loud and clear message to foreign tyrants and terrorists, "DON'T MESS WITH OUR U.S.A."

The only other reason I can imagine why we were suddenly locked-out of being selected for Round 3 was that our message wasn't funny or stupid. Clever and intriguing advertisements I can understand, but people don't buy from clownish commercials. They may laugh, they may snicker, but they don't rush out to buy 'ha, ha' childishly presented products. Did the sponsor actually believe they needed a TV spot to hit someone's funny bone? Frankly, I don't know where the singular funny bone is located in our anatomy. Do you?

BACK-OUR-VETS might be considered too serious to play during Super Bowl in some people's minds. However, in this mind of mine, it is never too often to repeat, repeat and repeat a message worthy of hearing. Repetition is the keynote of muscular success in advertising.

My everlasting regret is that I may have blown the chance to have America's real heroes playing during the Super Bowl to get their message out to the millions of Americans to learn they can put in their common two cents to BACK-OUR-VETS.

You might be asking yourself: 'why can't I do more of the advertising and promotions yourself instead of trying to win a contest?'

Good question. Natalie and I have poured our souls and money into BACK-OUR-VETS without attaining our goals. Not yet, at least. We always remember that Thomas Edison tried 10,000 times before he finally invented the light bulb. We are not ready to surrender, though it gets more difficult to rob Peter to pay Paul, when we are both Peter and Paul.

"Then do as other non-profits do and seek grants."

Understandable suggestion, however from day one it was my decision to never compete with those sterling organizations involved with supporting our troops, veterans and their families. This conflict might hurt well established organizations as the grantor would have an excuse we have already funded our budget in support of the military. That is one of the main reasons we were more interested in establishing a grass roots fund raising effort that could spread like prairie fire across every state.

The money we would raise would be granted to vetted non-profits as explained earlier.

I must end this chapter simply by thanking everyone who voted repetitively to BACK-OUR-VETS, and hope they understand that I was not pulling their leg when I firmly stated how proud we were to be included in Round 2 of the Big Game contest. Somehow the scales of justice will favor us and our noble cause.

Our purpose in life is not to play games as we are trusted to win the support of every American to BACK-OUR-VETS and their families. That's the game we are determined to win, or 65 million lose.

Two to Tango

The United States today is divided into Red states being more conservative and leaning Republican, whereas the Blue states tend to be Democratic and liberal.

Mix equal parts of red and blue together and what color do you get? The usual answer is purple, but depending on the ratio of blue to red, the color may be anything from lavender to magenta. Simply meaning, that determining the color you need to acquire the best results you have to learn to mix and match.

Compromise is the mixing and matching of firm ideas to formulate common ground.

Is it easy? No! Is it impossible? No! Is it important to work together for the common good? YES! Not only is it important-it is imperative for our great generation to lead to be even grander in deed and accomplishment.

Now, with your blessings, I will try to examine some of the important issues facing America today. Of course, the solutions to these problems are not ever easy, as many of these wounds have been festering for years searing our minds and souls. I don't want you to turn away because some of my suggestions may irritate you to the point where you want to throw up. Remember, I may feel precisely the same way about what I think are your irrational ideas. Using COMMON SENSE is the best way to find common ground on which we both can stand firm knowing we haven't compromised our principals.

I have expressed some of my thoughts on the hungry, the homeless and the need for jobs. Together we can search through these subjects, and address some of the major issues which need to be examined, explored and exchanged between the blue and the red to form a more perfect United States of America.

Are you with me? O.K., then let's plunge ahead with open minds. You already know my position on most social issues as being, what Rush Limbaugh would accuse as being a Marxist, Communist, Socialist. On the other hand, there are few people more aligned with conservative support of the military than where I stand.

Being flexible, and willing to see both sides of an issue can lead us to break bread while breaking barriers.

Only today I heard the Mayor of Salt Lake City explain on TV how the private sector joined hands with the government and have practically eliminated any veterans and their families from the binds of being homeless. I also learned that Phoenix also found housing for their homeless. These exceptions should become the rule, so I think we should turn to those leaders and follow in their steps. No one would be happier than me, should every city start with seeing that their veteran population has a roof over their heads. I know once you feel the taste of victory, you won't stop by making certain everyone of your community finds a home of comfort to sleep other than a sidewalk or a culvert.

The Houston Food Bank is a wonderful example of how to reduce the number of people whose stomachs cry an ocean of tears to have something to eat. In addition to collecting the non-perishable foods donated by caring shoppers that drop a can of soup, or a box of cereal into the Red Barrels, the Food Bank collects donated foods from restaurants to help feed the hungry. The Bank pays a unique interest to especially feed the children through a wide network of community houses-of-worship and pantries. Please feel free to contact them and from the small acorn which we planted over 25 years ago, every dot on the map of America can be able to tuck their kids to bed with smiling stomachs.

The Americn tragedy of veterans taking their lives at the rate of nearly one per hour is a crisis calling for a cure. There is a new medical treatment that holds the promise of helping sufferers of post traumatic stress disorder (PTSD), and from traumatic brain injury (TBI). Dr. Pail Harch, director of LSU School of Medicine's Wounded and Hyperbaric Woundcare and Hyperbaric Medicine Department, believes hyperbaric oxygen therapy should be made available to America's wounded warriors as it holds the key to a therapy that could be saving lives. Meanwhile the Department of Defense and the VA are blocking access to a successfully tested therapy that could save lives. I am not expert enough to go into the details of how this treatment works, but Dr. Eddie Zant, who has treated many veterans , says, "HBOT works. Of those I have treated, 99 percent are almost back to where they were before they were injured. The VA gives them medications, and these guys are like zombies. With HBOT, they really do get better, and many get off the drugs. HBOT could save a lot of lives."

Please scratch your memories to remind you of Juan who was one of the veterans we took out fishing during the Wounded Warrior Weekend in Port O'Connor. He was a perfect example of a sufferer of post traumatic disorders – excruciating head-aches, depression, fatigue, memory loss, and anger – leading to further tragedies of joblessness, divorce , and all too often suicide, as reported by Clayton R. Reid in a recent article he wrote in NEWSMAX magazine.

If the delay in approving and extending this treatment is due to the Defense Department being cash strapped then let America's consumers step up and do what's right for the veterans. It makes common cents to BACK-OUR-VETS with the 2 cent consumer donations to do the right thing to solve this moral issue. Isn't it common cents to relieve the pain and suffering that over 300,000 veterans of the Iraq and Afghanistan wars are suffering? Their crisis is our call to duty to save a lot of lives. There is the other issue – the moral issue. Our men and women in uniform sacrifice their all for us, and we are willing to turn our backs on them when we could raise billions of annual dollars as we BACK-OUR-VETS.

What I am about to propose next will probably sound as if I have lost my mind. My idea may further guaranty my scattered brains land somewhere in Canarsey or fantasy-land.

I have never been able to understand the Supreme Court making the judgment that a corporation is a human being which entitles it to fund candidates running for election to office. If a corporation is supposedly a human entity then why not allow tigers, lions and alligators vote in our elections? That makes about as much sense to let all the animals in the zoo to vote to make a monkey of one citizen – one vote.

Those corporate donations are no more than someone paying a prostitute for favors. And, their lobbyists are no more than their pimps pumping self-centered interests into the politicians' ears and pocket books that have been bought with "do what keeps you elected and loads your pockets with cash, benefits and payment for life." It's not only wrong, but it needs to be stopped if we expect the people that are elected to work for us rather than their major contributors.

The solution is simple, but will probably never be passed because the legislators who are supposed to follow the will of the people will only follow the cash of their major donors. Nevertheless, I will suggest a simple solution to level the election playing field. A law needs to be written and passed that only citizens qualified to vote can donate $100 to a candidate running for a local office, $250 for a statewide office, and $500 for a national office such as Congress or the Senate. Any candidate chosen by their national party running for the U.S. Presidency or Vice President's office is eligible to receive $1,000 per legitimate citizen. There would be no allowance to pay for a parties support as it again opens the door to trickery and confusion. It's the person, and not the party, we should be choosing to represent our best interests. Earning the right to represent us is not a commitment to blindly follow an obstructionist party rule. I am hoping we can find intelligent, honest people who want to work for what is best for all the people, all the time. It would be a crime, punishable in the harshest manner, for someone to pay another's fees to vote.

I am concerned that some people may take this recommendation as punishing those that cannot afford to pay the election fees. They are not mandatory; they simply limit the amount a candidate can spend. Anyone who chooses to can elect to pay up-to-the maximum amount in small and repetitive payments.

Is it the end of supporting political parties? No, as they do serve a legitimate purpose but any contribution would be limited to a total of $1,000 a year per citizen. None of these particular funds can be used for any mass media at all including the production of materials for individual candidates. Grass roots efforts would be encouraged especially if the "grass" is individuals planting the seeds of contentment for their candidates, by knocking on neighbors doors, holding home rallies or using social media. I can already hear the howls of discontent by the media, the printers, the producers and advertising agencies that spew out their spiel of how great their candidates are when they hardly know them other than to collect the checks for their drivel. There must be a way to clean-up the uncontrolled lies, distortions and accusations made by some desperate and desperado characters running for an elected office. We need patriotic men and women pledged to act, and be one of 'We The People' working for our common good. It may never happen in my lifetime, but it is just common sense.

The winds of change are blowing across the world including America with Pope Francis being revealed as a messenger of mercy and reform. The "Pope of the poor," is indeed an icon as his mandate is to lift the underprivileged and disenfranchised. He faces the backlash of non justified capitalists who claim the Pope's words are pure Marxism coming out of the mouth of the Pope. Pope Francis practices what he preaches, as widely reported he slips out of the Vatican at night dressed in regular priestly garb to meet with the poor and the homeless.

I can't fault him for his missionary church of mercy which moves out of the sacristy and into the streets to deliver a message of love and care to wounded men and women. God Bless Him and God Help his Critics! If only some of our politicians and media loud-mouths would also reach out to understand that capitalism is an investment to help the poor so that they too can share the fruits of comfort. Then everyone benefits which makes common sense to this observer.

Now I can expect to hear about the "welfare queen" who is living in her luxury apartment while watching TV on her 76" screen, and munching on caviar sandwiches…all on YOUR tax dollars. Could be that there's one in a million, but I can guarantee you that there are multi-millions living below the poverty level that are clawing and scratching simply to exist. You respond, "It's not my fault they are too lazy to get a job. Too spoiled to want to make something out of themselves except complain and bitch, and want more free stuff handed to them." Brother, try doing what the Pope does rather than for an evening, but for a month, or more. Put away that dark suit, tie and shirt, shiny new shoes and live in squalor, filth and hunger with no credit cards, and stand in long lines to find a job in your dirty hand-me- down clothes, or waiting for some food stamps. When you are robbed of your dignity you are robbed of your destiny to climb out of the gutter. Maybe you are more courageous than I am to be in the 1.7 million households living on $2 a person per day, or less. Be thankful for what you have and be less critical, and hateful to those less fortunate. Instead be responsible that you can share your bounty and blessings. Please don't shake your head and walk away from me thinking I must have a hole in my head thinking as I do. I will agree that my mouth, eyes and ears attest to the fact that I have the holes of which you accuse me, but it's better than having an open hole in your pocket without a penny on which to live.

The welfare cheat is no better, or worse than the smug corporations hiding their profits behind the screen of foreign deceit to avoid paying their share of U.S.A. taxes. Neither one deserves to be condoned. Instead both need to be condemned and corrected for conning all of us who may not like, but belly-up to Uncle Sam and pay our taxes.

Certainly both Democrats and Republicans should have a common interest to ending this chicanery. Collecting more in hidden corporate taxes which are rightfully due as well as stopping the gravy train of welfare waste, will help decrease our nation's debt. The dollars saved makes common cents to me as I hope both political parties can agree to this workable solution.

How can someone like me, and the millions of others who benefited from the G.I. Bill to help pay for our college educations, and by using the G.I. Bill to purchase our homes not recognize the value of the government to step-in to lift us through tough times?

Programs like unemployment insurance and food stamps are

keeping millions of families afloat. For poverty to decrease - the low-wage market needs to improve.

Should our do nothing Congress approve lifting the federal minimum $10.10 an hour minimum wage from its current $7.25 level, it would lift about 5 million people out of poverty. Our great hope is to have a stronger economic recovery which can decrease the unemployment rate to below the current 7 percent. An almost unbelievable statistic is that the poverty rate for full time workers is just 3 percent while it leaps to 33 percent for the unemployed. Wake –up America, and roll-up-our sleeves to create more jobs instead of wasting time bickering and not doing anything to put more people to be gainfully employed.

I previously suggested some job plans for the veterans, now expand those ideas to work for everyone…and we can relieve or eliminate joblessness.

Caring by sharing, makes common cents to being a righteous, united nation.

We keep stalling improving our immigration laws because some people think that the new immigrants will work for lower wages than what are currently being dished out to our low paid existing immigrant populations. I would guess that has been a common fear across the years. When my grandparents arrived on Ellis Island I guess they may have taken jobs below the pay scale of the then carpenters and moving truck laborers. What really happened is the blueprint for today. Their sons and daughters, and grandchildren became the entrepreneurs, lawyers, teachers, scientists, business men, bankers, brokers and builders of America...many of whom served in our armed forces. We are a nation of immigrants and have been since a Jewish Italian named Christopher Columbus landed on these shores.

Surprised I referred to CHRISTopher as being Jewish? Some claim he was, others say not. Makes no matter to me. What does matter is that he and his crew discovered a new land of opportunity where everyone should have a fair chance to make something of themselves. It was not too long back when I can remember that we were afraid to use a person with black skin in our advertising commercials unless they were pictured as a servant or a train porter. I can also recall receiving an irate message from one of our hotel clients general manager's asking me how we can solve the public relations problem of a white customer eating a meal with a black man in his hotel's restaurant. What made him even more indignant was that the white man was a top executive of our advertising agency. Thank our lucky stars that we have 'come a long way, baby' since those days of stubborn prejudice. Turn on your television and within the hour you are likely to see people of every race, and color, acting, performing or participating in advertising, the news and the talk shows. It's not unusual to be dining in public with families, and singles or couples of every race and breed wherever you go in America, and everyone all seem to be eating heartedly, minding their own business, which is precisely the way it ought to be.

America is the land of the free and you should be able to practice your own religious beliefs without impositions. Which simply means don't try to shove your religious tenets down the throat of any other person. Obey the law and keep the separation of church and state. Your birth, or choice of religion belongs in your heart, your family and congregation. That doesn't need

to be interpreted that I can't enjoy looking at Christmas deco-
rations up and down my neighborhood of homes and apartments, nor should you object to seeing a lighted up Menorah,
but not on public grounds or institutions where some may see
it as proselytizing.

The glory of America is the respect we must have for one another.

What I am about to say will make some in our population
furious. But I must be honest with you as well as with myself.
Unless you are a true American patriot, willing to give your life
for this country, please don't expect me to bow to your beliefs
that you plan to change our American way of life by wanting
to overthrow our government and impose your beliefs and ancient traditions. I do not want to tolerate your public speaking
in a foreign language when English is our tongue. I do not
want to tolerate your imposing restrictions on women where
they are second hand pawns to be restricted to a foreign way of
dress, denied education and equal opportunities. I do not want
to be subjected to your using our public streets or parks for you
to bow to your God. I do not want you to invade our schools
to teach the tenants of religious hatred. I do not want you to
stone, mutilate or harm disbelievers or those who you believe
violated your strange and inhuman laws. You are welcome here
to worship, prosper and live in peace as Americans first and
foremost. I and others will welcome you and extend our hands
in friendship only when we see by example, and act, that you
will keep your customs private, but assimilate into our family
of citizens.

How can I take such a strong stance? Only by personal example, both Natalie and I were born Jewish and will remain and practice in our faith until our deaths. We have never objected privately or personally when all three of our children made their choice to either marry people of other religions or chose to adopt another faith. As parents we gave them the best of Jewish education and full involvement in our faith, however when they are grown-ups they have the right to choose independently whether it be by love of someone or by choice of finding comfort and solace. To be truthful, it gives both Natalie and myself the joy of participating in both Protestant and Catholic ceremonies and holidays as one close family. The best of three out of three isn't bad. It does make you believe that there is a universal God who looks after all of us including the atheist and any non-believer.

The words may differ, the music, ceremonies and testimonials may vary, but the basic beliefs of each religious persuasion - to love thy neighbor and walk humbly with your God, remain sacred and the same.

Our "Do Nothing" Congress won't take matters into hand and use common sense to agree to help fix what ails our county. Only this morning as I was eating my bowl of oatmeal and raisins I read Thomas Friedman's column which headlined, "Compromise: Not a four-letter word that the country's biggest challenges could be solved by adopting a hybrid of best ideas."

Thank you, Mr. Friedman for your erudite thoughts and hybrid solutions that can make a difference. I must agree with your suggestions as to how we can get the derailed train back on the track, but until we voters wise-up, and throw out-of

-office the members of the TEAr Party, who are determined to TEAr aPart our nation, we will continue to drift in an ocean of daffiness.

Republicans and Democrats can Compromise to make common sense for the good of every American.

When that happens I won't shed a tear for the disruptive tear apart dissidents who will be parted from destroying progress.

The End Is Only the Beginning

Was it Yogi Berra, the famous baseball star who said, "When you get to the fork in the road — take it." I am not sure I can interpret accurately what Yogi was instructing, but I think he was advising us to take it and move forward. Standing still and stonewalling will never get you where you need to go!

Since the beginning of the American Revolution more than 43 million men and women have served in the U.S. military during wartime. There are only something like 86,000 veterans from World War 2 still living as we are a fast dying breed.

How fortunate I am to be amongst this group of honored men and women to have had the privilege of serving, and I am able to share my personal observations with you and others.

Yogi, the two forks in the road, of which I have taken both, are what happened after World War 2 and what is occurring today with the aftermath of Iraq and the continuing war in Afghanistan. I invite you to be patient and allow me to share my overview of the differences, dissensions and advances.

I've enjoyed success as exhilarating as flying to the moon, with some painful disappointments that hurt like the dentist drilling an abscess tooth. But I survived, just as Natalie is a cancer survivor – lucky for me to have the good fortune to have lived through these times to be able to tell the truth, troubles and tumbles.

Let's look back to the end of World War 2 when we had a crippled President who never crumbled under the pressure of millions of veterans returning to a country going into a deep economic nose dive due to the closing down of the biggest war machine the world had ever seen. He had to live with the typical do nothings in Congress that were crying tears that we can't afford to spend another penny as we are a nation overloaded in debt. "We are about to go broke. Cut! Don't spend or we will be bankrupt. Our debt ceiling will soon be crashing down."

President Roosevelt coddled and cajoled Congress, and made them swallow his advice to invest in the nation's future. We began to rebuild our infrastructure, build our schools and repair our streets, and means of transportation. We didn't just survive, we pulled ourselves out of despair and misery by working together and helping new businesses create jobs with prosperity replacing poverty of mind and matter. We passed the G.I. Bill, Social Security, Medicare, despite the howling and the objections of the opponents whose echoes we still hear today.

I can't speak for the millions of others during those post war years, but those government investment programs saved many a life then, and continue to this day (69 years later) to help keep us alive and living supported by a strong and true safety net from falling into the crevice of an overwhelming avalanche.

I can only comment as just an ordinary common citizen that bleeds red, white and blue, I am thoroughly thankful for the foresight of our leaders in government to have extended a much needed helping hand.

The G. I. education, the home were the supports of my career, but more importantly are the foundations of our family lives. This experience has made me understand that government has an important role to shore up the nation and the people that can prosper under its protective roof.

We have had great, good and ordinary Presidents, but what really matters and takes advantage of the challenges is when all the political leaders of responsibility, whether it's local, state or national, work in harmony for a common cause. America doesn't have to only unite solely when we have a war. Every day we have the obligation to fight poverty, homelessness and diseases of all kind. We must continue to invest in new technologies, invest in new frontiers in space, invest in new entrepreneurial businesses, invest in science to help avoid controllable catastrophic disasters, as well as research and develop new frontiers that open up new doors to a better future. Invest in our children as they are our future. They need a head start, and continuous support, so stop kidding ourselves by cutting education funding.

"Good ideas, so where is all this money going to come from?" The answer is so simple, it makes common cents. The more productive we become, the larger our middle-class, the greater our wealth which creates the affordability of whatever we must do to stay ahead of the curve, and remain the world's leader.

Money doesn't trickle down from the top like pennies from heaven. It comes from the bottom, the middle and the wealthiest sharing, fairly and squarely for one nation under God providing liberty and justice for all.

Speaking words like these must make me sound like the village idiot to lots of folks. "We want it now. The heck with the other guy. It's me, and only me that I care about. Why share anything? I made it. I want to keep it all. Forget about being my brother's keeper. I got enough trouble keeping myself alive. Don't bother me about abortions, civil rights. Let me smoke my pot and take my own risk that I am killing my brain." I've heard them all…and I am appalled.

I am appalled to see how some of our young boys and girls dress. Bill Cosby said it better than I when he addresses the young punks who think it's cool to have your baggy pants hanging down below your behind, your cap going backwards as if you are walking from where you just had come, drooping a cigarette out of browning teeth and wearing more tattoos than a jungle tribesman . .. and, you complain nobody is gonna' give you a job. I am not suggesting you have to look like Little Lord Fauntleroy, but man, you have got to clean up your act. Be presentable. Be responsible so that the employer knows he can trust you. You are not a gangster. You are no better, or worse, than a U.S. Marine, so act like one. Stand-up tall, be erect, don't slouch and shuffle. Speak like a gentleman. Earn your stripes and you will earn respect and a job where you can prove you are worth more than you are being paid. I may be old-fashioned, but that is the American way to get ahead instead of falling on your face and being a disgrace to whatever your race.

Someday, possibly when it's too late, and you have watched your friends go to prison, or see some other guys who made the effort to be accepted into society, you will realize the advice from this old codger makes common sense.

Young ladies you are not immune. During my long years in advertising I probably sold millions of dollars of every type of ladies fashions, from lingerie to outerwear through our numerous department stores and specialty shops. I am not queer, but I still enjoy going into a store and looking at the latest fashions, and seeing who made them and how much they cost. I'll also admit to looking over every lady I see to check them out as to what they are wearing as it's part of my DNA.

School is not the place to see who can outdo a Las Vegas showgirl strutting her stuff on a stage. You can look absolutely stunning and alluring by being modestly clothed. Nothing can replace good taste. It's not the money you spend, but the common sense you apply to dress yourself. There's no earthly reason to make your outfit shout and scream at everyone when your smile can do that for you. You are not in competition to try to make the other girls cry because you spent the most money, or poured on more face disguise than Dracula. If you are going out to some place more exotic, or fun, then use your own wise discretion whether you need to overdress or under dress. Remember you are not a female under stress so that you have to flash your wares like a stop light. Believe it or not, guys like to find the proverbial girl next door where they can build a long relationship. It can become a good friendship or a lasting marriage like mine and Natalie's. When two people discover a gem in the rough they both want to tie a knot, so what's not to want that? It's part of the American dream that it's up to you to make come true.

After listening to the young ladies in the Alternative School I thought it might be a good idea to have everyone in school wear a tidy uniform. It eliminates the competition of who out-did the other, as well as keeping the cost down. Maybe you can suggest that to your school and lead the student fashion parade. Makes common sense to use common cents that you can use for more important things than wasting money on fashion conscience clothes you wear one time, and "wouldn't be seen in that old thing" again.

When you are rich and successful then it's the time to flash your fashion style from your pretty little heads to your high spiked shoes.

Found the Money

Mel Gross and I share many things in common. We are both loyal members and supporters of the Anti Defamation League where I first met him. Mel, through his Rotary Club activities is involved in supporting the military, and has been kind to invite me to their luncheons honoring the veterans and current military members.

We sit on opposite sides of the sea-saw between conservatives and liberals; however, we do have common agreement on how to end the waste in government. Recently he shared an email with me which expresses our common sense agreement that our government can reduce wasteful spending.

Here is how (and I quote);

"Both Democrats and Republicans say, 'We're broke' and can't help our own SENIORS, VETERANS, ORPHANS, HOME-LESS, etc. ??? BUT, over the last several years THEY have provided DIRECT CASH aid to ..... Hamas - $351 M ..... Libya - $1.45 BILLION..... Egypt - $397 M..... Mexico - $622

M…. Russia - $380 M….. Haiti - $1.4 BILLION….. Jordan - $463 M….. Kenya - $816 M….. Sudan - $870 M….. Nigeria - $456 M….. Uganda - $451 M….. Congo - $359 M….. Ethiopia - $981 M….. Pakistan - $2 BILLION…. South Africa - $566 M….. Mozambique - $404 M….. Zambia - $331 M….. Kazakhstan - $304 M….. Iraq - $1.08 BILLION….. Tanzania - $554 M….. …with literally BILLIONS of DOLLARS – and they STILL hate us!!!

Our retired seniors living on a 'fixed income,' nor do they get any breaks, while our government and religious organizations will pour HUNDREDS OF BILLIONS of $$$$$$$$$'$ and tons of food to Foreign Countries!

Someone needs to explain to them that CHARITY begins at HOME!!!

And another atrocity…We have Hundreds of adoptable AMERICAN children who are shoved aside to make room for THE adoption of *FOREIGN* orphans.

AMERICA: A country where we have: Countless Homeless without shelter; Children going to bed hungry; Elderly going without needed medication; and the Mentally ill without treatment – etc. YET….they will have a 'BENEFIT SHOW' for the people of Haiti, on 12 TV stations, plus, ships and planes lining up with food, water, tents, clothes, bedding, doctors and medical supplies.

NOW JUST IMAGINE if OUR OWN gave 'US' the same support they give to foreign countries."

Personally, I have little fault in the U.S.A. rushing to give aid to any country suffering a natural disaster, but we must STOP paying CASH to countries sworn to crash and burn the land that I love – AMERICA.

This should not mean we won't help, aid and support other democratic countries when we share a common interest. We are our brother's keeper, but not if foreigners pick- pocket our money with one hand, and have a knife in the other, to stab us in the back.

Saviors – YES!

Suckers – NO!

I hope you agree that it makes common cents to better use the cash (we give to support un-democratic foreign countries) to boost our own American people.

Please stop crying we can't afford to provide help to our less fortunate unless we cut education, health and welfare and aid to those less fortunate. Take the money we are pitching away and let's strike out poverty to build prosperity. You don't have to be a Wizard to use common sense for OUR common good.

The Tidal Wave of History

Gather 'round now, and make believe we are in the war room planning our next mission. Spread before us is a giant map taken from a satellite which shows the U.S.A. from the Atlantic and the Pacific, and the land between the border countries - Canada to Mexico. To our left it's marked 1945, and to the right is 2014.

The leader speaks, and he says we need to know more about this land and history before we invade it with our latest ideas and ideologies. He begins to tell that after the Americans blasted two Japanese cities practically to kingdom-come the Japanese surrendered on September 2, 1945.

A Japanese delegation headed by foreign minister Mamoru Shigemitsu and General Yoshijiro Umezu of the imperial general staff boarded the U.S.S. battleship "Missouri" to sign the document that officially ended World War 2, six years and one day after it had started. The Victory over Japan was no picnic.

The Japanese fought with fanatical fury and disregard for death.

The number of casualties and losses of life were astronomical on both sides.

Thus began a kaleidoscope of change in America. I can only tell it through my own eyes. Because so much has happened I will be limited to quickly thumbing through the pages of a history book and only highlight few of the most important changes. I can begin with America opening its arms cheerfully and as wide as possible to every returning service man and woman. Hugs and kisses were implanted soon to be measures of gratitude in the form of assistance to get higher education, skills to acquire jobs, help to pay for mortgages on new homes, and providing medical care to the thousands of wounded and maimed. Everyone was not only rejoicing in our victory, but they wanted to enjoy the fruits of our sacrificing during the war years to join together to build a better and bigger America. There was a dream and everyone wanted to share in it both individually and collectively.

Yet the one big cloud hanging above the land of the free was that discrimination was still part of the fabric across the tapestry that was America. I will skip to February 1, 1960, in Greensboro, North Carolina, when four determined young black men sat down at the lunch counter of the F.W. Woolworth store to order a cup of coffee...which never came. They came back each day with more and more fellow students, and the tidal wave spread across the land. And, little by little, first in one community and then another, because of nameless and numberless people who gave a damn, the color bar began to edge downward.

On June 25th, 1950 Korea was attacked by invading Communist forces from North Korea. The Security Council of the United Nations called upon its members, including the United States to give the Korean Government troops and support. President Eisenhower, haunted by the specter that nuclear power would not only end war, but life on earth as well. Experts were to be mobilized to apply atomic energy for peaceful pursuits such as providing energy to the power starved areas of the world, and to the needs of agriculture, medicine and other safe applications benefiting mankind.

John F. Kennedy became President in 1961, and shortly thereafter he approved a plan for the invasion of Communist Cuba by Cuban exiles. The operation failed miserably. Subsequently the United States discovered the Russians had made the island a base of intermediate range missiles. Kennedy announced an arms "quarantine" and ordered the Navy to intercept any arms being shipped to Cuba. It worked and the missiles were removed.

When J.F.K. was assassinated, President Johnson took office and sent to Congress a law designed to eliminate illegal barriers to the right to vote. He addressed Congress with these words, "For Negroes are not the only victims. How many white children have gone uneducated? How many white families have lived in stark poverty? How many white lives have been scarred by fear, because we wasted energy and our substance to maintain the barriers of hatreds and terror? These are our enemies, not our fellow man, not our neighbor. And these enemies too – poverty, disease and ignorance –we shall overcome."

Over the war in Vietnam was the deepening shadow of Communism in all of Asia. President Johnson explained… "Over many years we have made a national pledge to help South Vietnam defend its independence. And I intend to keep that promise. To withdraw from one battlefield means only to prepare for the next. We must say in Southeast Asia, as we did in Europe, in the words of the Bible, "Hitherto shalt thou come; but no further."...

Vietnam era was a conundrum. Johnson had set in motion the most ambitious program of social improvement in 30 years, under the slogan of the "Great Society", including a landmark education bill, a major civil rights bill and a series of anti-poverty project. On the other hand, as the casualty lists from Vietnam mounted the American populace's, already timid support, began to tumble. To our everlasting disgrace, upon the return of our soldiers from Vietnam, they weren't welcome home but spat upon by a disgruntled nation. I am ashamed to admit that even today we do not properly respect and treat those who fought for America while in Vietnam.

There was a long period in America of hippies, drugs and riots. By 1968 middle America who President Richard Nixon called "the forgotten Americans" began to stand up and be counted. A patriotic wave of flags and decals swept across the country. The high flying decade of the sixties brought fame and fortune to athletes in every sport and competition. From former low scale wages, Americans watched their favorite sport heroes play at the game of big business. The unmarrieds of the 60's started a search in the dating game where a singles bar would be a zoo where everyone wanted to grab you. And Americans began thinking serious thoughts about pollution and the population explosion.

The miracles of technology conjured up computers that could calculate millions of times faster than the human brain, laser beams to light up the planets above, and vehicles to deliver man to the depths of the ocean. It was man's first step to another heavenly body with the firing of moon bound Apollo 8 on December 21, 1968.

July 1969 men from the planet earth first set foot on the moon while astronaut Buzz Aldrin planted a nylon American flag on the moon surface. "We came in peace for all mankind."

Whoa!! As much as I love history and doing the research, it just dawned on me that if I continue exploring these events in any detail I will be writing this description of 70 years of history for the next 70 years, or more. When I went to school boys went to woodworking or the gym, and were never taught to type, so I have to resort to putting the words down on paper by using one finger at a time after I search carefully for where each letter is located on the keyboard. My new conclusion is to simply highlight the years between World War 2 and today, in capsule form, because few of you may have had the good fortune to celebrate or meditate over the daily happenings. With the help of the computer I have attempted to select what are signifying events in each year. Some may seem insignificant, while others will scream of their importance. My purpose is to give you a quick travel tour through these momentous years, however if any item strikes a chord of interest please dive into researching the event more thoroughly. They each hold a Pandora 's Box of fascinating interest.

1941   Japanese attack Pearl Harbor; Jeep invented; Mount Rushmore completed

1942   Anne Frank goes into hiding; the Bataan Death March; T-shirt introduced

1943   Warsaw Ghetto uprising

1944   Ball point pens go on sale; D-Day-June 6th invasion of Normandy

1945   F.D.R. dies; first computer built; Germans surrender; Microwave oven invented; Slinky toy hits shelves; United Nations founded

1946   Bikinis introduced; Nuremberg trials; Dr. Spock's book on baby care is published

1947   Dead Seas Scrolls discovered; MARSHALL Plan; Polaroid cameras invented

1948   Berlin airlift; Gandhi assassinated; State of Israel founded

1949   First non-stop flight around the world; NATO established; Soviet Union has atomic bomb

1950   First modern credit card introduced; first organ implant; first "Peanut's" cartoon strip; Korean war begins; President Truman orders construction of Hydrogen bomb

1951   Color TV introduced; South Africans forced to carry I.D. cards identifying Race; Winston Churchill reelected Prime Minister of Great Britain

1952   Car seat belts introduced; Polio vaccine created

1953   DNA discovered; first "Playboy" magazine; Hillary and Norgay climb Mt. Everest

1954   First atomic submarine launched; report says Cigarettes cause cancer; Roger Bannister breaks 4 minute mile; segregation ruled illegal in the U.S.

1955   Disneyland opens; McDonald's Corp. founded; Rosa Parks refuses to give up her seat on bus

1956   Elvis gyrates on Ed Sullivan show; Grace Kelly marries Prince Rainier lll of Monaco; TV remote invented; Velcro introduced

1957   Dr. Seuss publishes "The Cat in the Hat;" Soviet satellite Sputnik launches Space Age

1958   Hula Hoops become popular; LEGO toy bricks introduced; NASA founded; Peace symbol created

1959   Castro becomes dictator of Cuba; "The Sound of Music" opens on Broadway; U.S. quiz shows found to be fixed

1960   First televised Presidential debates; Lasers invented; the birth control pill is approved by the FDA

1961   Adolph Eichmann on trial for role in Holocaust; Bay of Pigs invasion; Berlin Wall built; JFK gives "Man on the Moon" speech; Peace Corps Founded

1962   Andy Warhol exhibits Campbell soup can; Cuban Missile Crisis; First James Bond movie; First Wal-Mart opens; Johnny Carson takes over "Tonight" show; Marilyn Monroe found dead

1963   First woman in space; JFK assassinated; March on Washington; Martin Luther King, Jr. makes his "I have a dream" speech

1964   Beatles become popular in the U.S.; Cassius Clay becomes World Heavy Weight Champion; Civil Rights Act passes; Hasbro launches G.I. Joe action Figure; Japan's first bullet train opens; Nelson Mandela sentenced to life in prison

1965   Los Angeles riots; mini-skirts first appear; U. S. sends troops to Vietnam

1966   Black Panther Party established; National Organization for Women (NOW) Founded, "Star Trek" TV series airs

1967   First heart transplant; first Super Bowl; Six-day war in the Middle East; Three U.S. Astronauts killed during simulated launch

1968   Martin Luther King, Jr. assassinated; My Lai massacre; Robert Kennedy assassinated; spy ship U.S. Pueblo captured

1969   ARPANET the precursor of the Internet is created; Neil Armstrong becomes the first man on the moon;

Rock-and-Roll concert at Woodstock; "Sesame Street" first airs

1970   Beatles breakup; computer Floppy Disks introduced; Kent State shootings

1971   London Bridge brought to U.S.; VCR's introduced

1972   M*A*S*H* TV show premieres; Mark Spitz wins seven Gold Medals; Pocket calculators introduced; Watergate scandal revealed

1973   Roe vs. Wade legalizes abortion in the U.S.; Sears Tower built; U.S. pulls out of Vietnam; U.S. Vice President resigns

1974   Halie Selassie Emperor of Ethiopia is deposed; Patty Hearst kidnapped; U.S. President Nixon resigns

1975   Arthur Ashe, first black man to win Wimbledon; Microsoft founded

1976   Nadia Comaneci given seven perfect tens; Tangshan earthquake kills over 240,000

1977   Elvis found dead; "Star Wars" movie to be released

1978   First test-tube baby born; John Paul ll becomes Pope; Jonestown massacre

1979   Iran takes American hostages in Tehran; Mother Teressa awarded the Nobel Peace prize; Sony introduces the Walkman

1980   John Lennon assassinated; Pac-Man video game introduced; Rubik cube becomes popular; Ted Turner establishes CNN

1981   Assassination attempt on President Ronald Reagan; first woman appointed to the Supreme Court; millions watch Royal wedding on TV; new plague identified as AIDS; personal computers (PC) introduced by IBM

1982   E.T. movie released; Michael Jackson releases "The Thriller;" Vietnam War Memorial opens in Washington, D.C.

1983   Cabbage Patch Kids are popular; Reagan announces Defense Plan called "Star Wars;" Sally Ride becomes the first American woman in space; U.S. Embassy in Beirut bombed

1984   Indira Gandhi, India's Prime Minister killed by two bodyguards

1985   Hole in the Ozone layer discovered; new "Coke" hits the market; wreck of The Titanic found

1986   Space shuttle "Challenger" explodes; Chernobyl Nuclear Disaster; U.S. bombs Libya

1987   DNA first used to convict criminals; N.Y. Stock Exchange suffers huge drop on "Black Monday"

1988   Pan Am Flight 103 is bombed over Lockerbie; U.S. shoots down Iranian airliner

1989 Berlin Wall falls; Exxon Valdez spills millions of gallons of oil on coastline; Students massacred in China Tiananmen Square

1990 Hubble Telescope launched into space; Nelson Mandela freed

1991 Collapse of the Soviet Union; Operation Desert Storm; South Africa repeals Apartheid Laws

1992 Official end of the Cold War; Riots in Los Angeles after the Rodney King verdict

1993 Cult compound in Waco, Texas raided; use of the Internet grows World Trade Center bombed

1994 Nelson Mandela elected President of South Africa; O.J. Simpson arrested for double murder

1995 Oklahoma City bombing; Yitzhak Rabin assassinated

1996 Unabomber arrested

1997 Hale-Bopp comet visible; Princess Diana dies in car crash; tallest building in the world built in Kuala Lumpur; Tiger Woods wins Masters

1998 "Titanic" most successful movie ever; Viagra on the market

1999 The Euro the new European currency; fear of Y2K bug; JFK, Jr. dies in plane accident; killing spree at Columbine High School; Panama Canal returns to Panama

2000   "I Love You" virus hits thousands of computers; Microsoft ordered to split; U.S. Cole bombed

2001   Wikipedia is launched; George Bush sworn in as 43rd President; the world's first space tourist; Apple launches iPod

2002   Apple introduces the iMac G4; the dwarf planet Quaoar is discovered

2003   Space Shuttle Columbia disaster; the invasion of Iraq; the Human Genome product is completed; My Space is launched

2004   The emergence of Web 2.0; Hubble ultra deep field; Mars exploration with Rovers; Facebook is launched

2005   You Tube is launched; USB flash drives replace floppy disks; Hurricane Katrina floods New Orleans

2006   Twitter is launched; Pluto is demoted to 'dwarf planet" status; Saddam Hussein is executed

2007   Global economic downturn ; Apple debuts the iPhone; Amazon releases the Kindle; Google Street View is launched

2008   Oil prices hit record high; the Internet continues to boom; breakthrough in facial CGI

2009   Barack Obama is sworn in as President of the USA; major breakthrough in cancer research; scientists engi-

47....

neer new plastics without the use of fossil fuels; water is discovered on the moon; mind controlled headsets enter into the video game market; 3D scanning enters the consumer market

2010 Haiti is struck by a devastating earthquake; Apple debuts the iPad; Macular degeneration is curable; speech-to-speech translation is common in mobile phones; robotic manipulation of non ridged objects

2011 The death of Osamar bin Laden; worsening economic crisis in Greece; the world's first synthetic organ transplant; Global population reaches 7 billion; nanometer chips enter mass production; consumer level robotics are booming; world's first commercial spaceport

2012 Windows 8 is released; Quad-core smart phones and tablets; Nintendo Launches the WiiU

2013 North Korea conducts its third nuclear test; the first creation of human embryonic cells for cloning; the NSA documents are leaked; birth of Royal baby; China overtakes the USA in scientific research; the first gene therapy in the Western world; highly flexible touch sensors are appearing in a range of gadgets; launch of Xbox one and the PS4.

From "Whoa" to "WOW" we have covered a number of earth shaking events in this great big, wide wonderful world we live in. Just as the Hubble Space telescope gazes at the galaxies we have taken a snapshot of our lifetime since 1941 through today. Though things continually keep forming and evolving from good to worse and back to good, some things remain constant. Babies are born. Lives are lost. The butcher, the banker, the software maker are not created equal. Our DNA's prove that.

What is equal is sunrise and sunset. Our mission is to make the best of the lives we are given. We must understand we are not all given the brains of an Albert Einstein or Stephen Hawkins. Few of us can sing like Sinatra or Pavarotti. And I know Natalie and I can't dance like Fred Astaire with Ginger Rodgers. Yet, everyone should have a personal mission to be the best they can be with the attributes given to us, and pledge to help the less capable or unfortunate to be able to enjoy their moments in life. Plurality in life is an obligation for people and nations to make every effort to live in peace and shared comfort. There's room enough in this world house to be friendly neighbors that watch out for another with a common goal to be our brother's keeper.

We leave no one by the wayside.

We boost one another to the moon and to the galaxies beyond.

In looking at the progress, as well as the regressive wars and disturbances, during these past 72 years (1941 through 2013) I couldn't help but wonder at the miracle of development that has swiftly launched us from the Tinker toys to today's technology. President Kennedy had told us that change is inevitable, and we must not only live with it, but promise to promote the future.

I believe the teachings of Moses with the Ten Commandments, and Jesus with the gospels were right for their time and followers of which are the foundations and precursors of our later generations. Yet, you and I must adopt and adept to the evolution from living in a tent like structure to working in a skyscraper with your body, heart and soul, reaching out to the towering stars above. Time waits for no one, and we must not be left at the station watching the train you missed speed by. Stonewalling, standing still isn't an option as it can only lead to failure because some other person or country is running a Roger Bannister faster mile to win the big prize.

To quote my sonnet, "Bullets are for battle. War is for peace." Leave the bullets for law enforcement and the military. Keep your guns for hunting, and protecting your possessions. End the wars and battle for peace among all people. Bring our troops home from the hell hole of Afghanistan. Today! We should have learned our lesson in Iraq that we can't impose peace if their native tribes can't figure out that killing one another solves nothing except continuous lost lives, and lost prosperity.

I admire, and am not afraid to admit it, that I revere F.D.R. and his wife Eleanor for creating the "New Deal"; John F. Kennedy who led us to the moon; Lyndon B. Johnson's "Great Society;" Martin Luther King, Jr. that broke the binds of discrimination; Nelson Mandela whose prison terms didn't break his courage; and Pope Francis who is the People's Pope. My apologies to the many other leaders who have made a difference as the world is constantly forming and evolving as it revolves in our celestial heavens.

I am a proud product, and beneficiary of the "Greatest Generation."

Who is this progressive liberal that is preaching to me? I hear it from my immediate family members; friends and business associates; the pundits on the conservative media; my fellow gym rats; and even from my military veteran brothers and sisters. I am simply a product of my parents' practices of providing food and help to their family members; my military experience of knowing we fight a common enemy who wants to take away our liberties and way of life, so we are willing to put our lives on the line as our duty and responsibility to our country; to the teachings of my and other religions to love thy neighbor; having the honor to work to feed the hungry; trying to indoctrinate our youth that illegal drugs kill; assisting the sick and mentally disturbed; learning the horrors of alcohol abuse, and the potential cures; wrestling against the demons of discrimination, hatred and intolerance; seeing the joy of providing food, clothing and housing to the less fortunate and particularly for veterans; and building jobs so that everyone can be gainfully employed to contribute to the greater good of society.

I am not a Priest, Pastor, Rabbi, or Politician. I am just like all 7 billion inhabitants of this earth who has not accomplished extraordinary things. When I look in the mirror I think of myself as a common, ordinary guy who loves his wife, family and friends that is dedicating his remaining purpose in life to BACK-OUR-VETS, troops and their families – all 65 million true patriots and Americans.

What continues to amaze and puzzle me is how the people who are enjoying all the luxuries of the good life think they are the ones whose taxes need to be cut. Are they afraid they will miss a meal or be thrown out to the wolves on the street?

Am I so egotistical to think I have all the answers when our government and political experts can't come up with common sense solutions to our local and national problems? My answer would be, "Yes, and No", as I believe I have offered some quick and relatively easy solutions to put many of those problems to bed, once and for all's benefit. Nothing good will come of them unless people cooperate in a spirit of consensus to make common sense for the good and welfare of all the people. Individuals, and parties, must join together and find common ground to benefit the plurality of all the people if we are to enjoy the American pursuit of happiness. Makes common sense to me – an ordinary guy.

Agreed -- some problems are more complex than others. I have my personal thoughts in regard to abortions, gay rights, marijuana, mixed marriages, penal rulings and the death penalty, but I am in the same ballpark as Pope Francis...

"Who am I to judge?"

Excuse me, but I can't let the subject of abortion and planned parenthood slip away into the sunset without me digressing for a moment. The governors and judges are not fooling anyone when they try to pull their will- over- our eyes by claiming they are protecting women's health by shutting down Planned Parenthood services and abortion clinics. They are eliminating proper attention to the needs of millions of women who have chosen to abort an unwanted fetus due to rape, or not being able to properly provide for a child. Forcing women to try to find a provider hundreds of miles away is an undue burden, especially if you don't have the money or access to a vehicle to pay for the trip. Asking the Doctors to have approved admission in a nearby hospital is creating another hurdle as many of the hospitals prohibit abortions due to their religious affiliations.

Requiring new or existing abortion providers to meet the requirements of Emergency Facilities is mixing apples and oranges. Because a service station repairs cars do they need to teach people how to drive...or vice versa? If anyone prefers to turn the clock back to the back alley use of wire clothes hangers as the available solution to a human being women's problem, then go hang your head in shame with these retroactive laws. Plain old common sense is giving women options of their choice, but not stone throwing tortuous walls of camouflaging your real political driven intensions. Live and let live women to decide and choose. It's simply freedom of choice which is a guaranteed right.

Women have not only broken through the glass ceiling, but I believe many of them will ban together to crash your political seat. You have been warned.

I do believe we can't let our government stagnate by not approving wage increases; by facing another government "closed-for-business" folly; cutting education and employment boosting efforts. I am all for cutting the waste in our government, our military and our corporations and businesses, but just because it is mandatory to invest in growth does not mean we have to cut off our nose by cutting necessary and much needed expenses. When we lop money off programs like head-start we are lopping off our future scientists, engineers, physicians, and business leaders.

My back does straighten and I do get a little nervy when political hacks want to hack-away at our lawfully approved Obamacare health program which gives more people the insurance to protect, improve and care for their lives while they are here among us. Are they blind to the benefits which Americans enjoy due to Social Security and Medicare that are proven safety nets that benefit the majority of our population? Is it unreasonable to expect errors in the introduction of a complex, new program?

Over the years I have watched the giants of industry fail in the introduction of new products. Don't you remember the catastrophic introductions of the "Edsel" auto by Ford, or the changed formula of the new "Coke" by Coca-Cola? Only recently both Wal-Mart and Chick-Fil-A put their foot in their mouths by making misleading statements that made Americans turn purple with rage. We all make mistakes, I have admitted to mine. These examples didn't have the effect of changing the lives of all 310,000,000 Americans like the Affordable Healthcare Act (Obamacare) whose introduction had to depend on the computer network over the Internet. Troubles had to be expected, and may continue, but that does not negate the benefits this program is providing for 'We The People'. Sure, some Doctors may be affected, and insurance companies along with health providers will have to adjust their profits temporarily. Over the long run, with more customers, everyone will benefit. That is the way capitalism works.

If you are like me your computer is interloped daily with messages from companies and people you hardly know. Typically I wear my fingers out hitting the "Delete" button numerous times over and over.

Once in a blue moon something strikes me as being apropos. I want to share this cartoon comment which came in today from a cousin of Natalie's who resides in Dallas. It's titled

"Coffee."

"An Indian walks into a café with a shotgun in one hand and pulling a male buffalo with the other. He says to the waiter: 'Want coffee.' The waiter says, 'Sure Chief. Coming right up.' He gets the Indian a tall mug of coffee. The Indian drinks the coffee down in one gulp, turns and blasts the buffalo with the shotgun, causing parts of the animal to splatter everywhere, and then just walks out.

The next morning the Indian returns. He has the shotgun in one hand, pulling another male buffalo with the other. He walks up to the counter and says to the waiter, 'Want coffee.'

The waiter says, 'Whoa, Tonto! We're still cleaning up the mess from yesterday. What was that all about anyway?'

The Indian smiles and proudly says, 'Training for a position in UNITED STATES CONGRESS...come in drink coffee, shoot the bull, leave mess for others to clean up, disappear for rest of the day."

My common sense advice to "Commander-in Chief TontOBAMA, use BULLy pulpit and shoot straight with Congress to clean up this mess. Rest for the day."

Steak of the Union

When it comes to junkies there are those that abuse drugs and then there is me. I rightfully can be accused of being a political junky.

I can't really account for which one is worse as I probably squander too much time following and cursing how our do nothing Congress is wasting our tax payer money by sitting on their hands and fighting amongst themselves like juvenile bullies in the school yard.

I plunked myself down in front of the TV and had eyes glued to the set watching President Barack Obama enter the Chambers just before delivering the anticipated State of the Union address. He's relaxed and smiling broadly while shaking hands with admirers or exchanging a quick pat on the back and a hug or two. Many of the ladies get a quick brush of a kiss on the cheek while Sheila Jackson Lee makes sure the camera will capture her five seconds of fame with the Commander-in-Chief. Personally I am surprised to see the two Secret Servicemen leading the President through the admirers being more mature than what is usually expected of those men who are sworn to put down their lives to protect our President. But, they are equally alert as they help open the wave of politicos that want to give President Obama their encouragement and maybe some last minute advice as if the President can, or will, heed their well meaning words.

He walks over to the representatives of the military who stiffly stand and firmly shake his hand as if they have been Commandeered by their Chief, then President Obama approaches the members of the Supreme Court and I am pleasantly surprised to see Justice Ginsberg reach up and give him a warm hug followed by the other ladies of the Court and the gentlemen are equally courteous in their greetings though none tried giving him a hug or a hearty clap on the back.

The President climbs to the podium and turns to shake the hand of the Vice President and the as usual sun tanned Speaker of the House. The noise in the Chamber continues to escalate until the Speaker raps the gavel repeatedly too close to the Vice President's hand, and calls for attention. The President is formally introduced and he steps in front of the microphone.

He smiles broadly and appears perfectly relaxed and at ease. He speaks with boundless enthusiasm. I imagine myself in the same situation and would be dying from fright knowing that half the audience is praying he will stumble and fall flat on his face where the other half is expecting miracles to come rolling out of his articulate mouth. The office of the President of the United States could make a fortune by going into the hair bleaching business. It doesn't take very long once someone accepts that position that their hair turns to gray and becomes whiter from one public appearance to another.

At each State of the Union address it appears as if they are following a scripted movie. The President, no matter who he is, delivers a political promise which members of his party will immediately acknowledge in a chorus of approval by clapping like trained 'patty-cake, patty-cake' babies. The opposing party members sit like they are paralyzed and glued to their seats. Looking at their expressions as the TV scans their side of the aisle you see frowns as they wrinkle their faces while turning their heads from side-to-side indicating disapproval, and even signs of disgust and disbelief. If this was the night of the Academy Awards the judges would have a difficult time as to which politico won the Oscar for best actor on the floor to be applauded by his adoring constituents.

This isn't just a one-time scene. It's repeated over and over again as the President delivers his ideas as to how to combat poverty, to build jobs, to solve the immigration problem, to increase the minimum wage, to end the disparity between the income levels, to offer equal pay to women, to create better education opportunities, to lower or raise the debt depending on the subject, while the list drones on and on. Nothing changes in the audience. The clowns on both sides of the aisles perform on cue. They either rumble or they tumble as their faces freeze red or blue. There's either glee and approval or glaring disapproval and gloom depending on which side of the aisle you have been assigned to sit. The only ones who show no emotion are the stone faced Supreme Court justices while the highly decorated members of the military stand only when the President graciously praises the armed forces.

I excuse these honored Generals and Admirals lack of approval of some of the proposals as all the medals and chest of ribbons they are each wearing load them down to make it difficult to rise out of their seats. What is absolutely a sign of ignorance and disrespect was when one Congressman from Texas stormed out of the Chamber as a signal of disagreement with some of the President of the United States of America's pronouncements. It is just his customary misbehavior by rarely attending Congressional sessions while secretly cavorting to Egypt and Russia. You have the right to disagree, but in my opinion, Mr. (?) Congressman, do not disgrace your elected office and the people who elected you to do the nation's business for the common good of all.

In this homogenized society of America has civility and compromise flown out the window or walked out the door of the Chamber?

Most politicians today, to help emphasize the point they are trying to propose have invited someone to attend the speech who is an example of voluntarily raising the minimum wage of his employees, or a woman who has succeeded to break through the glass ceiling and is now running our nation's largest automobile manufacturing company. It just makes good staging and is proof that in America there are people who have and continue to achieve success no matter the height of the hurdles they must bound over. Even in many of these worthwhile examples there was never universal approval throughout the listening audience. Are we so constrained by our ideologies that we can't recognize and applaud achievement?

Can we so easily forget where this nation was when our nation's

STEAK OF THE UNION

President Obama first came into office? It was a deep recession. High unemployment. Greater numbers of homeless, hungry and despair for the future. He has been elected twice by a majority of We The People. I urge you to THINK and stop being the United States of Amnesia. Learn to join the UNITED States of AMERICA!

It was interesting to keep watching the comparison of reactions by the Vice President and the Speaker of the House. They both win the award for best supporting actor...or, if it were the Super Bowl they would get the prize winning ribbon for outstanding or sitting-out cheer leader.

I was reminded that this type of ill-mannered behavior is not unusual. If it were Presidents Kennedy, Reagan, Eisenhower, Truman, Clinton, Johnson or either of the two Bushes the gathering of brain washed puppets on both sides react with no difference as if they are being pulled by the puppeteers wireless strings. Thank you Hedy Lamarr for your wireless invention that helped the Allies win World War 2, and is obviously being employed during State of Union addresses by the various Presidents and their political parties to control their loyal robotic followers.

When President Obama explained his position on getting our troops out of Afghanistan as soon as possible you could see the stare of disbelief on some of the hawks perched in their seats. Even a mention of easing the sanctions on Iran, while watching them like a hawk that they keep their word not to develop nuclear weaponry, was greeted by stone like solemnity as on the Mt. Rushmore faces of former Presidents.

Iran. It is a dilemma. Can we really trust them? Should we believe, relieve and reduce the sanctions or are we ready to go once again to war? In watching the reaction of some of the Senators and Congressmen who were staring blank-eyed with lips clamped in opposition to what the President was proposing, I couldn't help but think of my experience in trying to help Michelle avoid going to prison for a long term. She was marked as a felon and couldn't get or hold a job. If she served wouldn't it be better if the tattoo of "felon" would be erased and she could regain her place in an accepting society? Maybe we need to give Iran a chance to prove they will keep their promise before rushing to battle and leave more American bodies bleeding on their soil. But, we won't be felon- fooled and taken for suckers. Just one violation and the wrath of the free world will descend to their everlasting demise. That's not a threat. It's a pledge and a promise if Iran even blows a single nuclear "test".

It was interesting to watch the reaction to the President's proposal to reinforce and strengthen our borders, yet open our doors to immigrants and include a path to citizenship. What is of interest is to note that the Republican reaction to his proposal has taken a turn for the better within days from the speech. The speaker is indicating they might negotiate with some differences they can accept. "If the speaker proposes something that says right away: Folks aren't being deported, families aren't being separated, we're able to attract top young students to provide the skills or start businesses here and then there's a regular process of citizenship, I'm not sure how wide the divide ends up being," Obama said.

Republicans are objecting to a pathway to citizenship, because in my humble opinion, they fear that immigrants will vote

Democratic. It stands to reason that if they take a firm stand to allow immigrants to come into America to find jobs, pay fines and taxes and slam the door shut to citizenry so they can vote is a loud and clear message they are willing to accept slaves without the power to vote. It's a sure fire signal we don't like or want you while claiming they love Hispanics and are wooing their votes. Other immigrants who have come to these shores and prospered vote Republican and support them generously with their time and money. Look, listen and learn from your own Ted Cruz, Marco Rubio and other Americans of Hispanic heritage about their family history and experience. Accept compromise, and include a principled legislative process of earning citizenship with the right to vote. It just makes common sense.

Just as I wrote earlier about love letters written in the sand at Port O'Connor, countless letter carriers filled the Chamber hall with love, admiration and respect. I am aware that I could not do justice to reporting this momentous event so I am taking the liberty of quoting Becky Bratu, Staff Writer, NBC News.

"Sgt. First Class Cory Remsburg's story of struggle and survival had the entire room in ovation near the end of the State of the Union as President Obama recognized the nation's wounded heroes as a symbol for our own resilience.

Praising the 30-year old Army Ranger, that "like the Army he loves, SFC Cory Remsburg never gives up, and quit."

The unifying moment—which made both Republicans and Democrats, some misty eyed, stand and applause in unison – was the emotional highlight of a speech marked by Obama's vows to use executive powers to sidestep Republican road-blocks on Capitol Hill.

As he introduced Remsburg to the audience, Obama described his first impression of him; "A strong, impressive young man, with an easy manner, sharp as a tack."

Remsburg, who has met Obama three times, joined the Army on his 18th birthday and was first deployed in 2003.

Since then, he's been on 10 deployments to both Iraq and Afghanistan. It was on his last deployment, in Oct. 2009, that he was nearly killed by a roadside bomb in Kandahar, Afghanistan.

The blast propelled him into a canal, face down in water with shrapnel in his brain and a head wound. One of Remsburg's fellow Rangers perished in the explosion.

The bomb left Remsburg in a coma for three months, partially paralyzed, barely able to speak and brain-damaged.

But after enduring dozens of surgeries and hours of rehabilitation therapy over the years, Remsburg is now able to walk and speak, although he still struggles on his left side and is blind in his right eye.

Last year, Remsberg was finally able to return home to Phoenix, Ariz., where he continues working on his recovery and enjoys cycling.

Among his many honors, Remsburg has been awarded the Purple Heart, the National Defense Service Medal and the Bronze

Star. On the night of the State of the Union address it also brought him a nation's gratitude.

Obama said Remsburg acknowledged his recovery has not been easy, as "nothing in life that's worth anything is easy."

But the commander-in-chief equated Remsburg's strenuous path to recovery to the nation's own struggle to uphold its ideals of freedom and democracy.

"Sometimes we stumble; we make mistakes; we get frustrated or discouraged," Obama said in his speech. "But for more than 200 years, we have put those things aside and placed our collective shoulder to the wheel of progress."

As for one guys' sitting at home who was mesmerized by this unity of tribute to a fellow veteran I had to wipe my tearing eyes and remember "nothing in life that's worth anything is easy."

This display of unity and respect for our military and veterans demonstrated to me that Americans, all Americans, are patriotic and would gladly put-in their 2 cents to BACK-OUR-VETS. "Sometimes we struggle" to reach our goals; "but when we put our collective shoulders to the wheel…we can uphold the ideals of freedom and democracy."

Please, I plead you to stop sitting and stand-up for our 65 million veterans, troops and their families. Ask the retailers where you shop; "When will you join to BACK-OUR-VETS?" When it happens and you shop at a store where they are participating in this noble cause please don't hesitate to thank them and be

sure to voluntarily add your 2 cents on top of your total bill.
Three hundred million citizens using their common 2 cents
will be able to help the millions of Cory Remsburg's throughout America. Join me in our united effort to BACK-OUR-
VETS.

Together we can learn from the State of the Union speech that
by using our common 2 cents we can change platitudes of
promises into platters of steak and potatoes nourishing the lives
of our needy veterans and their families while forming a more
perfect UNITED States of America. We can do it!

Now as I finally tuck this book to bed and fold the covers closer
together I hope you may have found some warmth and comfort in using common sense for our collective good.

My common 2 CENTS advice to every American;

"Don't forget to BACK-OUR-VETS."

My common SENSE advice is God Bless America, and bless
my eternal love – the ever beautiful, romantic, sweet – Natalie
(BooBoo) Littman.

POST SCRIPture:
Who Is the Wizard?

The Wizard is me. It's you. It's every one of the 300 plus million 'WE THE PEOPLE' of the UNITED States of America.

We are all born with the capability to use our common sense. We all inherently know what is right and what is wrong. We are taught the simple "Do's" from the "Don'ts." For people of faith, we understand what is our moral responsibility. We have been instructed to love thy neighbor, and to walk humbly.

The world has changed, and will continue to advance and progress as it has for centuries. We must march into our future together. Determined to progress. Medicine has changed, communication has changed, transportation has changed… but, our moral compass must remain steady and true.

Partisan brinkmanship and stonewalling doesn't open our Hope Chest for a better, stronger and safer America. Fighting among ourselves whether inside our families, or with our personal, business or social relationships can be solved using our God given common sense to compromise for the common good. Sometimes you have got to give a little to gain a lot. It's simply common sense. Use it!

Nothing should reach deeper into your hearts than the universal message to love, respect and practice what we preach.

How, you might question is one quick and easy place we Americans can start - that won't cost us or cause any sacrifice that will deliver a common good?

Allow me to suggest we use our common 2 cents by uniting our local, state and federal government along with businesses, and WE-THE POWER OF THE PEOPLE to show our love and gratitude to 65 million troops, veterans and their families when we BACK-OUR-VETS. Then God WILL shower blessings on each of you under one nation, indivisible, with liberty and justice for all- forming a more perfect **UNITED** STATES OF AMERICA.

God Bless America

EARL LITTMAN
America's PREACHER for PATRIOTISM
BACK-OUR-VETS, Inc.
info@backourvets.com
www.backourvets.com

CPSIA information can be obtained at www.ICGtesting.com
Printed in the USA
BVOW05s0856220414

351354BV00001B/81/P